TEXTXET

Studies in Comparative Literature 55

Series Editors
C.C. Barfoot and Theo D'haen

Re-Thinking Europe
Literature and (Trans)National Identity

Edited by

Nele Bemong, Mirjam Truwant and Pieter Vermeulen

Amsterdam - New York, NY
2008

Cover photo: Mirjam Truwant

Cover design: Pier Post

The paper on which this book is printed meets the requirements of 'ISO 9706: 1994, Information and documentation - Paper for documents - Requirements for permanence'.

ISBN: 978-90-420-2352-9
© Editions Rodopi B.V., Amsterdam - New York, NY 2008
Printed in The Netherlands

Acknowledgements

Early versions of the articles assembled here were presented at the Hermes International Seminar "Re-Thinking Europe" that took place in Leuven in June 2006. We want to thank Theo D'haen, who organized the seminar with us and whose expertise greatly facilitated the composition of this book.

The editors of the present volume are grateful to Academia Europaea and the Editors of the *European Review*, and to Cambridge University Press, for permission to re-use the following materials: David Damrosch. "Global Regionalism." *European Review* 15.1 (2007): 135-143; Lieven D'hulst. "Comparative Literature versus Translation Studies: Close Encounters of the Third Kind?" *European Review* 15.1 (2007): 95-104; Herbert Grabes. "*Prodesse et delectare*: The World of National Literatures and the World of Literature." *European Review* 15.1 (2007): 105-114; Bart Keunen. "Rethinking European Identity through a Triptych of Literary Heroes." *European Review* 15.1 (2007): 125-134.

Kleinefenn Photographie's photo of Kader Attia's installation *Arabesque* (p. 129) is reprinted with permission of the Palais de Tokyo, Paris (France) © Palais de Tokyo/Kleinefenn, 2006. Copyright the artist and Galerie Kamel Mennour, Paris.

Table of Contents

Introduction: Europe, in Comparison
Nele Bemong, Mirjam Truwant, and Pieter Vermeulen   7

Part I. Beyond the Nation? Inter-, Trans-, and Hypernational Identities

Europeanism in One Country: August Vermeylen, Paul van Ostaijen, and the International Approach to Nationalism
Matthijs de Ridder   21

The *Histoire anglaise*: Towards a Cosmopolitan View of the Other?
Beatrijs Vanacker   33

Global Regionalism
David Damrosch   47

Why the World Is Never Enough: Re-Conceptualizing World Literature as a Self-Substitutive Order
Michael Boyden   59

Translation and Its Role in European Literatures: Some Questions and Answers
Lieven D'hulst   81

The (Im)Possibilities of a European Literary History: The Case of Flanders
Ben van Humbeeck   93

Part II. Performing Transnational Identity

Re-Thinking Ottoman Empire: East-West Collaboration in Orhan Pamuk's *The White Castle*
Nagihan Haliloğlu   111

Kader Attia's *Arabesque*: Inscribing Islam in a Provincialized Europe
Mary Stevens   123

The Old World through a Baroque Mirror: Europe in the Work of Alejo Carpentier
Reindert Dhondt   139

Cultural Hierarchies, Secondary Nations: The Tension between Europe and "Minor" Cultures in Witold Gombrowicz and Jorge Luis Borges
Silvana Mandolessi   151

Arriving in Eurasia: Yoko Tawada Re-Writing Europe
Kari van Dijk   163

Part III. Conjuring the Past, Imagining Europe

Staging a European Republic of Letters: (Supra-)National Concepts of Literature in Arno Schmidt's Early Prose
Iannis Goerlandt   179

Epistle to the Europeans (On Not Reading Kipling)
Ortwin de Graef   195

Prodesse et Delectare: The World of National Literatures and the World of Literature
Herbert Grabes   209

The Late Europe: Elias Canetti and the Ordering of Time and Space in *Auto Da Fé*
Jeppe Ilkjær   223

Prague in Victorian Fiction: An Imagological Approach
Iulius Hondrila   237

European Identity from Normality to Immanence
Bart Keunen   253

Notes on Contributors   265

Nele Bemong, Mirjam Truwant, and Pieter Vermeulen (K.U.Leuven)

Introduction: Europe, in Comparison

Ever since the beginnings of the discipline of comparative literature in the 19th century, the relation between comparative literature and the idea of Europe has been an intricate one. It is because, for reasons that we will come to explain, this connection no longer seems so self-evident today that it becomes an open question, a question that the contributions to this volume will approach in their different ways. When the first projects for comparative literature emerged in 19th century Europe – foremost in Germany and France, but, as David Damrosch and Herbert Grabes remind us in their contributions to this book, also in Britain and in culturally less dominant countries – the term "comparative" was to be understood in contrast to the term "national": while the latter term held connotations of partiality and parochialism, "comparative literature," as Susan Bassnett explains, "carried with it a sense of transcendence of the narrowly nationalistic" (21). Comparative literature, then, was always more than a value-neutral research project, as its vocation to overcome bias and opposition also carried the political and ethical promise of peace and cooperation beyond national and ethnic lines. In practice, however, and in spite of such lofty vocational claims, early comparative studies all too often tended to conclude their comparisons of their own literature with the literature(s) of other nations by declaring the superiority of the masterpieces of their own literary history. Also, in the rare instances in which they ventured beyond the small set of major nation-states, they generally ended up reinforcing the privilege of these major players. Not only were early comparative practices Eurocentric, then, by their negligence of non-(central-)European literatures, they also tended to reinforce the division of Europe in different nation-states that they set out to transcend. Indeed, because it insisted on comparing literatures along national lines, the Eurocentrism of early comparative literature was not only due to the fact that it almost exclusively limited itself to the study of European literatures, but also to the fact that it studied these literatures as *national* literatures, and therefore reproduced the 19th- and early 20th century European political status quo, which further effectively blinded it to the rest of the world (Appiah 54).

It is no surprise, then, that when American comparative literature really took off after the Second World War, it motivated its claim to offer a more genuinely *comparative* kind of comparison by underlining the distinction between the characteristically European picture of a multiplicity of different nations opposing each other and the uniquely American success of an all-embracing national unit that had managed to integrate ethnically and culturally very different groups of immigrants (Reese-Schäfer 261). The American melting pot seemed to provide a more promising model to realize the comparative ideals of interdisciplinarity and universalism than the multidirectional oppositions between the different parts of Europe (Bassnett 33). It is on the strength of this alleged American impartiality that Werner Friederich, one of the pioneers and untiring missionaries of the American comparative creed, in an address to the Australasian Language and Literature Congress in 1964, could declare the superiority of the American approach to comparative literature. Friederich took to task "[t]he most unworthy among the European comparatists" who "ignore the fact that comparatism [...] constitutes a political creed, an abjuring of all forms of racism," by publishing "so-called comparative books only to underscore all the more bigotedly the alleged superiority of their own national literature" (48). Friederich voiced a basic conviction of his field when he claimed that the American situation lent itself particularly well to the promotion of "cosmopolitan cross-fertilization" (37). Already in 1948, when Europe still found itself in the midst of its self-perpetrated ruins, Friederich declared in an address in Paris that "[a]way from the national rivalries of strife-torn Europe, [Americans] have no special axe to grind and can weigh the debits and the credits of the various national literatures justly and with detachment" (9).

What this proclamation of a blissful removal from the constraints of a partial national viewpoint should not be allowed to obscure is the realization that the very ideals of universality and cosmopolitanism that Friederich promotes reflect decidedly European ideas (Aseguinolaza 423; Bassnett 1-5). Friederich seems to admit as much in the sentence following the one just quoted from the Paris address: "Furthermore," we read, "with the blood of most European nations flowing through their veins, [Americans] have a possibility of achieving a tolerance and a level-headedness in their outlook which at times is missing among militant European scholars" (9). American comparatism thus paradoxically seems to derive its capacity to supersede Europe's residual provincialism from the fact that it belongs to the very lineage that it at the same time claims to correct. By filling in what "at times is missing" in European comparatism, American comparative literature did not so much offer an alternative to European comparatism, but rather saw itself as the completion of what remained unfulfilled in Europe. The impulse animating postwar American comparative literature was still recognizably the European dream of cosmopolitanism that had migrated across the Atlantic in order to come to fruition in that more welcoming climate. In this respect, it is useful to remember that many of the early sponsors of American comparatism were displaced Europeans – we can think of such giants as Erich Auerbach, Leo Spitzer, René Wellek, and indeed of Werner Friederich himself. At the very end of his Paris address, Friederich underlined this conception of the United States as the furthest province of Europe by inviting his (European) audience to think of "what we are doing" as "part of the deeper meaning of the Marshall Plan," as part of an effort to restore and perpetuate Europe's grandeur in order to save, in the words of Friederich's closing call, "the great cultural heritage that belongs to us, the Western World" (10). The idea of Europe here served as the invisible border of the imaginary realm in which the dream of even-handed comparison could be acted out. Because the idea of Europe remained invisible *as* a limit, it was mainly considered as a benevolent supranational principle that allowed the study of the traffic of a limited set of literary devices, themes, and topoi between a limited set of European literatures to be perceived as a model of global cooperation and universal tolerance.

If we want to appreciate how Europe only gradually became visible as also a *limit* to the cosmopolitan hopes of comparatism, a good place to look is in the successive "reports on standards" that the American Comparative Literature Association (ACLA) has solicited from a committee made up of some of its most distinguished members at different times in its development (in 1965, 1975, 1993, and 2004). When read in sequence, these documents offer us a clear narrative of the discipline's changing self-image, and specifically of the changing place of Europe in this image. The first report from 1965 contains an emphatic call to reaffirm the "belief in the internationalism of [the] field." This internationalism, however, will be sufficiently established, or so this committee believes, if American comparatists only honor "what has been validly established by our predecessors and colleagues across the sea" – a sea that, as the rest of the document makes clear, is most definitely the North Atlantic, and most definitely not the Gulf of Mexico or the Pacific ("The Levin Report" 25). The 1975 report, at least, begins to acknowledge the existence of these waters, without therefore abandoning the priorities of the earlier report. The report states that "[t]he growth of interest in the non-European literatures is another development we can welcome, while cautiously searching for ways to accommodate this interest to our own traditions." The reasons for this caution are assumed to be obvious, as "[i]t goes without saying that we cannot begin to absorb the wealth of exotic literatures before firmly possessing our own" ("The Greene Report" 36).

It is only in the 1993 report, written by a committee chaired by Charles Bernheimer, that we find a frank acknowledgement that the "impulse to extend the horizon of literary studies" that had motivated postwar comparatism "did not often reach beyond Europe and Europe's high-cultural lineage going back to the civilizations of classical antiquity" ("The Bernheimer Report" 40). Indeed, "[t]he apparent internationalism of the postwar years sustained a restrictive Eurocentrism that has recently been challenged from multiple perspectives" (41). The Bernheimer report testifies to a shift in the idea of Europe that goes together with the fact that, in the age of multiculturalism, Europe is no longer just considered in opposition to "narrow, warring nationalisms," but increasingly also from the perspective of its non-European others (Suleiman 268). While from the former perspective, the idea of Europe recalls a venerable tradition of peace and tolerance, it now increasingly refers to an imperialist force propelled by claims of racial and cultural superiority. The report acknowledges that the idea of Europe no longer only functions as the implicit *horizon* of comparative thinking, but that it also serves as the explicit *target* of many attempts to move beyond this horizon and to render the world lying beyond that horizon visible. The multicultural correction of the tradition of comparison consists in the double gesture of, on the one hand, a critique of the inherent link between comparison and Europe that earlier attempts at comparison often took for granted and, on the other, the affirmation of particular identities that had found no place within the European horizon that had circumscribed the interests of these earlier versions of comparative studies (Chow).

While this revisionist picture has certainly informed much identity-political and multicultural work, it is important to realize that the 1993 report's acknowledgement of the validity of the contributions of non-European and non-Eurocentrist perspectives does not lead to an outright dismissal of the tradition of comparative literature that such perspectives critique. Such a condemnation would simply repeat the binarist thinking of Europe that these perspectives object to in that tradition. In its conclusion, the 1993 report states that it has attempted to put forward some proposals "in order to expand students' perspectives and stimulate them to think in culturally pluralistic terms" (47). This ambition can easily be recognized as a continuation of the pluralist agenda that already motivated both the early European versions of comparatism and the later American uptake of these attempts. The report's recognition of the validity of the challenges to comparative literature's Eurocentrism does not signify a call for the wholesale abandonment of the dream of universalism that informs comparative studies, but is rather an indication of its hope to be more true to the promise of tolerance by transforming the tradition from within. The danger that the report is only too aware of is that, if we simply condemn the very ambition to transcend ethnic and national particularities, the different localities that are clamoring for recognition in the multiculturalist wake of Eurocentrism will remain separated as so many stable, closed-off, sectarian particularities. If we refuse to even attempt to strategically engage the "European" temptation to transcend boundaries in order to open these boundaries to the rest of the world, this may well result in a disabling opposition between distinct cultures that exist fully-formed in splendid isolation from each other. In order to avoid such an impasse, it is necessary not only to explode the alleged self-sufficiency of projects that are explicitly or implicitly Eurocentric, but also to underline the mobility and the fluidity of the multiple perspectives that perform a critique of Europe – not only for commendable political and moral reasons, but also because such a flexible and dynamic picture is much more adequate to describe cultural movement. It is here that the comparatist's commitment to transcending the constraints of his or her culture becomes an advantage. As the 1993 ACLA report notes, "[c]omparatists, known for their propensity to cross over between disciplines, now have expanded opportunities to theorize the nature of the boundaries to be crossed and to participate in their remapping" (43).

In one of the documents that Haun Saussy assembled to function as the multivocal 2004 ACLA report on the state of the discipline, Djelal Kadir expresses his fear that such a fruitful multiplicity of perspectives no longer exists, and that comparative literature is now fatally co-opted by what he refers to as "an age of terrorism." Having moved from Friederich's Marshall Plan-conception of comparative literature to "the era of the Martial Plan," we now find ourselves "beyond the need to domesticate dissensus," as in the United States today "[t]he actual possibility of dissensus itself may be an illusion" (69). While this reign of terror is of course first of all an effect of the United States' National Defense Strategy, Kadir also underlines the close affinity between this terror and the insistence on incomparable difference that the Bernheimer report resisted. Kadir notes that "[i]ncomparability is the dynamic, not of criticism or of comparatistic counterpoint, but a handmaiden of terror. Terror thrives on unbreachable difference, on exceptionalism, on the cultural and political monads that lie beyond the plausibility of dissensus and outside the possibility of the negotiable consensus." Terror, for Kadir, feeds on "the eradication of difference through the hyperbole of self-differentiation into Self-Same" (74). Comparative literature, for Kadir, finds itself immobilized in a globalized world marked by an all-pervasive opposition between those who are "with us" and those who are "against us." Because of the 2004 report's emphasis on the closely connected phenomena of globalization and U.S. militarization, the idea of Europe no longer figures prominently in it, except as a missed opportunity: when David Ferris returns to the 1993 report, he recognizes that Bernheimer's attempt to think a comparative literature beyond Eurocentrism still relied on a right that Europe has traditionally claimed for itself, "the right to compare without restriction" (83). For Ferris, it is not a question of renouncing that right, but rather of understanding the archive of comparative literature as "a constant struggle between the project of comparison and what continues to evade that project, namely, the world" (86). Comparative literature, then, exists in the attempt to negotiate the impossibility of the ambition of boundless comparison. As such, the Eurocentric temptation still holds out the hope for a future comparative literature that will finally be able to "take up the question that the project of comparison has historically been unable to confront, the question of an incomparable impossibility" (94). For Ferris, it is through such contradictions and contaminations that a way beyond the terror of selfsameness can be envisioned.

It is the contention of the present volume that what warrants reflection on the role of Europe in literary studies today, apart from the history which we have told here, is the fact that Europe is readable as such a site of contradiction and self-differentiation, and that it therefore offers a promising place from which to address the challenges facing the study of culture today. That Europe is not as self-identical and as unified as it might once have thought itself – and as its critics who conceive of it as a well-circumscribed target may think – is today perhaps clearer than ever. If we only look at such issues as the concerns about the inclusion of Turkey in the European Union, the social inequality that the enlargement of the Union only seems to make more rampant, and the crisis following the Dutch and French rejection of the European Union draft constitution, it becomes very hard to recognize this reality of division and self-doubt as the powerful, self-contained monolith that Europe is often taken to be. And while this discrepancy may at first seem like the harsh reality check that the postwar dream of European integration was bound to encounter sooner or later, we may well remember that already in 1919 Paul Valéry noted a distinction between what Europe is "in reality" and what it "seems." In reality, Valéry writes, Europe is merely "a little promontory on the continent of Asia"; yet what it *seems* is "the elect portion of the terrestrial globe, the pearl of the sphere, the brain of a vast body" (31). For Valéry, the appearance of Europe's pre-eminence was slowly giving way to the harsh reality of Europe's limited geographical size, but because this opening up of a quantitative perspective was a European achievement, Europe's decline was, for Valéry, paradoxically still a consequence of Europe's "seeming" superiority. The tension between reality and ideality is thus inherent to Valéry's idea of Europe. The current situation, in which the cultural and social unification of Europe lags behind the purely economic achievement of a common European market (Segers and Viehoff 16-17), is then not so much the inversion as the continuation of a tension that already marked the idea of Europe for Valéry.

European unity remains today an "un-actualized" possibility. Without a constitution, uncertain about its borders, deeply divided about its relation to religion, and without an army to defend it, Europe today consists in the tension between simultaneous tendencies toward the local and toward the supernational (Segers and Viehoff 13-15). To the extent that its present make-up differs significantly from that of the United States – where the constitution does serve as a constant touchstone of political practice, where the borders are natural (give or take a crystal frontier), and where talk of one nation under God is made to support pre-emptive attacks on "rogue states" as an appropriate form of defense – and to the extent that it persists in an uneasy tension between centralization and dispersal, the idea of Europe can serve as a figure for the problems that are central to comparative literary studies today. In a commentary from 1990 on Valéry's declaration of Europe's constitutive self-division, Jacques Derrida translated this condition into a double and contradictory injunction. On the one hand, Derrida writes, European cultural identity "cannot and must not be dispersed into a myriad of provinces, into a multiplicity of self-enclosed idioms or petty little nationalisms, each one jealous and untranslatable"; yet, on the other hand, neither must it accept a centralization that would "control and standardize, subjecting artistic discourses and practices to a grid of intelligibility, to philosophical or aesthetic norms, to channels of immediate and efficient communication, to the pursuit of ratings and commercial profitability" (38-39). For Derrida, it is a question of "renouncing neither of these two contradictory imperatives" (44) and of moving beyond a binarist thinking of Europe.

Literature offers a privileged domain where we can test possibilities to respond to Derrida's double injunction. While the study of literature in the last two decades has convincingly demonstrated how literature aids the construction of cultural identities, it has at the same time not forgotten that literature is also often (and perhaps even constitutively) subversive of such attempts to enlist it in the service of the articulation of a distinct identity. Indeed, if it is the constitutive tension the term Europe implies that makes Europe a privileged term through which to approach the question of comparison, it is literature, and the work of reading that it calls for, that can bring out the affinity between Europe's self-difference and the oscillations between universality and locality that define comparative literature. As Gerhard Richter has observed, it is "once we begin to read closely the rhetorical strategies that have been mobilised to engage 'Europe' [that] the concept becomes visible as a site of self-differentiation upon which key questions concerning the shifting relations among power, politics, culture and figurative language converge" (55). Literature's multifarious responses to Europe's double injunction demonstrate in an exemplary way that, as Klaus Eder has remarked, the attempt to realize a European identity simultaneously disenchants the very idea of constructing a collective identity (176).

In this volume, three sets of essays engage the double injunction to rethink Europe. These essays do not assume that Europe is a pre-given essence, nor that abandoning such essentialist thinking means that we can simply dispense with the work of thinking altogether. A first group of contributions opens up the archive of European literature and investigates a number of critical concepts and methodologies that have been coined in order to give shape to the ambition to transcend national borders. These essays show how these transnational ambitions must always be understood in relation to the locality or context from which they hope to depart, but which they never completely succeed in leaving behind. These essays show how the idea of Europe mediates (without resolving) the tension between universalist ambition and irremediable particularity – between cosmopolitanism and national stereotypes in the case of the 18th century genre of the *histoire anglaise* (Vanacker), between the global and the regional in the project of world literature (Damrosch and Boyden), and between Europe and the subnational in the case of Flemish literary history (de Ridder and van Humbeeck). Lieven D'hulst's contribution shows how the concept of translation and the field of translation studies currently present an important new version of the attempt to affirm and to describe the dynamic and fluid relations that hold between different cultural formations.

A second set of essays reminds us that the dialectic between the national and the international that the first group of essays focuses on has itself often served thoroughly Eurocentric ambitions, as our overview of the place of Europe in the history of comparative literature has shown. These essays disturb Europe's comfortable conviction that it has successfully transcended every constraining particularity by confronting it with one or more of its non-European others. By bringing the idea of Europe in a constellation in which it must negotiate its residual particularity, these essays show how non-European critiques and mobilizations of the idea of Europe challenge its exclusionary logic while receiving (and returning) the critical potential that the idea also contains. The essays of Reindert Dhondt and Silvana Mandolessi present Latin American mobilizations of the concept of Europe in the works of Carpentier, Borges, and Gombrowicz, while Mary Stevens and Nagihan Haliloğlu show how Islamic engagements with Europe in their turn manage to contribute to the work of re-thinking the meaning of Europe. Kari van Dijk's essay shows how the work of Yoka Tawada stages a confrontation between Europe and Asia that ends up producing an enriched model of European identity. These essays thus test the capacity of literature to forge models for transnational identity, and of the notion of Europe to contribute to the imagination of such identities.

A third and final group of essays returns from the non-European re-thinking of Europe to cases in which Europe, as it were, re-thinks itself and addresses aspects of its own past in order to retrieve opportunities for future renewal. As such, they take on the task of what Emily Apter, when she characterizes Edward Said's generous return to the avowedly Eurocentric work of Erich Auerbach, has called "[m]ining the humanist tradition for a utopian politics – despite the association of humanism with Eurocentrism and Orientalism" (81). In this "activist" return to Europe's past (80), literature's constitutive self-difference appears not as a failure, but rather as an opportunity to keep the question of cultural identity resolutely open. The essays of Iulius Hondrila and Bart Keunen investigate the logic of literature's contribution to the formation of cultural identity, while the essays of Iannis Goerlandt and Ortwin de Graef more dramatically show how the *reading* of literature reveals literature to be subversive of the dream of coercive identity formation for which it is enlisted. Herbert Grabes' impassioned return to the history of European comparison argues for a renewed engagement with the notion of literary pleasure as an occasion to move beyond the constraints imposed by this history. This is not all that different from Jeppe Ilkjær's explanation in his essay on the work of Elias Canetti of how Europe's constitutive lateness opens up unexpected literary resources. Both Grabes and Ilkjær find in Europe's difference from itself a remainder that holds the promise for a future that demands to be re-thought. It is to this work of re-thinking Europe that this volume hopes to contribute.

Works Cited

Appiah, K. Anthony. "*Geist* Stories." *Comparative Literature in the Age of Multiculturalism*. Ed. Charles Bernheimer. 51-57.

Apter, Emily. *The Translation Zone: A New Comparative Literature*. Princeton: Princeton University Press, 2006.

Aseguinolaza, Fernando Cabo. "Dead, or a Picture of Good Health? Comparatism, Europe, and World Literature." *Comparative Literature* 58.2 (2006): 418-35.

Bassnett, Susan. *Comparative Literature: A Critical Introduction*. Oxford: Blackwell, 1993.

Bernheimer, Charles, ed. *Comparative Literature in the Age of Multiculturalism*. Baltimore: Johns Hopkins University Press, 1995.

Bernheimer, Charles. "Introduction: The Anxieties of Comparison." *Comparative Literature in the Age of Multiculturalism*. Ed. Charles Bernheimer. 1-17.

Chow, Rey. "The Old/New Question of Comparison in Literary Studies: A Post-European Perspective." *ELH* 71.2 (2004): 289-311.

Derrida, Jacques. *The Other Heading: Reflections on Today's Europe*. Trans. Pascale-Anne Brault and Michael Naas. Bloomington: Indiana University Press, 1992.

Eder, Klaus. "Integration durch Kultur? Das Paradox der Suche nach einer europäischen Identität." *Kultur, Identität, Europa*. Ed. Reinhold Viehoff and Rien Segers. 147-79.

Ferris, David. "Indiscipline." *Comparative Literature in an Age of Globalization*. Ed. Haun Saussy. 78-99.

Friederich, Werner. *The Challenge of Comparative Literature and Other Addresses*. Ed. William J. DeSua and David H. Malone. Chapel Hill: University of North Carolina Press, 1970.

Kadir, Djelal. "Comparative Literature in an Age of Terrorism." *Comparative Literature in an Age of Globalization*. Ed. Haun Saussy. 68-77.

Reese-Schäfer, Walter. "Supranationale oder transnationale Identität: Zwei Modelle kultureller Integration in Europa." *Kultur, Identität, Europa*. Ed. Reinhold Viehoff and Rien Segers. 253-66.

Richter, Gerhard. "Sites of Indeterminacy and the Spectres of Eurocentrism." *Culture, Theory, and Critique* 43.1 (2002): 51-65.

Saussy, Haun, ed. *Comparative Literature in an Age of Globalization*. Baltimore: Johns Hopkins University Press, 2006.

Segers, Rien and Reinhold Viehoff. "Die Konstruktion Europas: Überlegungen zum Problem der Kultur in Europa." *Kultur, Identität, Europa*. Ed. Reinhold Viehoff and Rien Segers. 9-49.

Suleiman, Susan Rubin. "Introduction: The Idea of Europe." *Comparative Literature* 58.2 (2006): 267-70.

"The Bernheimer Report, 1993: Comparative Literature at the Turn of the Century." *Comparative Literature in the Age of Multiculturalism*. Ed. Charles Bernheimer. 39-48.

"The Greene Report, 1975: A Report on Standards." *Comparative Literature in the Age of Multiculturalism*. Ed. Charles Bernheimer. 28-38.

"The Levin Report, 1965: Report on Professional Standards." *Comparative Literature in the Age of Multiculturalism*. Ed. Charles Bernheimer. 21-27.

Valéry, Paul. "The Crisis of the Mind." *History and Politics*. Trans. Denise Folliot and Jackson Matthews. New York, Bollingen Foundation, 1962, 23-36.

Viehoff, Reinhold and Rien Segers, eds. *Kultur, Identität, Europa: Über die Schwierigkeiten und Möglichkeiten einer Konstruktion*. Frankfurt am Main: Suhrkamp, 1999.

PART I

―――――

Beyond the Nation?
Inter-, Trans-, and Hypernational Identities

Matthijs de Ridder (University of Antwerp)

Europeanism in One Country: August Vermeylen, Paul van Ostaijen, and the International Approach to Nationalism

In September 1916, the Flemish poet Paul van Ostaijen (1896-1928) wrote the following: "The most important duty of Flanders is to stay closely in touch with the youngest phase of the European evolution. [...] We have to stay informed, and therefore our first and foremost task is to change our national focus: less history, more future" (14).[1] Van Ostaijen refers to the new generation of German expressionist artists who gathered in magazines like *Die Weißen Blätter* and *Die Aktion* and wrote about the First World War as the beginning of a new era. Until then, the self-conscious Flemish nationalist Van Ostaijen had primarily been confronted with a different approach. The dominant discourse in the Flemish Movement was not focused on a new future, but rather on the restoration of a historical situation. In this traditional view, Flanders is pictured as a nation with a proud (medieval) history, which finds itself on the verge of inevitable regeneration. This sense of inevitability was – to a certain extent – the big seller of Flemish nationalism. In the years prior to World War One, it caused an unprecedented enthusiasm throughout the population for causes that concerned only a small percentage of the people, such as the adoption of the Flemish language at the university of Ghent. This only seemed possible because of the infectious and unambiguous optimism that accompanied this political program. In the newspapers, a modest manifestation would be eagerly depicted as a demonstration of a determined army and an even moderately successful rally would often be called a great victory in the Flemish Battle. Criticism within the Flemish Movement of its policy or the effect of this policy on Belgian politics was very scarce indeed. People who did criticize the movement were immediately accused of 'unflemish' behavior. While the lack of real criticism and the undiscriminating support for everything the movement produced resulted in a relatively high number of supporters, this situation also paralyzed the movement completely, for it left no space for discussion, let alone for a different approach to the problems at hand.

---

1   All translations from the Dutch are the author's.

The First World War changed everything. Mass manifestations were history. The main concern of the majority of the Flemish population was the German occupation. Most of the former leaders of the Flemish Movement remained relatively silent, and those who continued writing articles on the issue either argued in favor of a temporary 'cease-fire' or became more radical, to the point where they became separatists. In this different landscape, some youngsters took the opportunity to launch a different kind of *flamingantisme*, of sympathy for the Flemish Movement. In the midst of the war, in 1916, Paul van Ostaijen argued that his generation should reconsider its nationalism. Would they be nationalists just because their predecessors had made it seem self-evident to be nationalist? Should they fight for the emancipation of Flanders just because they were Flemish? Van Ostaijen argued that they should not. They first had to analyze the situation for themselves and then had to come up with solutions of their own. Although their first and foremost concern remained the emancipation of the Flemish people, the outcome of this generation's political analysis differed greatly from that of the analysis of their predecessors. According to Van Ostaijen, Flemish emancipation, autonomy, or even independence should not be the final goal of the movement. It would only be the first step in the process of becoming a self-conscious entity within Europe. It was in order to be able to join the international brotherhood of peoples that one should be allowed to know, love, and express one's own identity.

Van Ostaijen's reflections appear to be a quite drastic renovation of the traditional position of the Flemish Movement; indeed, why would Van Ostaijen, and with him an entire generation of Flemish writers, not only try to update Flemish nationalism, but also attempt to turn it into a form of internationalism at the same time? And subsequently, did they in fact do so? To answer these questions, we will first have to look at the essays of Van Ostaijen's main inspiration, the Flemish writer and essayist August Vermeylen (1872-1945), who introduced the European perspective for the Flemish Movement some twenty years earlier in his (albeit with some delay) influential "Critique of the Flemish Movement" (1896). In this text, Vermeylen not only introduced an international view on national politics, he initiated a whole different way of thinking as well. In contrast with the dominant discourse in the Flemish Movement, Vermeylen put aside the logic of inevitable regeneration and came up with a philosophy of transition instead.

This philosophy was loosely inspired by Hegel's triadic pattern of the human experience. In its most abstract form this pattern looks something like this (read this from left to right and from the bottom up):

                reason
consciousness   self-consciousness

or:

              absolute spirit
subjective spirit   objective spirit

In Hegel's dialectic the opposition between thesis and anti-thesis results in a synthesis. Subsequently, this same synthesis can start to function as the first term (the thesis) in a new triad, enabling ever new syntheses to be made. On the highest level, the pattern would eventually lead to a state of absolute spirit. Although Hegel was not an evolutionist at all, some of his (left wing) followers turned his dialectic into a path of evolution. Famous examples are the path "history-present-future" or "childhood-youth-adulthood." This last schema was used by the 'left Hegelian' Max Stirner who divided the history of humanity in the following three parts in his book *Der Einzige und sein Eigentum* (*The Ego and his Own*, 1844):

nature – spiritual age/epoch of the tyranny of Ideas – egotism/absolute freedom of the individual

Mankind was believed to find itself in the second stage of this three-way evolution and had yet to reach the phase of absolute freedom. In Stirner's view, the individual should in fact be in-dividual, indivisible. No religion, nationalism, nor institution should supersede the individual.

Stirner's extreme adaptation of Hegel had a great influence on Vermeylen's writings. Vermeylen used Stirner's three-way evolution of the human being as an analogy for the history of the Flemish Movement. In his view the movement had had its brief moment of childhood, followed by the phase of self-consciousness or, in the Stirnerian terms used by Vermeylen, the romantic age. In 1896 Vermeylen found the Flemish Movement stuck in this phase, with no real signs of progress. His "Critique" was meant to make a difference in this respect. Although Vermeylen showed a lot of respect for his (literary) predecessors who had shown "character" in the necessary romantic phase (47), he argued that the period of meaningless slogans was over. The Flemish Movement now badly needed absolutely free individuals who would not try to cure the negative *effects* of their suppression, but rather the actual *causes* of oppression itself. For instance: for years and years the movement had been focused on language and language alone. During the 19th century, Dutch was not allowed in administration, law, education, and so on. But the inequality of languages in Belgium was only the effect of a fundamentally corrupt system. It would therefore be foolish to fight for the adoption of Dutch as an official language, if that would only mean that, as a result of this so-called victory, the Flemish laborer would now be suppressed in his own language. The fact itself that he was being suppressed, was, of course, the main issue. Vermeylen's main concern was the freedom of the individual, and in his Stirnerian view, this individual freedom was absolute. No philosophy or belief system, let alone an institution such as the state, could overrule the integrity of the individual.

Vermeylen's philosophy is fundamentally anarchistic and essentially incompatible with nationalism. Yet, his pamphlet was not meant as a piece of criticism from an outsider. In fact, he had no intention whatsoever to criticize the Flemish Movement as such. He condoned this nationalistic movement and even placed himself within its boundaries. He too was a nationalist, or at least someone who was concerned about the social and cultural position of the average Flemish individual. The main difference between Vermeylen and the traditional Flemish Movement was the direction they thought improvement should take. Traditionally, the nationalists were focused on history: the restoration of the past was believed to bring about a better future. In Vermeylen's view, this would literally mean that Flanders would take a step back in time and even in evolution. Instead of returning from the "Epoch of the Tyranny of Ideas" to the era of ignorance, Vermeylen argued that his people should take a leap into the phase of "egotism." Or, in plain English, to the phase in which the world would no longer be reigned by moral or economic powers, but by clusters of organically united and absolutely free individuals.

Four years after his "Critique of the Flemish Movement," the man who argued against meaningless slogans summed it all up in one powerful slogan of his own: "To be something, we should be Flemish. We should be Flemish in order to become Europeans" (170). While over the years this slogan has arguably become rather meaningless itself, it remains as intriguing as it was on the verge of the 20th century. Compact as it is, it still bears the Stirnerian scheme in it. One should in fact first be something if one wants to be able to become something else. At the time when Vermeylen published his essays, this 'something else' proved to be a major issue. The idea of becoming something that superseded the Flemish identity was revolutionary enough to provoke numerous furious reactions. In the view of the more romantic forces of the Flemish Movement, Vermeylen and his co-workers were degenerate. And ever since, they have been known as posh cosmopolitans with no apparent bond with Flanders. In a way, this is not even an exaggeration: Vermeylen would not have shed a tear if he had been forced to say goodbye to the Belgian state and he did not care much for a republic of Flanders either. He had a more or less universal view on the world. But at the same time, it is a bit odd that this alleged degenerate cosmopolitan not only narrows the cosmos down to the earth, but further all the way down to Europe. Apparently not every individual was fit to join the unity of individuals.

This observation is not that striking when we look at it from a Hegelian perspective. According to Hegel, one could only reach the final phase of absolute spirit as a result of the clash between the subjective and the objective spirit. Europe was virtually on the verge of the stage of reason, but large parts of the world were thought to be unable to even get to this point, for they were supposedly lacking the basic conditions. These regions were unhistorical. Africa, for instance, could not be fit into Hegel's scheme at all. In Hegel's view, the people in the inlands were still savages, and while the people in the coastal areas might be more civilized, their culture was imported from Europe. Hegel believed Africans to have no culture of their own and to be unable to develop. The exception to the rule – the civilized African – had, in a way, become European, and could not lift his continent out of its misery either (Bernasconi).

This Eurocentric view was quite common in the 19th century. Moses Hess for instance – like Max Stirner a 'left Hegelian' and someone who had a great influence on the young Karl Marx – situated his utopian and prophetic socialism explicitly in a European context. Moreover, Hess is the author of what is perhaps the most extreme pro-European statement the world has ever seen:

> Europe is a holy sanctuary [...] there is no other land like it on earth! Like Christ, its model, Europe has sacrificed itself for mankind. It has had to drink deeply of the cup of sorrows. It is still livid, and the blood still trickles from its wounds. – But, in three days, it will celebrate its resurrection! [...] One More Day like the first two, and Christ's victory in the history of the world will have been achieved! Roman-German Europe is the chosen continent and stands under God's special protection [...] it is the apple of God's eye, the center from which the destiny of the world is directed. (quoted in Kouvelakis 126-27)

August Vermeylen was far too down to earth for this kind of fanaticism. Besides, the predestination of Europe as the Promised Land was largely incompatible with the philosophy of his main inspiration, the left Hegelian and individual anarchist Max Stirner, who argued that no Idea, not even that of Europe, should supersede the individual. Still, in his texts Vermeylen does seem to adapt the idea of the privileged position of Europe. As broad-minded as he was, his idea of a unity of organically grown communities could only exist within a European context – although Hegel's and Hess's prediction that the classical triarchy of Germany, France, and Great Britain would lead Europe to its destiny of an earthly paradise could not serve Vermeylen's program: he faced the classical opposition in the Flemish Movement between the Roman and the Germanic world, where France was considered the archenemy of the Flemish, whereas Germany was one of its most obvious allies. Great Britain, for its part, was the odd one out: England was of course part of the Germanic axis, but had discredited itself by starting a war against the (more or less) Dutch-speaking Boers in South Africa.

In Vermeylen's view, these traditional alliances and hostilities were part of a rather paralyzing romantic discourse that the Flemish Movement had to abolish. In the same vein, he thought it unwise for the Flemish to close their eyes to the cultural achievements of French artists, while on the other hand he argued that Flanders' natural bond with Germany had to be reconsidered. Although the *Heimat* of Hegel and Stirner had dominated the 19th century with outstanding art and philosophers of great importance, by the end of the century it had become the home of industrialism and militarism. Moreover, late 19th century Germany seemed to be heavily influenced by the United States of America and had thus lost its position as a European role model (Vermeylen 53). The only truly organic community that Vermeylen deemed possible was the Flemish-Dutch community. He believed that this was the largest unity that could exist within the utopian United Peoples of Europe. Vermeylen's internationalism, then, was still rather local. Although he foresaw a completely different world, in which there was no place for a repressive state, he believed that the newborn, free, and international individual would be very likely to form alliances only with its close neighbors.

Vermeylen's ideas shocked the bigger part of the Flemish Movement when they were first published in 1896. The "Critique of the Flemish Movement" was considered to be too radical and – even worse – untraditional. But how modern was Vermeylen, really? His ideas were rooted deeply in the tradition of German Idealism and showed no real influence of Karl Marx's critique of these fundamentally metaphysical philosophies. He also seemed to deny the arrival of the industrialized age. Should we then say that *even* Vermeylen was not ready to accept the devastating experience of the modern *time out of joint* just yet? Instead, he criticized the new, far too industrialized Germany (once the *Heimat* of great art and important thinkers) and kept dreaming of an organic society within an irreversibly industrialized world. In his own "enlightened" way, Vermeylen was, while certainly radical, also still rather idealistic (see Humbeeck, *Geschiedenis* 427). Nevertheless, after the publication of the "Critique of the Flemish Movement" he found himself two steps ahead of the movement which he had left behind in confusion. But what had proven to be far too great a leap for the Flemish Movement seemed only a small step from a European perspective. It is, for instance, striking to see that Vermeylen, who proclaimed internationalism and considered himself to be a socialist, operated in almost complete isolation; his ideas seemed to be too progressive for the Flemish people and too exclusively Flemish for the rest of Europe. Moreover, there are no accounts of attempts by the internationalist Vermeylen to join the broader scene of international socialism.[2]

---

2   In comparison: the Dutch novelist and utopian thinker Frederik van Eeden, who shared the disadvantage of the marginality of his mother tongue with Vermeylen, was acquainted with many important left wing artists such as Romain Rolland and Upton Sinclair, and some leading politicians, such as Karl Kautsky.

In 1916, twenty years after Vermeylen's text, little had changed, and the new generation's version of Vermeylen's ideas still sounded fresh and 'new' to Flemish ears. Just like Vermeylen, Paul van Ostaijen and the members of his peer group confronted a rather isolated and complacent movement that was in need of modernization. Since nothing had really changed, Vermeylen's texts still seemed useful for these youngsters. There was only one problem: during the Great War the two kindred spirits Vermeylen and Van Ostaijen fought – so to speak – on different sides, as the war divided the Flemish Movement in two parts. On the one hand there were people who thought it wiser not to fight for Flemish rights as long as the country was occupied – the so-called 'passivists.' On the other hand there were people who argued that they had no obligations towards the kingdom of Belgium and therefore had no reasons to put their struggle on hold. Some of these so-called 'activists' were even willing to collaborate with the Germans. Van Ostaijen, as most young poets, was an activist, whereas Vermeylen was a self-proclaimed passivist.

It could be argued that Van Ostaijen's adaptation of Vermeylen's ideas was very consistent indeed. If you follow the "Critique" to the letter, it makes no difference which regime you are facing, as all regimes are equally corrupt. This is the way we should look at Van Ostaijen's early writings, because only then can we understand why he neglects the horror of the military violence and why he writes about the importance of poetry in mid-war. Along the same lines as Vermeylen, Van Ostaijen argued in favor of the internationalization of the Flemish Movement, in favor of a new Flemish literature (a literature on a European level), and finally he argued against the repressive state. The main distinction between the two seems to be a difference between generations. August Vermeylen was very much a product of the 19th century, whereas Van Ostaijen embraced the new art of what we now call the historical avant-garde. While the philosophical influence of the latter was not very different from that of Vermeylen and company, the way this philosophical input was transformed into literature differed quite strongly. Both in terms of content and form, Van Ostaijen's new poetry became more and more radical. In contrast with the aesthetical principles of Vermeylen's literary work, Van Ostaijen's early poetical program is very political or 'pragmatic' indeed. One might even say that his poetological ideas root in his political ideal.

Elsewhere, this political and poetical project has been captured by the term 'activism' (Humbeeck, "God geve"; Buelens and De Ridder).

For Van Ostaijen, the First World War had uncovered the fiercely mechanized and fundamentally corrupt nature of the 20th century. It had underlined the destructive force of imperialism and emphasized the importance of the internationalization of the nationalist movements. The Russian Revolution and the peace negotiations in Versailles seemed to be two promising attempts to come up with a persistent solution. And there was even more good news: the young Flemish poet moved from Antwerp to the center of modern Europe, although not deliberately. Van Ostaijen's political activism forced him to flee the country just a few weeks prior to the armistice of 11 November 1918. The young poet went to Berlin, capital of the aggressor and center of the avant-garde, where he came into contact with at least part of the international avant-garde. He became friends with the expressionist painter Fritz Stuckenberg, attended at least one meeting of the German Communist Party, and witnessed the Spartakist Uprising in January 1919. One might say that Van Ostaijen went to the right place at the right time. In Berlin he had access to the international center of both arts and politics. Still, he did not turn into the international revolutionary one might have expected him to become. Although he had tasted the flavor of proletarian uprising and had dipped his toe into the pool of communism, Van Ostaijen remained a mere spectator to the world revolution. At the same time his writings became as political as they would ever get.

During his stay in Berlin, Van Ostaijen's work dealt almost exclusively with Flemish politics. One of the texts he wrote in Berlin is a rather elaborate overview of Flemish nationalist politics after the Great War. The article is entitled "About the Flemish Problem." It was written in September 1920 and published in the communist review *De Nieuwe Tijd* (*The New Era*) in February 1921. In this article, Van Ostaijen shows his sympathy for the communist revolution – as a hard-boiled bolshevist he even defends the Soviet Russian campaign to install Soviets in Poland. According to Van Ostaijen the campaign could not be seen as an instance of foreign aggression, for nationality was no issue for the bolshevists; it was, in fact, the liberation of the Polish proletariat. No foreign power or language was forced upon the Polish people; the Polish revolution was, in other words, nothing less than a blessing for an oppressed nation.

We now know that this is a rather romantic view on the Soviet Russian version of communism. What is even more remarkable is that Van Ostaijen does not seem to care a whole lot about the European revolution. He does not express the wish that the Russians would come and rescue the Flemish as well, nor does he reflect on the possibility of an actual, unprovoked revolution. Just like August Vermeylen, Paul van Ostaijen narrows international politics down to the local movement. And in this case the result of the process is rather astonishing. Van Ostaijen in so many words urges the Flemish communists not to focus too much on the world revolution, but to concentrate on the struggle of the Flemish proletariat. He moreover considers the radicalized Flemish Movement to be revolutionary in itself:

> Communism will find a collaborating force of great importance in the flemish movement, in terms of spreading the communist idea in Flanders. [...] The Flemish have been awakened from their quietism as a result of the suppression. The flemish movement has become a revolutionary force. (125)

The idea of Flemish internationalism seems to have been inverted here. Instead of viewing Flemish emancipation as the first phase in the quest for a Communist Federal Republic of Europe ("we should be Flemish in order to become Europeans"), this international project is now asked to be of aid for a local cause ("let's not become Europeans yet, since we are still not Flemish"). This does not mean that Van Ostaijen completely abolishes the idea of a Communist Europe. A united Europe remains his final ideal. But in the meantime, it is really a matter of what is most likely to happen. The European revolution seemed too far away and, thus, Van Ostaijen opted – as an opportunistic Stalin *avant-la-lettre* – for Europeanism in one country: "The essential point is: 1) to convince the Flemish of the fact that they cannot count on the present european conjuncture; 2) to convince the communists not to neglect the flemish problem in Flanders" (126).

Both August Vermeylen and Paul van Ostaijen made important attempts to broaden the scope of the Flemish Movement. They tried to open up to the future the eyes of those who had been staring at the past for too long. On both occasions this attempt met with strong resistance. The explicit rejection of a paralyzing tradition combined with an explicitly international focus resulted in accusations of 'high treason.' Yet we must not forget that their internationalism was ultimately not all that international. First of all, their internationalism was deeply rooted in an elitist (Hegelian) concept of the evolution of mankind, which resulted in a Eurocentric vision (although the Greek and Icelandic proletariat, to name only those, were probably the least of their concerns). Second, both Flemish intellectuals were primarily occupied with typically Flemish issues, which kept them from teaming up with foreign movements. They probably did not have a whole lot to offer, either. As the Flemish nation was, in their view, not yet fit to play a role on a European level, their internationalism was mainly designed to have an effect on a national level, as a broad-minded antidote for a popular *Blut und Boden* discourse.

There is an ironic epilogue to this story. The first real attempt to internationalize the Flemish Movement was made by *Internacia*, a magazine that was founded in 1930 as a Flemish reaction to the celebration of the hundredth birthday of Belgium. This magazine was published in five languages, including Esperanto, and was meant to raise support for the Flemish Movement abroad. What began as a 'left wing' initiative, gradually changed into a forum of the extreme right. As from 1933 *Internacia* was called *De Aanval* (*The Attack*, after the German paper *Der Angriff*) and became the most vehement anti-Semitic review in Flanders. Europeanism suddenly meant something completely different.

Works Cited

Bernasconi, Robert. "Hegel at the Court of the Ashanti." *Hegel after Derrida*. Ed. Stuart Barnett. London and New York: Routledge, 1998. 41-64.

Buelens, Geert and Matthijs de Ridder. "''t Is allemaal een boeltje': Over activisme, frontisme, zaktivisme, arrivisme, neo-activisme, Vlaamsch idealisme, jusqu'auboutisme, Nieuw-Aktivisme, post-activisme en naoorlogs activisme." *De trust der vaderlandsliefde: Literatuur en Vlaamse Beweging 1890-1940*. Ed. Geert Buelens, Matthijs de Ridder, and Jan Stuyck. Antwerpen: AMVC-Letterenhuis, 2005. 162-98.

Humbeeck, Kris. *Geschiedenis, een roman: De komst van de trein in de Nederlandse letteren*. Wilrijk: Universitaire Instelling Antwerpen, 1991.

———. "'God geve dat wij Staatsgevaarlik wezen!': *Mijn kleine oorlog* en de retoriek van het linkse activisme." *Avantgarde! Voorhoede? Vernieuwingsbewegingen in Noord en Zuid opnieuw beschouwd*. Ed. Hubert F. van den Berg and Gillis J. Dorleijn. Nijmegen: Vantilt, 2002. 103-12.

Kouvelakis, Stathis. *Philosophy and Revolution: From Kant to Marx*. London and New York: Verso, 2003.
Stirner, Max. *Der Einzige und sein Eigentum*. Stuttgart: Reclam, 2003.
Van Ostaijen, Paul. *Verzameld werk 4: Proza: Besprekingen en beschouwingen*. Amsterdam: Bert Bakker, 1979.
Vermeylen, August. *Verzameld werk: Tweede deel*. Brussel: Manteau, 1951.

Beatrijs Vanacker (K.U.Leuven)

The *Histoire anglaise*: Towards a Cosmopolitan View of the Other?

In Montesquieu's *Réflexions sur la monarchie universelle en Europe* from 1727, we read the following:

> Europe is no more than a Nation made up of several others; France and England need the affluence of Poland and Moscow, just as any one of their provinces needs the others: and the State which thinks to increase its power by ruining neighboring states normally diminishes along with them. (quoted in Michaud 5)

As Montesquieu's words already indicate, the European dream was, to a certain extent, already conceivable in the age of Enlightenment, long before the concept was concretized by the emergence of a European Union. Yet, when we take a closer look, questions about the nature and the extent of this early modern sense of 'Europeanness' soon arise. If in the 18th century a certain cosmopolitan breeze did flow through various European courts, it was generally based on the somewhat selective logic of "a shared cultural space that favored exchanges within an enlightened community of educated aristocrats, writers, and scientists" (Fontana 119). And besides the explicitly elitist nature of 18th century cosmopolitanism, its importance was furthermore restricted by the existence of diametrically opposed nationalist tendencies. Biancamaria Fontana remarks that "'European' did not mean anything other than French, English, Spanish and so on. In the collective imagination of the century, European nations were separate entities, connected by close commercial and cultural exchanges but still divided by economic, dynastic and territorial rivalries" (119). More than that of other 'nations,' it was primarily the position of France that was of particular interest in this interplay of antagonistic powers. Although it had dominated the continent for a long time, in passing through a profound identity-crisis in the 18th century, France gradually came to acknowledge that the period of its political and intellectual hegemony was coming to an end. If in 1784, the academy of Berlin still raised the question of "what had made French the universal language in Europe" (Hazard 230), the rise of other political and cultural centers forced France to reposition itself.

Among these new centers, England soon revealed itself as one of Europe's new crucial poles of attraction. And instead of counteracting the fashionable Anglomania, the French rather "accepted, invited and celebrated it" (Hazard 243), thereby seemingly contributing to Europe's liberation from French supremacy. In the literary field, this shift from a dominant position to an apparently more humble and cosmopolitan attitude gave rise to an exchange of literary models and features between France and England, especially regarding the well-publicized 'rise of the novel.'[1] It is partly through this interaction that French and English writers to a certain extent *co*-constructed the new genre on both sides of the Channel. Simultaneously, this dynamic of mutual influences also generated, or at least intensified, another play of cultural interfaces: throughout the 18th century, both nations often founded the (re-)construction of their national identity on (their own perception of) their neighbors on the other side of the Channel.

Besides the amount of non-fictional writings on national character, this identity-building became, in its turn, a constituent aspect of novel writing.[2] Especially in France, literature took part in the *Anglomanie*-movement which dominated the country throughout most of the 18th century. In the first decades of the century, the admiration for English culture expressed itself in translations from English novels. However, these translations were often very 'frenchifying,' since most of the translators adapted the novels' so-called 'Englishness' to French taste. In the second half of the century other – one could say parasitical – literary phenomena made their appearance. While at first French authors confined their anglophile literary practice to "spurious translations from the English" (Grieder 55), from the eighties onwards one can distinguish a sudden increase of what seemed at first sight an even more far-reaching imitation of English literature, the *histoires anglaises*. This 'genre'[3] not only claimed to imitate certain poetological features pecu-

---

[1] To name but a few of these literary models, we can mention the model of the *roman-mémoires*, the vogue of sentimental epistolary fiction, the gothic novel, or the autobiographic novel, which was heavily influenced by Rousseau's *Confessions*.

[2] See David Fausset: "Stereotyping is one manifestation of the process by which cultures are constructed or demarcated, a process in which literary activity plays a role along with other forms of communication. Not only that, but literature makes this process of construction often its explicit object of interest, or theme" (133).

[3] Throughout the 18th century, some 25 *histoires anglaises* were published in France.

liar to 18th century English prose fiction, such as the emphatic attention to social detail, but it was also presented to the readers as a genuine re-creation of English character. While written by avowedly French pens and specifically intended for a French public, the stories were (mostly) set in England and often staged English narrators. Through the eyes of these narrators, the reader was supposedly allowed a direct view on specific English mores and manners.

As such, however, the *histoires anglaises* seemed to be founded on a fundamental tension. On the one hand, by the very fact that these stories pretended to be exponents – or at least (trust-)worthy imitations – of English literature, they presumed the capacity to embody English fiction. As was already announced by their use of the label *histoire anglaise*, French authors claimed to write their novels *à l'anglaise*, which implied both the adoption of literary features and the depiction of true Englishness. Thus without any real ground or justification, these novelists presented their external perspective as an introspective insight, in accordance with some sort of *contrat de lecture*, an implicit literary agreement, whereby author and reader agreed to act as if they were writing or reading an English story. This generally 'unspoken' rhetorical practice finds its most explicit expression in some notes by Madame de Bournon-Mallarme, one of the most prolific writers of *histoires anglaises*. More than once she openly encouraged her readers to take part in the fictional imposture by pretending to read the French text in English. So we read in one of her novels: "One should take into consideration that it is an English peasant woman who is talking; she calls Mlle de Beauchamps 'Miss,' since that is the expression which is commonly used. Mlle de Beauchamps and her mother speak English reasonably well" (*Milady Lindsey* 146). Yet on the other hand, given the fact that the stories were actually written in French instead of English, the *difference* and *distance* between French and English culture and literature, which were masked by the explicitly English setting of the stories, was never wholly eliminated. And so, despite its claim to Englishness, the *histoire anglaise* as such always seemed to include a certain tension between voice (French) and point of view (English). Moreover, as I will try to develop in this article, one could even consider this very discrepancy a

---

Whether or not to consider these novels as a genre *in stricto sensu* is a question that remains to be solved but that will not concern me here.

fundamental feature of the genre, through which, paradoxically, the very impossibility of its project is revealed.

Whether this literary construct of the other – this "hetero-image" (Leerssen 271) imposed *upon* the English while presenting itself as an "auto-image" coming *from* the English – had any relation to how the English *really* were or with the way they saw themselves is quite a hazardous issue that falls outside the scope of this article. How, after all, does one measure 'real' Englishness? The main question that will occupy me in this essay is rather whether the intensive contact with actual English culture could have softened the prevailing stigmatizing and simplistic fictional image of the Englishman, a depiction that was still widely spread at the beginning of the 18th century and that primarily implied the essential *difference* between the constructed other and the – equally constructed – French self. Did fiction still adhere to the binary representations that were so widespread at the beginning of the century, opposing 'gay' and 'refined' Frenchmen to 'melancholic' and 'brutal' Englishmen, or had it managed to release itself from this dichotomous cultural framework? Furthermore, did French prose fiction, by the end of the century, use devices (such as certain characters or tropes) in order to conceive of the idea of a transnational identity, to the extent that cultural differences between English and French identity could be transcended or at least minimized?

Josephine Grieder suggests such a progressive scheme in her monograph *Anglomania in France* (1985), when she claims:

> Disengaging from the fiction of these five decades their individual assessments will demonstrate, nevertheless, an evolution. The clichés appear, but largely in the earlier novels [...] Most important, the shift in values effected by the quasi-philosophy of sentimentality applauds qualities seen as distinctively British. By the eighties, the English have become moral models on whom the French might do well to pattern themselves. (83)

Following these assumptions, one could thus argue that it should be particularly in the *histoires anglaises*, most of which were published when this alleged evolution was nearly completed, that the shift in English identity-building becomes apparent. Yet, even if these stories do (or ought to) represent a more genuine attempt at imitation in comparison with earlier anglicized fictional writing (because of the internal point of view they claim), this analysis of four *histoires anglaises* allows me to present an alternative to Grieder's somewhat too straightforward evolutionary logic. I have chosen four works which were all written at the culmination of the Anglomania-movement: two *histoires anglaises* written by Mme de Bournon-Mallarme, *Mémoires de Clarence Welldone* (1780) and *Lettres de Milady Lindsey* (1780), and two works written by Mme Beccary, *Milord d'Ambi* (1778) and *Mémoires de Fanni Spingler* (1781). Moreover, all four works took part in the upcoming vogue of sentimental fiction, which, as Grieder points out, is also supposed to have played a distinctive role in 'softening' the image of the cultural other.[4]

As far as the 'Englishness' of the novels is concerned, one could argue that it is presented, on a highly superficial level, by a certain imitation of the features French readers generally attributed to 'real' English literature. Conforming to the widespread model of Samuel Richardson's *Clarissa* (1747), the novels consist of love stories in a polyphonic epistolary form; they demonstrate a special attention to the depiction of different classes and social detail; and they are charged with a moral message. Especially in the two novels by Mme de Bournon, the introduction of social details seems to provide the love stories with a more authentic English setting based on well-known places, such as Wauxhall and Hyde Park in London, which is markedly different from earlier *histoires anglaises*, where a realistic setting was hardly an issue. Indeed, in the first decades of Anglomania, the geographical surroundings were only referred to by means of the superficial name-dropping of toponyms such as London or Bath.

Still, these various allusions to a so-called typically English atmosphere contribute all the more to a very stereotypical and depreciative perspective on the English national character. Even though the "strange spectacle" (Bournon, *Welldone* 44) of these public places is much appreciated by the characters, they are also often linked to depravity. It is in Wauxhall that Clarence Welldone is chased by drunken English rakes, whose vulgar attitude is repeatedly underscored: "They [the rakes] asked us *in a very familiar tone* the permission to provide us with dinner; and as we refused to do so, they took the liberty of using *very rude words*. We moved away, [but] they were

---

4   Since the sentimental character of these novels generates a very 'traditional' plot, featuring innocent female protagonists whose happiness is threatened by the inconstancy of their male antagonists, I will make few distinctions between the different novels in the following analysis and treat them as a single corpus.

still following us, while assuring us that they would get their revenge for our dishonesty" (46, italics are mine). Hyde Park, for its part, is the scene where a secondary female character is kidnapped by another rake, who is "coincidentally" related to Clarence's pursuers. If in these cases the pejorative *mise en scène* arguably still remains rather subtle, it becomes more overt when the heroine of the novel visits the local theatre and the evening ends the same way as it did in earlier French fiction ... with a fight *à la manière anglaise*, a fist-fight. And even if the heroine, born from English parents but having spent most of her youth in France, points out that she does not have any strong opinions on this kind of behavior, she does mention her astonishment at the "strange liberty" which drives "the English crowd,[5] and even people of a certain distinction, to such indecent behavior" (116).[6] These quotes already show us that the general representation of English manners in some allegedly "mature" *histoires anglaises* still turns out to be remarkably similar to earlier accounts through its simplistic and stigmatizing tone.

Besides, as the story of Clarence Welldone indicates, a certain number of *histoires anglaises* represent, instead of a strictly English list of characters, also some French, or at least 'frenchified' protagonists. It thus becomes clear that the introspective point of view, which was supposed to be a constituent feature of this type of novels, is not always faithfully adhered to. More than once, the French point of view out of which the genre in fact emerged shines through the English setting, which reveals that the novel was written in a cultural system that apparently had still not entirely freed itself from its Anglophobic character. Still, this double cultural perspective, and the fact that the authors exclusively use French, do not seem to pose a challenge to the label "*histoire anglaise*." We could even state – and I will elaborate on this below – that it is mostly in these 'hybrid' *histoires anglaises*, which feature both

---

[5] The original French expression "la populace anglaise" expresses more clearly the character's contempt for this people. All translations from the French are the author's.

[6] Another example of a stigmatizing approach to English manners is to be found in Bournon-Mallarmé's "Milady Lindsey," where the (French) protagonist shows a certain disdain for the insolent attitude of the chevalier Wesper: "This is the chevalier Wesper. He made a deep bow in the most ungracious manner. Kiss him, my friend, kiss him, my uncle shouted. I presented my cheek with some reluctance. He had the boldness to press his lips against mine. I was extremely irritated, but my uncle assured me that it was an English custom. Oh mother, I will never adopt this habit!" (32).

English and French characters, that the representation of Englishness – in its relation to the French character – really becomes a theme, as they explicitly depict cultural interactions between the two nations.

Still, these contacts are generally represented in terms of radical and insuperable 'difference' and 'otherness,' and not as an occasion for "a happy shedding of prejudice" (97), as Grieder puts it. According to her, by the end of the Anglomania-movement, most novels referring to English culture divulge a cosmopolitan atmosphere, where the French and the English can be seen as sharing the same values and convictions. And indeed, only a few years before the publication of Bournon's and Beccary's novels, this was the case in *Milord Rivers*, written by Mme Riccoboni (1777), where the English protagonist overtly minimalized the cultural differences between the two nations, in conformity with the evolution towards "moral parity" which Grieder claims to discern. This more cosmopolitan attitude is illustrated in the following passage: "Even when examining them [the French] very attentively, I cannot discover these *extreme differences*, which have been noticed by some of our writers […] Nor can I perceive a single idea that should be different from ours" (Riccoboni 65). The fact that during the last decades of the Anglomania-movement certain authors did transmit an 'enlightened' view upon cultural differences is perfectly unquestionable; yet whether these individual expressions should stand for a more general evolution becomes uncertain when we take a closer look at the four novels under consideration here.[7]

In *Clarence Welldone* as well as in *Milady Lindsey*, most of the characters, both English and French, give proof of a sense of estrangement when they are confronted with the cultural other. While the French protagonists of both novels see their English relatives as radically different, and hence as opposite to their own beliefs and habits, some English characters also tend to underline the 'otherness' of French people and culture. This Francophobe attitude is, for instance, illustrated by the fact that Charlotte Lindsey is continually referred to as "cette française," "cette maudite française," or

---

7   Indeed, as David Bell puts it: "even to the extent that identity is defined as a highly subjective perception, it remains hugely unstable, constantly sliding between the many things people think they are (and think they are not), say they are […], what others say they are […], and what they think, and do despite all of the above. Identities change not only over time, but also according to where one is, and what one is doing" (20).

even "cette échappée de France." Correspondingly, when English characters cross the Channel, the representation of French social life (made, I recall, by a *French* author) mostly remains close to the stereotypical ideas from earlier decades and clearly indicates a 'dichotomous' approach. And so, French people are systematically restricted to their distinctive characteristics, be they rather negatively defined in terms of their 'lightness of being' and 'superficiality,' or distinguished by their 'gaiety' and 'refinement', as opposed to the coarseness characteristic of the English.[8] Even when the author does adopt the English point of view, in order to comment on French manners, these passages are also primarily based on the differential logic of 'otherness,' which brings along a feeling of alienation on both sides of the Channel. Most explicitly, the tendency toward differentiation and opposition takes the form of a pure lack of interest in intercultural contact.[9] This exclusion of the other becomes clear once more in a note added by Bournon-Mallarme, where she explains the – in her eyes – typically English notion of the "tavern"[10]: "These places are visited by very important gentlemen; they even organize meetings where no strangers are allowed. They have been given the name of 'clubs.' There, one freely eats, plays and talks about politics" (*Milady Lindsey* 55). The feeling of isolation and estrangement experienced in both nations is emphasized metaphorically in the story of Milady Lindsey, where the protagonist, a French girl who emigrates to go and live with her uncle,

---

8   For instance: "all the time we were eating we diverted ourselves with a good conversation and some jokes which, because they were very subtle, my thick mind [mon gros bon sens] had some difficulty understanding" (Bournon, *Clarence Welldone* 74).

9   This lack of interest in intercultural communication is shown in the following passage: "'Milord knows without any doubt some French lords.' – 'Not at all and I do not have any ambition to know one except for this man I have heard so much good things about'" (Bournon, *Clarence Welldone* 68). Furthermore, this communication problem is emphasized by the attention the author pays to the difference in language and to the incapacity or unwillingness of the English to speak French, in what are supposed to be 'francophile' times: "Try to learn English: from tomorrow onwards you will have a good teacher; almost all of my people talk only English" (Bournon, *Milady Lindsey* 19); "At dinner, I was seated between Miss Sara and her brother. Several of the people present did not speak French. I urged Milord to act as if I weren't there. And so, everyone spoke English" (100).

10   Besides, the very fact that even by the end of the period of Anglomania the author still considers it necessary to add footnotes explaining 'typical' English customs also underscores that real knowledge of English identity was still lacking at that time.

is literally cut off from her home country when her uncle intercepts the correspondence with her mother.

The only consistent 'cross-cultural' connection that seems to unite both countries is to be defined in rigorously negative terms. Instead of having become moral models to one another (Grieder), in all four novels, the English and the French still merely find a common ground in – mainly sexual – debauchery. Especially in the 'big cities,' mores and manners do not seem to be all that different: "The capitals are much alike I suppose, as well by their vices as their ridicules. It is natural to believe that the more people are gathered, the more misbehavior is developed and spread" (Beccary, *Milord d'Ambi* 16). Though the connection to France as a breeding-ground for debauchery is thus suggested in a few passages, throughout these specific *histoires anglaises*, licentiousness mainly determines the construction of (especially male) English identity. When we take into consideration the representation of the male characters in all four novels, it is remarkable how these can be divided in two diametrically opposed and conflicting groups: on the one hand, there is the melancholic and sober-minded gentleman, who is distinguished by his love of solitary retreat in the country, while on the other, there is the degenerate libertine, who is linked to 'gay' urban life. Following Grieder's reasoning, the presence of the former male stereotype indicates an evolution in French representations of the English, since, instead of stigmatizing Englishmen for their sober-mindedness and want of solitude, in the last decades of the 18th century this figure is 'revaluated' and charged with an explicitly positive connotation.[11] Still, this melancholic character never really appears in his 'pure' form – that is, totally free of depravation – as is illustrated by the person of the virtuous Milord D'Ambi. Even in this case, the character only opts for a peaceful life in the country after having lived a life of debauchery:[12] "It is on the countryside that I hope to free myself from all this uproar; from these amusements, [...] which do not have any value but the one that public opinion gives them and which leave behind them nothing but emptiness and

---

11   As Grieder already points out, this change in perception is to be linked to the "vogue de littérature sentimentale" in France. Obviously, Rousseau's *La nouvelle Héloïse* played a major part in this evolution.

12   The same observation applies to Milord Powers, whom Clarence Welldone marries in order to flee from her libertine pursuer, Henry Sandwick.

satiation" (13). To a certain extent, all – 'good' as well as 'bad' – characters are related to sexual inconstancy, either because they are already 'former libertines' at the beginning of the story or because they instead give themselves over to vice in the course of the novel. While Milord Lindsey is introduced as a faithful husband, for instance, he soon adopts a more volatile attitude when he seduces two very young girls.

While it is true that most of these libertines end up as converts to a more regular way of living, the construction of the male (English) character is essentially determined by the emphasis on inconstancy throughout these novels. Besides, the libertarians represented by Bournon-Malarme and Beccary are commonly captured in clichéd images of savagery, drunkenness, and rudeness, all features which already made up the *imageme* (Leerssen) of the Englishman as a 'primitive' in earlier decades.[13] Indeed, all libertines depicted in these novels are explicitly characterized by their abusive appeal to punch and by a tendency to violent behavior. More than once, these two classical libertine vices are linked together: "Extravagance seems to be going around, you all exhale it. I've just left an imbecile only to come and find an enraged man. You get drunk, you argue with a man, you kill him and then you run away; may you be doomed" (Beccary, *Milord d'Ambi* 211). On another occasion, difference of opinion is again resolved by a physical confrontation: "Let us go downstairs, he said to me coolly, let's fight; explanations will come afterwards. I liked his offer too much to refuse it" (Beccary, *Milord d'Ambi* 133). Moreover, this vulgar behavior is echoed in the linguistic register, given the libertines' frequent use of "plat verbiage" (Beccary, *Clarence Welldone* 183).

Besides this first set of features, another series of characteristics tends to appear when we look closely at the English libertine characters: there is their generally very passionate nature, which expresses itself through a choleric temperament;[14] moreover, following the example of Lovelace in Richardson's *Clarissa,* they are able to actually fall in love with their victims without giving up their volatile life,[15] while the libertines typically encountered in

---

13 Grieder remarks: "The English people are violent and bloodthirsty: so runs the cliché and so say the satirists, who spare no effort in inventing scenes to demonstrate it" (83).
14 "Never was one more restless than D'Orblac: the moderation of others irritates him; [...] my tranquility angers him, he follows the movements of his own exuberance and acts undoubtedly in a very imprudent way" (Beccary, *Fanni Spingler* 119).
15 As Milord Lindsey admits in the following passage: "while thinking all the time of

French literature more often approach their victims in a cold and calculating manner. As such, these English libertines subscribe to a sort of *literary Englishness*; most of these characters seem, in some way, to be inheritors of two English prototypes, as they combine, on the one hand, the stock character of the *rake* by their tendency to debauchery and rudeness, and, on the other, the tragic incapacity to remain faithful, despite their love, a characteristic that was introduced by Richardson's Lovelace a few decades earlier.[16]

One must never forget, however, that despite the influence of a literary or cultural 'legacy', all characters in Bournon-Mallarme's and Beccary's novels also remain literary constructions that are linked to a certain culture or a specific *ethos* and that are created by individual authors who attempt to transmit their personal views upon society to their readers. This very subjective 'constructedness' explains also why the libertine can appear in other prose fiction of the same period as a character explicitly linked to France. Indeed, both in French and in English literature characters appear whose depraved attitude is related to their Frenchness.[17] Very often, they give evidence of feminized behavior, which is a marked contrast to the (English) libertines represented in Beccary's and Bournon-Mallarme's novels.

What is more, in some of these other novels libertarian characters develop a mixed French-English nature, and these characters make a bicultural or even a transcultural character conceivable by blending, in a seemingly unproblematic way, their English origins with traits traditionally attributed to French culture. In this respect, one of the most fascinating characters

---

my wife, regretting her absence constantly, I was living with a woman who was not indifferent to me, and at the same time I felt a strong inclination to Rodzini's daughter. I'm not looking for any excuse, but the irresistible penchant I had for these two objects had never altered in my heart the feelings I owe to my virtuous wife" (143).

16   Colette Cazenobe suggests more or less the same idea in her study on libertinage: "[Lovelace] offers, compared with continental models, a remarkable originality on numerous points. An originality, moreover, which becomes total on a very crucial point: Lovelace is in love and does not deny it [...] and yet, he does not stop being a libertine. This complexity, if not contradiction, constitutes a considerable enrichment of the novel's view on libertinage" (166).

17   See, on this issue, Gerald Newman's description of the character of Bellarmine in Henry Fielding's *Joseph Andrews*: "The latter's principal attractions, apart from his equipage, flattering attentions, and lovely French-sounding name [...] are his speech – a mixture, particularly in his letters to Leonora, of English constructions interlarded with French phrases – and his fine gold-embroidered clothes [...]" (66).

of French literature is certainly Lord Chester, the devious protagonist in Crébillon's *Les heureux orphelins*, who, through the very complexity of his nature, puts into question the supposedly deep-seated differences between French and English character as well as, on a more general level, the justifiability of something like a national character *tout court*. It is only in this novel that the specific characteristics of the libertine become truly operational. As the libertine is often represented as a character for whom 'appearance' prevails over 'essence' and who, therefore, masters to perfection the art of taking other people's places, Chester in *Les heureux orphelins* can alternate, as a true chameleon, between French and English manners, sometimes even embodying both simultaneously. This capacity to reconcile, in one and the same character, two nations which are "made to esteem rather than to hate each other" (Crébillon 108), moves the debate over national identity up to a more complex level, where images of the self and the other tend to merge, thereby surpassing, to a certain extent, the differential logic that is so dominant in Bournon-Mallarme's and Beccary's novels. And when we take into account that Chester considers national character as a purely accidental feature that can be manipulated at will, we can even say that the novel raises questions of a more general nature by raising doubts about the very terms of the socio-cultural debate on national identity. Nevertheless, as Beccary's and Bournon's novels illustrate, writers of fiction did not always make the most of the emancipatory and creative potential that seemed to inhere in the libertine character. After decades of real-life contact between the English and the French, both authors represented a fictitious world where the question of surpassing national differences was hardly posed and where both peoples were *still* (or *again*) firmly tied to their separate, specific worlds.

"The French people are the first of all peoples and a model for every nation" (quoted in Fontana 121). These famous words from the Declaration of Rights of 1789, although published a few years after Bournon-Mallarme's and Beccary's novels had appeared, illustrate in an emblematic manner the nationalist beliefs that still occupied French minds at the end of the cosmopolitan age that the Enlightenment certainly was. Even if Enlightenment philosophers like Condorcet believed that "the progress of equality within a single nation would eventually lead to the disappearance of inequality between nations" (Fontana 120), to a certain extent this European dream still presupposed French supremacy.[18] Likewise, one could say, the Anglomania-movement that determined French literature – and culture in general – during the greater part of the 18th century never made a certain *francocentrisme* totally obsolete. While overtly admiring or even imitating Englishness on various levels, this intercultural exchange did not always lead to a realistic, let alone appreciative view of the cultural other. Even in a literary form like the *histoire anglaise,* where an alleged internal perspective on Englishness was recreated, the ability to give up stereotypes in order to build transcultural bridges over the Channel rarely materialized. Evidently, during the decade-long contacts between the two nations, first-class writers such as Prévost, Riccoboni, or Crébillon had adopted a more cosmopolitan attitude by promoting English values and by minimizing the binary oppositions between French and English manners. In one single case – that of *Les heureux orphelins* – the debate on national identity even reached a remarkable complexity by putting into perspective not only the dichotomous logic of the debate, which opposed self to other, good to bad, French to English, but also the necessarily arbitrary and constructed nature of the project of national image-building.

Still, we must not forget that the popular works of Bournon-Mallarme and Beccary arguably played as important a role in informing the general public on the life at the other side of the Channel as most of the names I just mentioned. Literature's emancipatory potential was certainly not always realized. The *histoires anglaises* discussed here do not, as they claim, offer a view from the inside, but rather an external, fundamentally French perspective on Englishness. Although writing for a public with a growing awareness of its European identity (Bell 93), these two authors still failed to – or maybe even refused to – transcend the dichotomous dynamics of the debate on national character. Rather than moving towards a potential space for a more adequate discourse on English culture at the end of the 18th century, as has often been suggested, the *histoire anglaise*, with only a few exceptions, proved to be anything but a realistic and illuminating 'passage' to the other side of the Channel and even less – in spite of the promise of an ex-centric perspective – a reassessment of French supremacy.

---

18 As Fontana indicates: "In the long run the empire became the only viable solution to these contradictions, the only formula that made it possible for Bonaparte to reconcile French supremacy with the vision of a peaceful sisterhood of European nations" (122).

Works Cited

Beccary, Mme. *Milord d'Ambi: histoire anglaise*. 2 vol. Paris: Gauguery, 1778.

———. *Mémoires de Fanni Spingler: histoire anglaise*. 2 vol. Paris: Knapen, 1781.

Bell, David A. *The Cult of the Nation in France: Inventing Nationalism, 1680-1800*. London: Harvard, 2001.

Bournon-Mallarme, Mme. *Mémoires de Clarence Welldone, ou le pouvoir de la vertu*. 2 vol. London and Paris: Cailleau, 1780.

———. *Lettres de Milady Lindsey, ou l'épouse pacifique*. London and Paris: Cailleau, 1780.

Cazenobe, Colette. *Le système du libertinage de Crébillon à Laclos. Studies on Voltaire and the Eighteenth Century 282*. Oxford: Voltaire Foundation, 1991.

Crébillon, Claude. *Les heureux orphelins. Œuvres complètes*. Ed. Jean Sgard. 3rd vol. Paris: Garnier classiques, 2001.

Faussett, David. "'Another world, yet the same': Ethnic Stereotyping in Early Travel Fiction." *Beyond Pug's Tour: National and Ethnic Stereotyping in Theory and Literary Practice*. Ed. C.C. Barfoot. Amsterdam and Atlanta: Rodopi, 1997. 133-44.

Fontana, Biancamaria. "The Napoleonic Empire and the Europe of Nations." *The Idea of Europe from Antiquity to the European Union*. Ed. Anthony Pagden. Cambridge: Woodrow Wilson Center Press and Cambridge University Press, 2002. 116-28.

Graeber, Wilhelm. *Der Englische Roman in Frankreich 1741-1763: Übersetzungsgeschichte als Beitrag zur französischen Literaturgeschichte*. Heidelberg: Universitätsverlag C. Winter, 1995.

Grieder, Josephine. *Anglomania in France, 1740–1789: Fact, Fiction, and Political Discourse*. Genève and Paris: Droz, 1985.

Hazard, Paul. *La pensée européenne au XVIIIe siècle de Montesquieu à Lessing*. 2 Vol. Paris: Boivin, 1946.

Michaud, Claude. "Présentation." *Dix-huitième siècle* 25 (1993): 5-10.

Newman, Gerald. *The Rise of English Nationalism: A Cultural History 1740-1830*. London: Weidenfeld and Nicholson, 1987.

Leerssen, Joep. "The Rhetoric of National Character: A Programmatic Survey." *Poetics Today* 21.2 (2000): 267-92.

Riccoboni, Mme. *Lettres de Mylord Rivers à Sir Charles Cardigan*. Ed. Olga B. Cragg. Genève: Droz, 1992.

David Damrosch (Columbia University)
Global Regionalism

Re-thinking Europe concerns relations of national identities and collective memories, and the collective memories on which nations build are often transnational in nature. These concerns are very current today, but from the beginning comparative literature as a discipline has been involved in re-thinking the cultural-political landscape of Europe, even as it has worked to see European literature within the broader world at large. If comparatists are striving for a more fully global vision today, this expansion also involves an expanded conception of Europe itself.

Comparative literature has often been accused of 'Eurocentrism,' yet during the past century, much of Europe has often been farther than China from the discipline's field of vision. In 1960, Werner Friederich, founder of the *Yearbook of Comparative and General Literature*, noted wryly that the term "world literature" was rarely being applied to anything like the full world, even the full European world:

> Apart from the fact that such a presumptuous term makes for shallowness and partisanship which should not be tolerated in a good university, it is simply bad public relations to use this term and to offend more than half of humanity. [...] Sometimes, in flippant moments, I think we should call our programs NATO Literatures – yet even that would be extravagant, for we do not usually deal with more than one fourth of the 15 NATO-Nations. (14-15)

If we now want to re-think Europe beyond the long-dominant great-power terms, this is not so much a new idea as a return to a crucial debate in the early years of our discipline's history, as comparative literature began to become an academic field in the third quarter of the 19th century. Here, I would like to consider the inaugural essay of the first journal of comparative literature, the *Acta Comparationis Litterarum Universarum*, founded in 1877 by the Hungarian comparatists Hugo Meltzl and Samuel Brassai. Turning from theory to literature, I will then look at a noteworthy literary example from Iceland, one of the peripheral regions of Europe long disregarded in most comparative studies, so often oriented to the work of a few literary 'great powers.'

In the 1870s, Hugo Meltzl was already fully alive to the problem of the dominance of major powers over minor literatures, and he exerted himself mightily to combat it. In 1877 Meltzl joined up with his older colleague Samuel Brassai at Cluj to found the *Acta Comparationis Litterarum Universarum*. In a programmatic essay announcing the journal's purposes, "Present Tasks of Comparative Literature," Meltzl set forth the editors' intention as nothing less than "the *reform of literary history*, a reform long awaited and long overdue which is possible only through an extensive application of *the comparative principle*" (56).[1] Meltzl argued that Goethe's cosmopolitan conception of *Weltliteratur* had been pressed into the service of narrowly nationalistic concerns: "As every unbiased man of letters knows, modern literary history, as generally practiced today, is nothing but an *ancilla historiae politicae*, or even an *ancilla nationis*" – a handmaid of political history or even of the nation itself (57).

Where Goethe had looked forward to German as taking a prominent role in cultural exchange, Meltzl and Brassai sought to showcase languages and literatures usually overlooked from great-power perspectives. This desire led to their most dramatic editorial decision: to admit no fewer than ten official languages for their articles. They printed the journal's title in all ten languages, though in a concession to identifiability, they printed the Latin title in large type, along with the German title (*Zeitschrift für vergleichende Literatur*), followed by seven others in smaller type. Last of all came the Hungarian title, in medium-sized type, "like a modest innkeeper following his guests" as Meltzl put it – in German – in a note "An unsere Leser" in 1879.

In keeping with their multilingual emphasis, Meltzl and Brassai established an editorial board of genuinely global scope, with members from Hungary, Germany, England, France, Italy, Switzerland, Holland, Portugal, Iceland, Sweden, Poland, the U.S.A., Turkey, India, Japan, Egypt, and Australia. By assembling so wide-ranging a team, and by founding their journal on "the Principle of Polyglottism," the editors sought at once to protect the individuality of smaller literatures and to explode nationalistic exclusivity altogether. As Meltzl said in his inaugural essay,

---

1 For further discussion of Meltzl, together with his Irish contemporary H.M. Posnett, see Damrosch, "Rebirth of a Discipline," from which the present discussion of Meltzl is adapted.

Today every nation demands its own "world literature" without quite knowing what is meant by it. By now, every nation considers itself, for one good reason or another, superior to all other nations. [...] This unhealthy "national principle" therefore constitutes the fundamental premise of the entire spiritual life of modern Europe. [...] Instead of giving free reign to polyglottism and reaping the fruits in the future [...] every nation today insists on the strictest monoglottism, by considering its own language superior or even destined to rule supreme. This is a childish competition whose result will finally be that all of them remain – inferior. (60-61)

The *Acta Comparationis Litterarum Universarum* was intended to set this situation right, both by its radical mixing of languages and also by its broad literary strategies. Meltzl and Brassai developed a two-pronged approach for their journal. First, they would compare masterpieces of global world literature (mostly composed in large, politically powerful and culturally influential countries). Secondly, they promoted the study of oral and folk materials. These could be found in every country and language, and so the study of folksongs became a centerpiece of the journal's project, a powerful way to level the cultural playing field for countries not yet on the map of world masterpieces.

In his inaugural essay Meltzl urged attention to "the spiritual life of 'literatureless peoples,' as we might call them, whose ethnic individuality should not be impinged upon by the wrong kind of missionary zeal." He went on to condemn a recent Russian *ukaz* that had prohibited the literary use of Ukrainian in the Ukraine. Meltzl was so outraged by this action that he denounced it with his own form of religious zeal: "It would appear as the greatest sin against the Holy Spirit even if it were directed only against the folksongs of an obscure horde of Kirghizes instead of a people of fifteen million" (60). It was evidently the Russian censorship of minor literatures that caused Meltzl to exclude Russian from the ten official languages admitted to his journal – a remarkable decision, really, to punish Russia by excluding its language from the pages of a young journal of enormous ambition but limited readership.

Discussions of globalization today sometimes use ecological metaphors to describe less-spoken languages and their literatures as endangered species; Meltzl was perhaps the first person ever to use such imagery: "In a time when certain animal species such as the mountain goat and the European bison are protected against extinction by elaborate and strict laws, the willful extinction of a human species (or its literature, which amounts to the same thing) should be impossible" (60). He was particularly concerned to distance his project from a leveling cosmopolitanism that would ultimately overwhelm smaller literatures: "It should be obvious," he wrote,

> that these polyglot efforts have nothing in common with any kind of universal fraternization. [...] The ideals of Comparative Literature have nothing to do with foggy, "cosmopolitanizing" theories; the high aims (not to say tendencies) of a journal like ours would be gravely misunderstood or intentionally misrepresented if anybody expected us to infringe upon the national uniqueness of a people. To attempt that would be, for more than one reason, a ludicrous undertaking which even an association of internationally famous scholars would have to consider doomed from the start. [...] It can safely be assumed that the purposes of Comparative Literature are more solid than that. It is, on the contrary, the *purely national of all nations* that Comparative Literature means to cultivate lovingly. [...] Our secret motto is: nationality as individuality of a people should be regarded as sacred and inviolable. Therefore, a people, be it ever so insignificant politically, is and will remain, from the standpoint of Comparative Literature, as important as the largest nation. (59-60)

Meltzl and Brassai's journal was a bold experiment, but how did their polyglottism work in practice?[2] Looking at their actual publication reveals a mixed situation of a pragmatic reality more constrained than the utopian polyglottism suggested by the journal's ten official languages. If it had truly been written in so many languages, the journal could not, after all, have been comprehensible to more than a handful of readers at most. In actual practice the journal's working languages were chiefly two: German and Hungarian. In examining the articles written in four volumes covering the years 1879-82, I find that half of all the articles were written in German, while another twenty percent were written in Hungarian. The remaining thirty percent of the articles were written mostly in three languages (English, French, and Italian), with also a handful of short items in Latin.

No articles appeared in such less-spoken 'official' languages as Icelandic and Polish. Poems from around the world were regularly given in the original, but always with a translation into one of the journal's dominant languages. So the journal's polyglottism was far more limited in practice than in theory,

---

2   For a valuable collection of essays on Meltzl – the first ever devoted to his work – see Fassel. Particularly useful are contributions by Horst Fassel and by Ildikó Tóth-Nagy that discuss Meltzl's complex, shifting relations to universalism and regionalism.

and yet even so it appears to have had a limiting effect on the journal's readership. In one of the few full-scale articles ever written on the *Acta*, Árpád Berczik has found that, in its best year, the *Acta* achieved a circulation of only a hundred copies, a number that actually declined in the journal's later years. For its select readership, however, the *Acta* provided a lively venue for the sharing of ideas and information among its far-flung correspondents, and the journal gave Meltzl an opportunity to work out his strategies for the promotion of Hungarian literature on the world stage. He pursued this goal with his double focus, both on transcendent masterpieces and on folk literature. In Meltzl's view, Hungary had produced one writer of genuinely world-class stature: Sandor Petöfi. In the *Acta*, Meltzl devoted a continuing stream of articles to Petöfi's work. Over the course of the journal's life, Meltzl arranged for translations of lyrics by Petöfi into no fewer than thirty-two languages, and his scholarly analyses were intended to show a broad European public that here was a Hungarian poet who deserved a prominent place at the table of world literature.

Rather than seek to promote other established Hungarian writers of (in his view) lesser literary merit, Meltzl placed his second great stress on his region's contribution to world folk poetry, showcasing lyrics not only in Hungarian but also in Romanian, and several times including Gypsy folksongs. In this effort he had some real success: the first English translation of Romanian folk poetry, by Henry Phillips, was published in Philadelphia in 1885, based on poems printed in the *Acta*. In his journal, Meltzl delighted in finding the circulation of folk motifs across wide geographical areas. In one article he discussed a lyric found in similar forms in Iceland, Sicily, and Hungary, concluding: "Das sind die Wunder der vergleichenden Literatur!" ("Volkstradition" 117-18). In the journal's second volume, Meltzl issued a call for contributions to an ambitious anthology (never realized), to be named *Encyclopaedia of the Poetry of the World*. Merging his two emphases, Meltzl asked his contributors to send in two poems from every possible country in the world: one folk poem and one literary work, each of them to be given in the original and in "a literal interlinear translation in one of the European languages" (177).

By these means Meltzl was working out a practical mode of comparison on a truly global scale, while at the same time he was creatively negotiating the cultural politics of relations between small and large literary powers. It is ironic, then, that his journal's impact was limited in his own time, and not only because of the polyglottism that would have made the journal difficult for many readers. Equally serious was the growth of comparative studies in France and Germany, for the scholars located in these great powers had little of Meltzl's interest in the literatures of smaller nations – and less interest still in working with scholars in those nations.

According to Árpád Berczik, "the death blow" to Meltzl's struggling journal was the appearance in 1887 of a rival journal, published in Berlin under the editorship of Max Koch, a professor at Marburg. As Meltzl himself complained, this new and better placed journal seemed intended to siphon off readers and contributors from Meltzl's journal, as Koch's title, *Zeitschrift für vergleichende Literaturgeschichte*, was suspiciously close to the *Acta*'s own German title, *Zeitschrift für vergleichende Literatur*. Though Meltzl had studied in Berlin and likely knew Koch, it was particularly galling that he learned of the new journal not from Koch himself but only through newspaper reports. In a plaintive editorial note, Meltzl tried to rally his readers, not precisely to boycott his new rival, but at least to remain loyal to his journal as well:

> We have recently learned from news reports that a journal of comparative literary history is supposed to be starting publication in Berlin. As pleased as we are that even in Goethe's homeland this great branch of comparative literature [...] is finding a freestanding home, we must equally lament the – surely coincidental! – choice of a title, which is bound to cause much confusion with the German title of the *Acta Comparationis*. We therefore wish here to plead in advance for care to be taken, so that at least the learned public may note the difference between the *Zeitschrift für vergleichende Literatur* (since January 1877) and the *Zeitschrift für vergleichende Literaturgeschichte* (since Summer 1886). (quoted in Berczik 98-99)

Koch's journal was not just a personal affront to Meltzl but a real step backward methodologically. Written entirely in German, its articles were contributed almost exclusively by German scholars, and their emphasis was heavily on German literary relations; the first issue, for example, included articles on Goethe, Uhland, Kleist, Lessing, and "Germanische Sagenmotive im Tristan-Roman," among other German-oriented articles, while also including articles on Chinese poetry and African fables. The Berlin journal did sometimes treat folk poetry as well. If Koch was trying to steal Meltzl's thunder, it may not have been a coincidence that the early issues of Koch's journal often focused on Transylvanian and Hungarian folklore. The very first issue included a short article on a theme from *Tristan* as found in Transylvanian Gypsy and Romanian poetry, while the second issue featured a prominent article "Zur Litteratur und Charakteristik des magyarischen Folklore."

Neither of these articles mentioned Meltzl or his journal at all, nor was the *Acta* mentioned in Koch's inaugural essay for his journal, although Koch discussed a wide range of previous efforts in comparative study. Koch's essay concluded by emphasizing comparative literature's national value: "German literature and the advancement of its historical understanding will form the starting point and the center of gravity for the endeavors of the *Zeitschrift für vergleichende Literaturgeschichte*" (12). Meltzl kept his journal going for another year after the Berlin journal appeared, but then gave up; Koch's journal had won.

The great-power perspective became dominant in comparative literature for a full century thereafter, but finally we may now be able to return to the perspective Meltzl was already developing a century and a quarter ago. We can pursue research that attends to regional as well as global concerns, studying minor literatures as well as great-power productions. In doing this, we can move beyond Meltzl's basic schema of global folk art versus great-power masterpieces, and can see that writers in all sorts of locations have very often been regionalists and globalists at one and the same time.

Current discussions of globalization often focus largely or exclusively on contemporary literature and culture, yet the global penetration of regional culture is not at all a new phenomenon. As a case in point, I would like to take the case of literary production in medieval Iceland. In converting to Christianity and making a parallel shift from runes to the Latin alphabet, the 11th century Icelanders set the stage for the explosion of vernacular writing of sagas and skaldic poetry in the ensuing three centuries.

A subtle but far-reaching orientation of local lore toward Christian and classical traditions came with Christianity and the Roman alphabet, and these traditions can be found in Norse texts where one might least expect it, such as in Snorri Sturluson's *Prose Edda* (c. 1240). This is the fullest medieval compendium of pagan Germanic myths, which Snorri has assembled, he says, as a resource for poetic allusions and tropes. He is anxious for young poets to know the stories behind the epithets and metaphors traditionally used in skaldic poetry, lest the old poetic language become obscure and die out. Yet in his preface he does much more than present the myths as a poetic repertory. Instead, he boldly connects the northern gods to classical history, euhemerizing them as legendary heroes later taken for gods, and he actually offers linguistic analyses to link them to Troy:

> Near the center of the world where what we call Turkey lies, was built the most famous of all palaces and halls – Troy by name. [...] One of the kings was called Múnón or Mennón. He married a daughter of the chief king Priam who was called Tróán, and they had a son named Trór – we call him Thór. [...] he traveled far and wide exploring all the regions of the world and by himself overcoming all the berserks and giants and an enormous dragon and many wild beasts. (25-26)

Snorri says that Thór's descendant Óðin journeyed north with his family and began to rule in Germany and then Sweden: "There he appointed chieftains after the pattern of Troy." Snorri even claims that the collective name for the Norse gods, the Æsir, derives from their homeland, "Asia" (27).

Iceland provides a fascinating and well-documented case of free choice to enter the new world of Christian Europe, and this was a new linguistic and grammatological world as well as a religious and political world. *Prose Edda* is in fact usually bound with grammatical treatises, most fully in the Codex Wormianus, which contains no fewer than four appended treatises, known today as the First, Second, Third, and Fourth Grammatical Treatise.

In the 12th and 13th centuries, Icelandic scholars freely experimented with the alphabet, adapting it to the sounds of Norse and theorizing the relation of speech to writing. They loved to make charts showing the possible combinations of vowels and consonants. With one chart, the writer of the Second Grammatical Treatise makes a musical analogy, inviting us to play the sounds on the chart like a musical instrument: "The mouth and the tongue are the playing-field of words. On that field are raised those letters which make up the whole language, and language plucks some of them like harp strings, or as when the keys of a simphonie are pressed." (Raschella 55) (Recently imported from France, a simphonie was a fiddle equipped with strings and a wheel.) The grammarian continues:

> Here there are eleven vowels crosswise on the page and twenty consonants lengthwise; the consonants are placed as keys in a simphonie, and the vowels as strings. There are twelve consonants which have a sound both when the key

is pulled and when it is pushed; but the eight which are written last have half a sound as compared with the former; some make a sound if you pull towards you, some if you push away from you. (73)

The First Grammatical Treatise shows a sovereign freedom in experimenting with the newly imported alphabet. It was probably written around 1170, in the second generation of Iceland's use of Roman alphabet. This grammarian insists that each country needs its own alphabet: just as the Greeks have theirs and the English and the Romans had theirs, the Icelanders need their own. But Latin, he asserts, is far poorer in vowels than Icelandic, and so he needs to invent a series of new ones. Moreover, Latin does not adequately distinguish between short and long consonants, often confusing meaning; so he proposes using small capitals for lengthened consonants. Altogether, the First Grammarian's alphabet contains fifty separate letters. Notably, he uses skaldic poetry as his prompt: readers won't get the meters right if they don't know just what sound each vowel and consonant has. At the end, the First Grammarian dismisses the reader with encouraging words – or a challenge: "Now any man who wants to write [...] let him use the alphabet already written here, until he gets one that he likes better" (Haugen 29-30).

Snorri Sturluson was thus operating in this world of sovereign grammatological adaptation, guided by poetry and by analogy to musical instruments imported from France. A similar freedom of invention is seen in Snorri's treatment of classical and Christian literary/cultural material as well. Though Snorri was a devout Christian and insisted that Thór and Óðin were mortal heroes, he opens the body of the *Prose Edda* with a virtual parody of the Christian Trinity. A Swedish king, Gylfi, goes to see the powerful Æsir who have created such a stir in the region, and when he comes to their castle he finds "three high-seats one above the other, and a man seated in each." Their names are Hár, Jafnhár, and Thriði – "High One," "Just-as-High," and "Third" (30-31). This parodic Trinity then answers his questions about ancient times, retelling the great Norse myths. Finally, the Æsir tire of all the questions and end the session – not by dismissing Gylfi but by themselves vanishing, with a final word of admonition from High One:

"And now, if you have anything more to ask, I can't think how you can manage it, for I've never heard anyone tell more of the story of the world. Make what use of it you can."

> The next thing was that [Gylfi] heard a tremendous noise on all sides and turned about; and when he had looked all round him, he was standing in the open air on a level plain. He saw neither hall nor stronghold. Then he went on his way and coming home to his kingdom related the tidings he had seen and heard, and after him these stories have been handed down from one man to another. (92-93)

As a writer from a peripheral region of Europe, Snorri was well aware that his traditions were in danger of being overwritten by the global traditions that entered Iceland in Christianity's wake. As a result, a concern over cultural memory pervades the *Prose Edda*. In his prologue, Snorri describes the early growth of the human race in terms of a material gain but also a memory loss:

> As the population of the world increased [...] the great majority of mankind, loving the pursuit of money and power, left off paying homage to God. This grew to such a pitch that they boycotted any reference to God, and then how could anyone tell their sons about the marvels connected with Him? In the end they lost the very name of God and there was not to be found in all the world a man who knew his Maker. (23)

Snorri is nominally talking about the ancients who forget the true God and fall into paganism, yet his own book is precisely devoted to telling young poets about the marvels performed by the pagan gods whose names are now being boycotted under Christianity. The concern for cultural memory is expressed within the *Edda* by no less a figure than the chief god Óðin:

> Two ravens sit on his shoulders and bring to his ears all the news that they see or hear; they are called Hugin ["Thought"] and Munin ["Memory"]. He sends them out at daybreak to fly over the whole world, and they come back at breakfast-time; by this means he comes to know a great deal about what is going on, and on account of this men call him the god-of-ravens. As it is said:

Huginn ok Muninn	Hugin and Munin
fliúga hverian dag	fly every day
iørmungrund ifir.	over the vast expanse of the earth.
Óumk ek Hugin	I fear for Hugin
at han aptr ne kome,	that he won't come back –
Þó siámk ek meirr um Munin	but I'm more concerned about Munin. (64)

Understanding the interplay of the local and the continental in early periods can give us a better understanding of the origins of our modern national literatures. Goethe formulated the concept of *Weltliteratur* in the 1820s, during the heyday of European nationalism, and it was natural for him then to speak of world literature as based in the interactions of established national literatures. As a result, Goethe treated world literature as a secondary or even future formation: "Nationalliteratur will jetzt nicht viel sagen," he announced to his young disciple Johann Peter Eckermann in January 1827; "die Epoche der Weltliteratur ist an der Zeit, und jeder muß jetzt dazu wirken, diese Epoche zu beschleunigen" ("the epoch of world literature is at hand, and everyone must strive to hasten its approach") (Eckermann 132). Yet as we can see in Iceland and many other regions, literatures have often developed in just the opposite direction: in most periods of history, local or national literatures have developed within – and, often, against – an existing regional or global world literature.

It is a rare country that develops its own script and its own literature in fundamental independence from other societies; ancient Egypt and Shiang China are more the exception than the rule. Most literatures – from Latin to French and from Hebrew to Icelandic – have been formed within broad systems grounded in the power of scripts to cross the boundaries of time, space, and language itself. Arising within a transcultural context, a local or national literature must negotiate a double bind: the new script that can help shape a people's traditions also brings with it the threat of the local culture's absorption into a broader milieu. As Snorri's case can suggest, regional European writers have repeatedly found creative ways to negotiate these continental and global tensions. Noah's raven could find nothing to bring back to him, but Óðin's ravens are more successful: they bring back news from around the world. God of wisdom, Óðin is blessed – and cursed – with foreknowledge, and he knows he can only use the ravens' reports for a time, until the gods enter their fated twilight and fade from memory: one day Munin will fail to return. Óðin is also the god of poetry, however, and perhaps he foresees the day when poets will adopt the script brought by the new dispensation that will displace him. Resisting the oblivion threatened by the advancing culture, these poets will use the foreign script to celebrate their former patron and his marvelous deeds, and their poems will keep alive the memory of the raven named "Memory."

Works Cited

Berczik, Árpád. "Hugó von Meltzl." *Német Filológiai Tanulmányok* 12 (1978): 87-100.

Damrosch, David. "Rebirth of a Discipline: The Global Origins of Comparative Literature." *Comparative Critical Studies* 3.1-2 (2006): 99-112.

Eckermann, Johann Peter. *Gespräche mit Goethe in den letzten Jahren seines Lebens.* Ed. Regine Otto. Berlin: Aufbau-Verlag, 1982; translated as *Johann Wolfgang von Goethe. Conversations with Eckermann.* Trans. John Oxenford. San Francisco: North Point, 1984.

Fassel, Horst, ed. *Hugo Meltzl und die Anfänge der Komparatistik.* Stuttgart: Franz Steiner Verlag, 2005.

Friederich, Werner. "On the Integrity of Our Planning." *The Teaching of World Literature.* Ed. Haskell Block. Chapel Hill: University of North Carolina Press, 1960. 9-22.

Haugen, Einar, ed. and trans. *First Grammatical Treatise: The Earliest Germanic Phonology.* Supplement to *Language: Journal of the Linguistic Society of America* 26.4 (1950).

Koch, Max. "Zur Einführung." *Zeitschrift für vergleichende Literaturgeschichte* 1 (1877): 1-12.

Meltzl, Hugo. "Present Tasks of Comparative Literature." *Acta Comparationis Litterarum Universarum* 1 (January 1877): 179-82 and 2 (October 1877): 307-15; reprinted in Hans-Joachim Schultz and Phillip H. Rhein, ed. *Comparative Literature: The Early Years.* Chapel Hill: University of North Carolina Press, 1973. 56-62.

——. "Islaendisch-Sizilianische Volkstradition im Magyarischen Lichte." *Acta Comparationis Litterarum Universarum* 3 (1879): 117-18.

Phillips, Henry. *Volk-Songs: Translated from the Acta Comparationis Litterarum Universarum.* Philadelphia, 1885.

Raschella, Fabrizio, ed. *The So-called Second Grammatical Treatise.* Florence: Felice de Monnier 1982.

Snorri Sturluson. *The Prose Edda.* Trans. Jean I. Young. Berkeley: University of California Press, 1954. The full Codex Wormianus was published in the 19th century, with facing Latin translation, as *Edda Snorra Sturlusonar.* 3 vols. Hafniae: Sumptibus Legati Arnamagnaeani, 1848-87.

Michael Boyden (K.U.Leuven Research Fund / University College Ghent)

Why the World Is Never Enough: Re-Conceptualizing World Literature as a Self-Substitutive Order

The turn of the 20th century has witnessed a remarkable resurgence of the concept of world literature in the North American context and, by extension, in the rest of the world. This debate is equally remarkable for its violent intensity as for its lack of theoretical conceptualization. To "theorize," as Gerald Gillespie once put it in a perhaps all too pessimistic mood, now often merely means that one is stating a political preference (212). It is in this present conjuncture that I would like to break a lance for a systems-theoretical approach to world literature. Thus far, Niklas Luhmann's systems theory has received scant attention in U.S. literary studies. This may be due to several factors, such as a lack of adequate translations – a projected translation of *Die Gesellschaft der Gesellschaft*, which I see as Luhmann's most definitive work, never materialized –, his seemingly dispassionate writing style, or the German stubbornness of his theoretical design (whatever that means). But perhaps the most commanding reason for the relative neglect of Luhmann's social systems theory is that, contrary to other approaches currently fashionable in literary studies, such as Immanuel Wallerstein's world systems theory or Pierre Bourdieu's field theory, Luhmann's perspective seems to resist easy capitalization in terms of a given political agenda.

Whenever he saw himself confronted with an apparently insoluble problem, Luhmann was in the habit of asking: "who is the observer?" It is precisely this refusal to adopt an otherworldly standpoint, i.e., the persistent attempt to theorize the reality of world society *from within* world society, that makes his social systems theory a useful vehicle for a thorough re-conceptualization of world literature in the present age. It does not, however, make it the only possible way of looking at the concept, since to assume as much would defeat the central premise of the theory. To put it very simply, this premise entails that, paradoxically, a valid approach to modern society has to involve a carefully staged *mise en abyme*, an unfolding of the world within the world. I assume that this point of view (which is basically the idea that every theory has to come from somewhere) is as mainstream as can be in the humanities today.

As I hope to make clear, however, the originality of Luhmann's approach lies not so much in this idea as such as in the consistency with which he pursues his difference-theoretical logic in all ramifications of modern society.

My immediate aim in this article is to offer a corrective to what I perceive as three equally widespread and equally erroneous notions about world literature. The first misconception is familiar enough, but somehow it continues to overshadow practically every discussion on the topic. It is the assumption that *world literature encompasses all literary works 'di tutti i tempi e di tutte le letterature.'* The attraction of such a megalomaniac point of view seems obvious enough: if we assume that world literature stands for everything that has ever been written on the globe, we disengage ourselves from the tedious problem of selection. This, no doubt, explains the perennial dream of the universal library, of which Google Book Search is but the latest manifestation. The fact that, despite intermittent disclaimers, the debate is continually redirected towards such impossible definitions indicates that, subcutaneously, world literature functions as a powerful selector, which serves to facilitate the process of social forgetting. In the era of optical character recognition and quasi-automatic translation, the urge to forget is more acute than ever. As I will argue, the category of world literature motivates selections precisely by continually pointing towards its own insufficiency, by suggesting that the world (as we know it) is not, and never can be enough.

A second misconception is the idea that, as can be read in the latest state of the art of the ACLA (the American Comparative Literature Association), *world literature "has a particular origin in the era of nationalisms"* (Saussy 6). This virtually uncontested assumption has great intuitive appeal, since it rests on the common sense inference that traditions need to develop a life of their own before they can start to circulate around the globe. In some respects, seeing world literature as a response to nationalism may work against the tendency to equate the notion with all the world's literatures (our first misconception), since, as comparatists never cease to remind us, the national model continues to exert its influence in departmental structures and elsewhere. Even though, therefore, world literature is in a sense as old as the world, it has not yet displaced the nation at the structural level and thus remains suspended in a state of perpetual becoming (which thus *a contrario* proves the continuing relevance of comparative literature study). So far so good. As I will try to show, however, the opposition between an age of nationalism and the "age of globalization," as the title of the Saussy report has it, proves rather unproductive when it comes to getting a better understanding of the workings of world literature. In what follows, I will turn the accepted view on its head by conceptualizing the nationalization of cultures as an anticipatory reaction to the gradual emergence of world society during modernity.

Let us call the idea that world literature represents all the world's literatures the Synecdochic Fallacy and the idea that world literature emerged in response to the development of national cultures the Adventist Fallacy. Now, I want to argue that, when these two fallacies work together and reinforce each other, they tend to produce a third, even more odorous fallacy, namely the inference that *world literature somehow presents a cure against narrow-minded nationalism or ethnocentrism*. I will call this third misconception, which in a sense represents the great foundational lie of comparative literature studies, the Therapeutic Fallacy. In an often-quoted phrase from his "Conjectures on World Literature," Franco Moretti states with great aplomb that world literature is nothing if not "a thorn in the side, a permanent intellectual challenge to national literatures" (68). In retort, I would suggest that world literature is nothing, if not an institution. So, here is *my* little pact with the devil: if, as Moretti convincingly points out, nobody has ever found a new method for approaching literary texts just "by reading more" (55), it is also true that no new method has ever had much direct impact on the overall drift of modern society.

In the first chapter of his 1940 *Preface to World Literature*, entitled "What Is World Literature?", Albert Guérard (a prominent representative of the "French school" in U.S. comparative literature, not to be confused with Albert Gérard, the editor of the ICLA series on *European Language-Writing in Sub-Saharan Africa*) comments on the linguistic and political fragmentation of the modern world, and the obstacles this poses for the comparatist. To which he adds reassuringly: "*Yet World Literature does exist:* Germany knows Shakespeare, and England knows Goethe. There is no more striking proof of Western unity than this victory, however incomplete, over what might seem an impassable barrier" (11, italics in original). Today, about seventy years later, such a statement may strike us as excessively presumptuous, if not completely ludicrous: in his hasty attempt to bolster the comparatist's morale, Guérard self-evidently equates world literature with the literature of the Western world, by which he actually means the literature of Western Europe, or more precisely the literatures of the dominant European nations, or rather a canonical segment of those literatures. Even while addressing the American student of literature, Guérard unproblematically defines world literature as "those works which are enjoyed in common, ideally by all mankind, practically by our own group of culture, the European or Western" (15).

During the last couple of decades, demographic changes in the comparative literature profession have driven a wedge between the practical and the ideal, or between "our own group," as Guérard saw it, and how this group relates to the rest of the world. Most current textbooks of world literature show a marked interest in so-called 'non-Western' literatures, to that extent that one could even claim that the established picking order as it applied roughly up to the mid-twentieth century, and of which Guérard and his generational fellows may have been the primary beneficiaries, has been turned upside down. Many observers, however, have noted the lingering Eurocentrism inherent in such attempts to reach out for 'the other half' of the globe. According to Waïl Hassan, for instance, the study of world literature now seems to resemble "a leisurely stroll in a global literary mall that is structured at once to satisfy and to reinforce Western modes of consumption and interpretation" (42). As Hassan argues, works such as *The Norton Anthology of World Masterpieces*, even while considerably broadening the horizons of world literature so as to include formerly suppressed or forgotten authors and texts, implicitly serve to perpetuate a form of imperialism inherent in global capitalism.

It is very well possible that, some seventy years from now, Hassan's harsh and perhaps rather facile verdict of the Norton textbook will strike comparatists (provided that there will still be such a species) as equally silly as Guérard's extremely limited conception of world literature appears to most observers today. What, I wonder, does Hassan understand by "Western modes" of reading? Does he not, even while going in the totally opposite direction, commit the same kind of category mistake as Guérard by conceptualizing the "Western world" as an amorphous whole, as easily localizable or penetrable as a shopping mall (is it totally absurd to define this quintessentially American institution as an offshoot of the Persian *bazar*?). However this may be, what seems clear is that it has become increasingly difficult in any discussion on the notion of world literature *not* to ask, as Djelal Kadir has put it, "who carries out its worlding and why?" ("To World" 2). One could argue that, currently, a canon of world literature can only validate itself by reflecting on its place in the world. More than ever, perhaps, world literature presents itself as a paradoxical concept: while it cannot shed its pretense to universality, which appears to be ingrained in its very meaning, it constantly frustrates the expectations it puts out – in a sense, it falsifies itself – by arousing suspicion as to its own capacity to be representative towards the world in its entirety. The question is: how do we respond to this development?

Let us move from Guérard's 1940 definition of world literature to the one offered by David Damrosch, undoubtedly one of the most vocal representatives of the new generation of comparatists in the U.S. In his *What Is World Literature?* (2003), Damrosch approaches the canon of world literature not merely as a list of masterpieces, but rather as "all literary works that circulate beyond their culture of origin, either in translation or in their original language" and that can be said to be "actively present within a literary system beyond that of [their] original culture" (4). As a matter of fact, this definition is merely a present-day reprise of (one possible interpretation of) Goethe's idea of world literature as "den Inbegriff derjenigen Werke fremdnationalen Ursprungs [...] die zu einer Zeit unter [irgendeinem Kulturvolk] lebendig sind" ("the totality of those works of foreign origin that have currency within a cultural community at a given point in time") (quoted in Beil 6).[1] Such a definition certainly has a lot to say for it: by drawing attention to the regional bias of accepted conceptualizations of world literature, Damrosch promises to go against the persistent tendency to take the world as we know it for the whole world, or what I have called the Synecdochic Fallacy. He attempts to do so by shifting attention from what constitutes the canon of world literature, a choice that will always to some extent reflect one's membership in a specific cultural tradition, to "the ways in which works of literature can best be read" (5). In this sense, the title *What Is World Literature?* is rather misleading, since what we are concerned with is no longer the *what* but rather the *how* of world literature, or as Damrosch puts it, its "phenomenology" (6), a phrase he may have taken from Curtius.

---

1   All translations from the German and French are the author's.

By analyzing the changing constructions of world literature in 20th century American textbooks, Damrosch convincingly shows how this concept has never been stable in the first place but has always entailed a negotiation between at least two focal points, that of the home culture at a certain point in time, and that of the foreign text, which serves to reinforce and put into perspective the values and ideals of the home culture. By analyzing this 'elliptical' process of continual give and take, Damrosch highlights how literary works move in and out of the category of the "timeless masterpiece" in accordance with the dynamics of cultural exchange and contestation. However, Damrosch's definition of world literature also raises a number of questions. Thus, for instance, he never truly addresses the question as to what it means for a literary work to be "actively present" in a culture. Does this entail that artists continue to tap from its themes or forms? A condition of survival for a literary work may very well be that it resists being re-read. Where lie the boundaries of a given culture (Damrosch uses the term culture more or less interchangeably with notions such as "system," "sphere," or even "world")? However suggestive and compelling, at points Damrosch's approach appears to me, as Auerbach would have phrased it, as "sehr ungoethisch" (40).

Despite its obvious merits, Damrosch's book is not always as rock-solid on the theoretical plane. This conceptual fuzziness would be a virtue rather than a defect, if not for the fact that it occasionally allows the Synecdochic Fallacy to sneak back in through the back door. Thus, when warning against the danger of cultural chauvinism through the imposition of "domestic" literary values on "foreign" texts, Damrosch without further ado equates these values with "Western critical theory" (4-5). In this way, the "West" is presented as a unitary addressee, while the appeal of "non-Western" texts derives primarily from the fact that they are observed as "foreign." A similar sloppiness affects his use of oppositions such as "provincial" and "metropolitan." The problem is that we can always apply these concepts to themselves, thus exposing the provincialism of the metropolis, or the cosmopolitan bearings of the province. In my opinion, Damrosch's a priori reification of analytical concepts precludes an adequate engagement with the slippery category of world literature, because it obscures the 'foreignness' inherent in each culture, or the tensions between different versions of such a culture. For another, such a perspective fails to bring to the fore the strategies by which 'foreign' ('non-Western,' 'provincial,' ...) texts get domesticated, or the ways in which their otherness is both accentuated and erased.

The geometrical figure of the ellipse does not offer much direction in this regard. Although it may be useful for highlighting the fact that world literature is always the result of a triangulation of different national or regional traditions, thus highlighting both the similarities and the differences between them, the ellipse also presents these traditions as simple focal points entirely identical to themselves. To my mind, however, the point to note is precisely that the canon of world literature does not merely appear 'foreign' from the perspective of the receiving culture, but rather takes the form of a twisted cylinder, whereby the outside is inside and vice versa. The hallmark of world literature is only accorded to those works that are expected to accentuate or finalize a culture's self-image. The canon of world literature is thus not only 'foreign' to, but also strangely at home in the culture that it serves to realize by injecting it with quasi-universal appeal. The residual foreignness of world literature – the fact that it remains partially outside the cultures which it helps to define – indicates precisely that the opposition between the 'domestic' and the 'foreign,' or between 'us' and 'them,' does not actually constitute the boundary of these cultures. Rather, such oppositions constitute a sort of filter mechanism *inside* the semantics of world literature, which serves to keep open the choice as to what belongs to it and what falls out of it, even while indicating that a choice needs to be made.

Damrosch further combines his untheoretical approach with an almost exclusive focus on the historical construction of world literature in the North American context (or rather the U.S.). To be sure, this is a limitation that the author acknowledges, but it does not prevent him from remarking in a rather offhand way that his reading method "can be suggestive for accounts of world literature elsewhere" (28). Here, it seems to me that Damrosch partly succumbs to the "implicit triumphalism" that he detects in such works as Pascale Casanova's *La république mondiale des lettres* (27). By focusing almost all attention on the American textbook market, Damrosch reproduces certain givens of that institutional context, such as the strong desire for inclusiveness and diversification that typifies the U.S. educational system. If this may be a commendable position to hold in itself, it does not amount to a full-blown phenomenology of world literature. Damrosch states somewhere that he wants to avoid "the hubris that we are the world" (28). For readers outside the U.S., such inadvertent statements (who, after all, is the addressee here?) may represent as much a symptom of as a reaction against American parochialism. I am convinced that the problem of world literature requires a more worked-out theoretical framework, which would allow us to analyze the interplay between different conceptions of world literature in different constellations, not just in the U.S., but elsewhere too.

David Ferris may be right when he claims that Damrosch's reconceptualization of world literature as a mode of circulation and reading entails that the imperative to be representative towards the world as a whole (or what I have called the Synecdochic Fallacy) is now "channeled through a mode rather than an object" (86). Why is it, Ferris asks, that comparative literature "must always be transfixed before the seduction of the impossible" (92)? To understand this dynamic, we need to tackle the second fallacy, or the idea that world literature is a response to the strictures imposed by the national organization of cultures. Despite its enormous temporal reach and intellectual bravura, a book such as *What Is World Literature?* can hardly conceal the fact that it issues from what Philippe Van Parijs would call "the ground floor of the world." By this phrase, Van Parijs means those areas of the globe whose official or main language coincides with a lingua franca and which therefore increasingly function as "regional attractor basins" draining intellectual energy from the "linguistic hills" of countries whose languages are less accessible (222). Damrosch's marked predilection for 'provincial' authors writing back to the center from the perspective of a dominated or marginal culture *a contrario* reflects the frog's view of a nation that has become globally dominant.

What is hard to visualize from such a perspective is the fact that the category of world literature may take on very different forms in the thinning air above the tree line. In their struggle to reassert a legitimate position in the academy in the face of all kinds of pressures, American comparatists have of late been very active redescribing their discipline's roots. Thus, Emily Apter discerns a "Spitzerian lineage" running through the heart of comparative literature studies, which would underscore the "Eastern" component in the emergence of the discipline (despite a lingering Eurocentrism, Spitzer is said to have shown a deep respect for the "foreignness" of Turkish culture), thus dissociating her ideal Saidian pedigree from its problematic Auerbachian legacy (60-62). Through this reconstructive activity, Apter is indirectly fighting rearguard battles with her immediate competitor Franco Moretti, the main proponent of the "distant reading" paradigm. In similar vein, Jonathan Arac distinguishes between the "critical" and the "theoretical" Auerbach in order to save his preferred method of "close reading" for prosperity: whereas someone like Said would pursue the former thread in Auerbach's schizoid character, Arac claims that Moretti's quantitative approach brings out his resemblance to "a German professor of the old days" (44-45).

What I find striking about this kind of origins theories is that, apart from the occasional reference to Goethe or Madame de Staël, they do not normally extend much further than the Cold War period, i.e., the period when the U.S. could no longer deny being a world power. This, I think, has considerable implications for the way world literature is conceptualized. In an established political framework, the literary system tends to react against the strictures imposed by the state, which will eventually result in a bifurcation of the nationalist and the universalist discourses, if one could call them that. Consequently, the canon of world literature will be formulated in counterpoint to the nation. In a constrained political space, however, where the state is at odds with the national or regional groups that it is supposed to represent (a predicament shared by the majority of the world's population), these two discourses are not fully differentiated and for the most part coexist without apparent contradiction. Here, the nation provides a vital supporting context for the universalist impulse. Vice versa, the cultivation of a body of world literature will serve to justify the existence of the contested political entity. This rather simple thought occurred to me while reading an article by the Croatian scholar Pedrag Matvejević, where it says: "Avec la réalisation de la consolidation nationale, la littérature perd, au sein de la nation dont elle émane, le sens qu'elle avait précédemment" ("With the consolidation of a national state, literature loses the direction it previously had at the core of the nation from which it flows forth") (38).

Once this is granted, it no longer makes sense to explain the emergence of world literature as a reaction against the nation. Obviously, this does not mean that I contest the right or the need to question national divides by going beyond seemingly closed-off traditions. All I am suggesting is that this antinationalist motive does not *of itself* result in a valid account of the operational logic of world literature in modern world society. The process of nationalization, I claim, is but one evolutionary trigger for the development of the idea of world literature. I hope that this will become clearer when looking at some of the fault lines running through alternative constructions of world literature in various (European and American) contexts. Such an exercise will doubtless bring out my own scholarly limitations and interests. As Damrosch phrases it in *What Is World Literature?*, echoing the Marvell epigraph to Auerbach's *Mimesis*, a single comparatist lacks "world enough and time" to acquire even a working knowledge of the complex interrelations between a couple of literary traditions, let alone to chart all the valleys and peaks on the literary globe (286). What the individual scholar *can* successfully analyze, however, is the self-liquidating impulse at the heart of world literature as an institution, which urges it to constantly invalidate its own selections and to reach out for the world as a whole.

The first histories of literature were written somewhere in the course of the 18th century, so to say in the middle of the nationalist frenzy in European politics. Examples are Massieu's *Histoire de la poësie française* (1739), Tiraboschi's *Storia della letteratura italiana* (1772-95), and Warton's *History of English Poetry* (1780). To be sure, it is possible to point out earlier attestations of national tradition formation, such as Fauchet's *Recueil de l'origine de la langue et poesie françoise, rymes et romans* (1581), or Puttenham's *Arte of English Poesie* (1589), but it seems to me that here the study of a nation's literary exploits remains largely undifferentiated from rulebooks for literary artists or the study of language and rhetoric. In Europe at least, the point of emergence for literary history *per se*, as distinct from poetics (although, clearly, a strict separation is untenable), can impossibly be separated from the gradual formation of national communities, the concomitant upgrading and generalization of metropolitan vernaculars, and the ensuing insecurity about the universal validity of classical standards (which is not therefore incompatible with a strong interest in and respect for the classics).[2]

---

2   It would be interesting to trace at what point in the institutional development of the modern university system the classical curriculum ceased to be regarded as the cornerstone of a commonly shared culture, and became merely one option among others. The downfall of the classics seems particularly apparent in U.S. universities, where their study is now often embedded in Departments of "foreign" languages and literatures. See such responses as Hanson and Heath's *Who Killed Homer* (1998), which both lament and exacerbate the

The historicization of literature – the dislocation of 'histoire' from 'règles' – thus has to be related to the self-promotion of modern literatures from the early modern period onwards and the concomitant need to make the 'new' traditions appear as old and as venerable as the classical heritage. At the same time, this development signals a growing sense that all valuation orderings are (at least in principle) replaceable. To put it bluntly, nations emerged from the realization that there are nations: *on est toujours le gavache de quelqu'un.* The nationalization of literature can thus be described as a means for countering the absence of legitimate criteria for the ranking of literary works in a time when increasing mobility and the spread of print culture were starting to eat away the foundations of the established order of things. National literary history is at once a symptom of the increased possibilities of comparison and an instrument for softening the impact of this development through the universalization of literary norms *within* a given national space. This national containment strategy, however, could hardly conceal the fact that, from now on, the legitimacy of a literary tradition could no longer depend on its correspondence to a god-given order, but rather paradoxically derived from its relation to *other* traditions loaded with *similar* universalist aspirations.

If the first national literary histories took shape in a struggle between ancients and moderns, it may not surprise that the 'universal' or 'general' history of literature actually developed apace with that of national literatures. Ludwig Wachler, whose work awakened Jacob Grimm's interest in the German folk tradition, was still undisturbed by the later division of labor between comparative and national literature scholars.[3] Before he published his *Vorlesungen über die Geschichte der teutschen Nationalliteratur*, he had already written a popular *Handbuch der Geschichte der Literatur* (1804). What I find interesting about the *Handbuch* is that, even while approaching the history of literature (significantly, Wachler did not see the need to add the epithet 'world') as an antidote against "krankhafte Einseitigkeit" ("sickly one-sidedness") (viii), the work does not therefore contest the validity of national traditions. Rather, national self-assertion constituted a *condition* for

---

foreignization of their discipline.

3   One notices a similar initial convergence when it comes to the differentiation of national traditions in formerly colonized states. The first histories of American literature were often conceived of as companions to histories of English literature. See my *Predicting the Past*.

membership in the world republic of letters, which, as far as concerns the modern periods, Wachler saw as the exclusive province of Europe (excluding the unassimilable Turks). In a remarkable turn, Wachler then explains the contemporary political fragmentation in his country as an asset rather than an obstacle for the growth of German literature, in that it would guarantee "die möglichst größte Mannigfaltigkeit geistiger Ansichten" ("the greatest plurality of intellectual views") (337). In this way, the "rich variability" of world literature, as Damrosch would phrase it, coalesces almost imperceptibly with the dream of a strong German nation.

This fusion of horizons is equally apparent in Johannes Scherr's influential *Allgemeine Geschichte der Weltliteratur*, which appeared in 1869 during the running-up phase of the Franco-Prussian war (within a decade, it went through six editions). In the introduction, Scherr commented on the growing importance of literary history and its overall significance for the history of mankind. He added, however, that this development had been particularly outspoken in Germany, "weil den Deutschen vor allen anderen Nationen die universelle Empfänglichkeit verliehen ward, die Weltsprache der Poesie zu hören und zu verstehen" ("because the Germans were granted the universal receptivity to hear and understand the world language of poetry") (4). By hinting at the superior receptivity of the German language to sounds of the most remote cultures in terms of both time and space, Scherr thus attempted to secure for Germany the role of *primus inter pares* in the world republic of letters. In all probability, this philosophy did not fall on deaf German ears at the time. After all, this was an age when Johann Gottlieb Fichte could claim in his *Reden an die deutsche Nation* (1807) that the German "can always be superior to the foreigner and understand him fully, even better than the foreigner understands himself" (quoted and translated by Edwards, 26). Scherr openly applauded a strong German nation and emphatically opposed socialist and realist art, which he thought of as merely "ein Kopirapparat" ("a copy machine") of common reality (13). All this makes it hard not to associate the universalist pretensions of Scherr's *Allgemeine Geschichte* with the unfolding German *Weltpolitik* of the Bismarck era.

What did the world look like on the other side of the shifting Franco-Prussian border? The first Frenchman to occupy a chair in comparative literature was Joseph Texte, a student of Brunetière whose promising career was aborted by his untimely death at age thirty-five. Texte is generally remembered for his *Jean-Jacques Rousseau et le cosmopolitisme littéraire* (1895), in which he describes the rise of the cosmopolitan spirit in French literature as a reaction against the authority of the classical tradition. Texte in particular stressed the role of the *émigrés* in this process, first of all the protestants in London after the revocation of the Edict of Nantes, and a century later those seeking shelter in the Northern countries from the revolutionary turmoil. The pivotal figure between these two waves was the Swiss born Rousseau, whom Texte saw as the personification of a cultural synthesis between the Teutonic North and the Latin South, and because of this, as the father of European literature (which Texte used more or less as a shorthand for "the literature of the world"). As the narrative moved into his own time, however, Texte increasingly stressed the importance of safeguarding the French tradition in the face of the challenge of a unified European literature. Texte's advocacy of the cosmopolitan spirit thus went hand in hand with respectful devotion to the 'genius' of the French tradition.

In the conclusion to the reworked English edition, Texte warns against the danger of a future "coalescence of tongues" and argues that French literature has to "uphold the time-honored position of influence it occupies in the world" (378). This message is perhaps even more pronounced in his later *Études de littérature européenne* (1898), in which he puts forward the ideal of a "United States of Europe," about a century before the official ratification of the European Union at the 1992 Maastricht Treaty. But Texte gives his ideal a decidedly French inflection: "l'idéal européen de demain sera voisin, en littérature comme ailleurs, de l'idéal français du XVIIIe siècle, en ce qu'il tendra à une fédération des peuples" ("the European ideal of tomorrow will be close, in literature as elsewhere, to the French ideal of the 18th century insofar as it will constitute a federation of peoples") (304). For Texte, the distinctiveness of the French tradition, that which set it apart from other traditions (and which would guarantee its future greatness), was precisely its universalism, its rejection of national single-mindedness in favor of a commitment to humanity at large. Written in a period of intense rivalry among the big European nations, Texte's history of European literature thus fused the dream of European unification with an at times barely hidden nostalgia for the French cultural dominance during the *siècle des lumières*.

This sacralization of the 'French' 18th century is still apparent about a quarter century later in Paul Van Tieghem's *Précis littéraire de l'Europe depuis la Renaissance*. In the preface to his book, Van Tieghem vigorously opposed those textbooks that, while pretending to be histories of universal literature, merely offer a juxtaposition of national traditions. Even while promoting an international perspective, however, Van Tieghem at the same time underscored the centrality of the French tradition in European literature (and, by extension, that of the world). He divided his history, spanning about six centuries in all, into three periods: the Renaissance, the classical age, and the modern period. He clearly felt most at home in the middle period, on which he had published widely (particularly the preromantic movement). Thus, indirectly, his internationalism served to bring out the international standing of French literature during that period. In fact, for Van Tieghem, the French classical tradition more or less coalesced with world literature as such: "L'âge classique est celui de l'hégémonie littéraire de la France; il commence et finit avec elle" ("the classical age is that of the literary hegemony of France; it begins and ends with it") (89).

Like most of his predecessors, Van Tieghem excluded the literature of Turkey (where Apter locates the origin of comparative literature!) but was much more welcoming towards that of the U.S., "qui s'ajoutent depuis le XVIIIe siècle au monde littéraire européen" ("who have joined the European literary world since the 18th century") (iv).[4] On the other side of the Atlantic, however, the canon of world literature acquired totally different overtones. Werner Friederich, one of the founders of comparative literature in the U.S., thought that his adopted country had a special duty to safeguard the European tradition from total destruction. In a speech delivered in 1948 at a conference in Paris, he states his view as follows: "For somehow we feel, with joy and with pride, that what we are doing is part of the deeper meaning of the Marshall Plan, that our vigorous activity somehow goes beyond the realm of mere book-learning, that we are here to help each other, and to save, together with you, the great cultural heritage that belongs to us, the Western World" (10). The analogy with the Marshall Plan indicates that after the

---

4 In fact, the only American author Van Tieghem discusses is Franklin, whose *Autobiography* he describes as an interesting contribution to the prose of the classical period despite "l'absence de style" (174).

Second World War the U.S. assumed for itself a key role in the transmission of the canon of "Western" literature (Friederich found world literature too presumptuous a term), but at the same time claimed the right to stipulate the future course of the world as a whole.

We seem to have come a long way from what to most observers in the U.S. may appear like the European 'prehistory' of comparative literature studies. Whereas for Wachler and company the history of world literature still to some extent served to articulate or consolidate the place of their national group in the world, now world literature seems to have become more of an instrument for radically questioning the validity of traditional national divisions.[5] At which point, one may ask, did world literature shift its meaning from the world as we know it to the world as we fail to (but should) know it? How can we explain this inflationary usage of the concept? Is it really true, as Wai Chee Dimock states in her *Through Other Continents*, that literature in today's world fulfills the role of "an NGO of sorts," which contradicts the institutionalized boundaries and the standardized time-reckoning of the modern nation-state (8)? I claim that such a view – I call it the Therapeutic Fallacy – is misguided in two respects. First, it is based on a false opposition between the nation and the world. As I have tried to show, the nation is a symptom, not a cause, in that it is always already postnational. That is why the proposal to go beyond the nation carries little or no explanatory value. Second, interventionist perspectives such as Dimock's, however useful for probing new research topics, fail to take into account the paradox that the idea of world literature came into being precisely at a point when the world was starting to lose the possibility of a unitary conception of itself.

In a globalized society, the world can no longer be adequately described as the totality of all things. Rather, it constitutes what Luhmann has called "eine selbstsubstitutive Ordnung" ("a self-substitutive order") (*Die Gesellschaft* 491-92). This means that the world has to take into account its own worldliness, and therefore has to abandon the illusion that it can offer a full picture of everything that it stands for. Put differently, the world has to represent itself as unrepresentable. Luhmann explains this semantic shift in terms

---

5   According to Djelal Kadir, we have now moved from the Marshall Plan conception of comparative literature of the post-World War II era to the "Martial Plan" conception during the age of terrorism ("Comparative Literature" 73).

of a number of structural changes in modern society which have dramatically multiplied communicative possibilities and, through this, the perspectives on the world: the spread of European colonialism since the 16th century, the introduction of world time since the second half of the 19th century, society's increasing reliance on the future rather than the past for its organization (and, hence, the need for historiography to disembarrass it from the past!), the growing autonomy and self-reflexivity of the different functional subsystems of society, and finally, the rise of new media which further trivialize the hold of traditional territorial boundaries. The nation, for Luhmann, constitutes one of those transitory semantics that accompany this gradual transformation, and which may now be in the process of deconstructing itself (1054).

In this context, world literature constitutes less a cure for nationalism than a machine for making the world appear within the world. In modern world society, world literature validates itself in a highly paradoxical fashion by indicating that, as James Bond would have it, the world is not enough.[6] Precisely this institutionalized self-negation is what allows such a category to mobilize enormous amounts of dissensus and self-criticism without disintegrating. But this guarantee for survival comes at a price. Literature is now locked into its own functional domain: in other worlds (in other function systems), it is of little consequence.[7] That is why the rhetoric of inclusivity and representativity that is currently dominant in literary and cultural studies will only accentuate the self-imposed incapacity to communicate with the world as a whole. Despite this fact, current discussions of world literature continue to be guided by a conception of the world as a *series rerum* (a more

---

6   In fact, the motto of Her Majesty's Secret Service in the Bond series is but the repetition of an old refrain going back to classical antiquity. "Non Sufficit Mundus" was inscribed in the Spanish monarchy's shield of arms at the end of the 16th century. Even here, one could argue, in a period of intense rivalry among the European colonial powers, the meaning of the phrase had already shifted from the insufficiency of the earthly world vis-à-vis the pre-ordained otherworldly order (*contemptus mundi*) to the insufficiency of the otherworldly in the face of an all too worldly world.

7   It is precisely because literature is autonomous in an operational sense (this means: its valuation orderings can no longer be imposed from the outside), that someone like Dimock is free to toy with the strictures of standardized time without being fired from her job for consistently missing appointments.

or less fixed quantity of things) that modern world society has had to give up. If Luhmann's systems-theoretical approach cannot cure the therapeutic urge of comparative literature studies (this, after all, would be to reinstate the rhetoric of self-improvement – it is this rhetoric, in my opinion, that severely limits the explanatory potential of most postmarxist theories), I claim that it does provide a sufficiently complex conceptual framework for understanding the self-substitutive dynamic of world literature as an institutional matrix.

Rather than embracing the "to come" as a *solution* for the problems besetting a decrepit discipline (Spivak 6 and passim), i.e., by suggesting a continually receding post-perspective (does not my admittedly tentative account of the emergence of world literature show that it has from the start projected itself into the future?), I propose to redescribe this "to come" logic as the constitutive *problem* of world literature, which ensures the necessary inadequacy of any kind of disease treatment (and, hence, the continuing connectivity of communication on world literature). What, then, explains the imperative mood of world literature, this communicative interest in ever more world (an interest rooted in an epistemology of ignorance)? In order to address this question, I think we need to abandon the current fixation on the effects of Anglo-globalism. The global dominance of a national culture and language is but one manifestation of deeper structural changes, just as the nation-state is but one way of segmenting the political system. By definition, every communicative act invites negation. Although some languages may be more successful than others, it is clear that this relative success has nothing to do with inherent properties of the languages themselves. Contrary to such media as money, power, the law, art, religion, and the like, language has a fairly limited potential for symbolic generalization (and this precisely because it makes understanding easier!).[8]

---

8   In his 1838 *Lectures on the History of Literature* Thomas Carlyle could still regret the fact that, despite French culture's "undeniable barrenness of genius," no ideas or inventions can possibly become popularized till they are presented to the world by means of the French language (10). Carlyle's unease at the priority of French as the language of science reflects the growing importance of English as a medium of international communication. At a similar juncture a century later, H.L. Mencken argues in the fourth edition of *The American Language* (1946) that one "must be a Bostonian to avoid open mirth" when hearing Oxford English (608). Here it is "Standard" English that represents the reviled norm and American English that functions as the democratic alternative (in Mencken's opinion, contrary to its

From this perspective, as Luhmann argued as early as 1975, all languages belong in principle to the same "Übersetzungsgesellschaft" ("translation community") ("Einführende Bemerkungen" 40).⁹ The problem that should concern us, therefore, is what motivates acceptance *in spite of* increasing possibilities of understanding (and, hence, of misunderstanding)? For this, I think we need to focus our attention on the paradoxical logic of the various symbolic media that have developed in modern society. In such a constellation, the world sustains itself through the institutionalization of its own refutation. It thus becomes clear that the vision of a 'planetary' perspective as opposed to the 'Eurocentric' standpoint of an earlier generation constitutes nothing but a replay of the earlier opposition between the 'cosmopolitan' and the 'classical' spirit that animated debates about a century ago. Although the coalitions have shifted dramatically, the dynamic remains more or less the same. Such asymmetrical counterconcepts as North/South, East/West, center/margin, or us/others can no longer demarcate the category of world literature; rather, they supply the semantic programs that facilitate the process of selection *inside* the contingent communicative space opened up by the various subsystems of a world society that insists on representing itself as unrepresentable.

Works Cited

Apter, Emily. *The Translation Zone: A New Comparative Literature*. Princeton and Oxford: Princeton University Press, 2006.
Arac, Jonathan. "Anglo-Globalism?" *New Left Review* 16 (2002): 35-45.
Auerbach, Erich. "Philologie der Weltliteratur." *Weltliteratur: Festgabe für Fritz Strich zum 70. Geburtstag*. Ed. Walter Muschg and Emil Staiger.

British variant, English in America had retained the Elizabethan libido for word-making). If anything, such shifting alliances show that the current fear regarding the growing standardization of culture through the spread of English is misguided insofar as every standard by definition invites contradiction.

9   Once again, this is not to deny the massive trade imbalances that exist between the world's languages (for this, see Venuti). Such discrepancies, however, do not depend on unalterable features of the languages in question, but on the ways in which they are put to use by symbolic media. Hence, the problem cannot be solved just by pleading, as Venuti does, for better, more "resistant" translations.

Bern: Francke, 1952. 39-50.
Beil, Else. *Zur Entwicklung des Begriffs Weltliteratur*. Leipzig: Voigtländer, 1915.
Boyden, Michael. *Predicting the Past: The Functions of American Literature*. (unpublished manuscript)
Carlyle, Thomas. *Lectures on the History of Literature*. Ed. Reay J. Greene. New York: Scribner, 1892.
Casanova, Pascale. *La république mondiale des lettres*. Paris: Seuil, 1999.
Damrosch, David. *What Is World Literature?* Princeton and Oxford: Princeton University Press, 2003.
Dimock, Wai Chee. *Through Other Continents: American Literature Across Deep Time*. Princeton and Oxford: Princeton University Press, 2006.
Edwards, John. *Language, Society, and Identity*. Oxford and New York: Blackwell, 1985.
Fauchet, Claude. *Recueil de l'origine de la langue et poesie françoise, rymes et romans*. Paris: Patisson, 1581.
Ferris, David. "Indiscipline." *Comparative Literature in an Age of Globalization*. Ed. Haun Saussy. 78-99.
Friederich, Werner P. "Comparative Literature in the United States." *The Challenge of Comparative Literature and Other Addresses*. Ed. William J. DeSua and David H. Malone. Chapel Hill: University of North Carolina Press, 1970. 1-10.
Guérard, Albert. *Preface to World Literature*. New York: H. Holt & Co., 1940.
Gillespie, Gerald. *By Way of Comparison: Reflections on the Theory and Practice of Comparative Literature*. Paris: Honoré Champion, 2004.
Hanson, Victor Davis and John Heath. *Who Killed Homer? The Demise of Classical Education and the Recovery of Greek Wisdom*. New York: Free Press, 1998.
Hassan, Waïl S. "World Literature in the Age of Globalization: Reflections on an Anthology." *College English* 63.1 (2000): 38-47.
Kadir, Djelal. "To World, to Globalize – Comparative Literature's Crossroads." *Comparative Literature Studies* 41.1 (2004): 1-9.
———. "Comparative Literature in an Age of Terrorism." *Comparative Literature in an Age of Globalization*. Ed. Haun Saussy. 68-77.

Luhmann, Niklas, "Einführende Bemerkungen zu einer Theorie symbolisch generalisierter Kommunikationsmedien." *Aufsätze und Reden*. Ed. Oliver Jahraus. Stuttgart: Reclam, 2001. 31-75.

———. *Die Gesellschaft der Gesellschaft*. 2 vols. Frankfurt am Main: Suhrkamp, 1997.

Massieu, Guillaume. *Histoire de la poësie française; avec une défense de la poësie*. Paris: Prault, 1739.

Matvejević, Pedrag. "Cultures et littératures nationales en Europe (concepts et pratiques)." *Littérature comparée / Littérature mondiale – Comparative Literature / World Literature: Actes du XIième congrès de l'Association Internationale de Littérature Comparée (Paris, août 1985) / Proceedings of the XIth Congress of the International Comparative Literature Association (Paris, August 1985)*. Ed. Gerald Gillespie. Vol. 5. New York: Peter Lang, 1991.

Mencken, Henry L. *The American Language: A Preliminary Inquiry into the Development of English in the United States*. 4th ed. New York: Knopf, 1946.

Moretti, Franco. "Conjectures on World Literature." *New Left Review* 1 (2000): 54-68.

Puttenham, George (Richard). *The Arte of English Poesie. Contriued into Three Bookes: The First of Poets and Poesie, The Second of Proportion, The Third of Ornament*. London: Richard Field, 1589.

Saussy, Haun, ed. *Comparative Literature in an Age of Globalization*. Baltimore: Johns Hopkins University Press, 2006.

Scherr, Johannes. *Allgemeine Geschichte der Weltliteratur*. 6th ed. Stuttgart: Conradi, 1880.

Spivak, Gayatri C. *Death of a Discipline*. New York: Columbia University Press, 2003.

Texte, Joseph. *Études de littérature européenne*. Paris: Colin, 1898.

———. *Jean-Jacques Rousseau and the Cosmopolitan Spirit in Literature: A Study of the Literary Relations between France and England during the Eighteenth Century*. Trans. J.W. Matthews. London: Duckworth & Co., 1899.

Tiraboschi, Girolamo. *Storia della letteratura italiana*. 11 vols. Modena: Presso la Società tipografica, 1772-95.

Van Parijs, Philippe. "The Ground Floor of the World: On the Socio-Economic Consequences of Linguistic Globalization." *International Political Science Review* 21.2 (2000): 217-33.

Van Tieghem, Paul. *Histoire littéraire de l'Europe et de l'Amérique de la Renaissance à nos jours.* Paris: Colin, 1941.

Venuti, Lawrence. *The Translator's Invisibility: A History of Translation.* Philadelphia: University of Pennsylvania Press, 1995.

Wachler, Ludwig. *Vorlesungen über die Geschichte der teutschen National-litteratur.* Frankfurt am Main: Hermann, 1818-19.

———. *Handbuch der Geschichte der Litteratur.* 1804. 3rd ed. Leipzig: J.A. Barth, 1833.

Warton, Thomas. *The History of English Poetry, From the Eleventh to the Seventeenth Century.* London: Murray, 1780.

Lieven D'hulst (K.U.Leuven)

Translation and Its Role in European Literatures: Some Questions and Answers

The image of Europe as a 'network' of literatures calls to mind quite different concepts such as distinct identities and interconnectedness. For many, the 'network' metaphor may appear nowadays as more fashionable than, say, the 'melting pot' metaphor or even the 'salad bowl' metaphor, since it seems to express more adequately the way they think cultures ideally should talk to each other. Yet, retrospectively, as we all know, the history of Europe has rarely lived up to this ideal. How, then, should we proceed from a research perspective? One might be advised to understand a network as an open, so-called 'heuristic' metaphor, one that might help to locate relationality between literatures on a scale that goes from 0% to 100%. Such an approach would at least imply the replacement of an 'either/or' (or 'yes/no') approach by a 'when/how' or a 'when/why' approach. In other terms, we better not start from *a priori* assumptions about the homogeneity and high relationality of the European space or, inversely, about its heterogeneity and low relationality. Instead, we should start from the assumption that it is possible to reconstruct types, contents, and degrees of relations on a diachronical axis: when, and under which historical circumstances, did the awareness of literary relations taking place between European literatures emerge? How did it materialize in different literary and critical traditions? How did it change and by which constraints?

Generally speaking, interliterary relations are established either in a direct way, through multilingual communication, or in an indirect way, through translational communication. One may safely assume that the latter has been, and probably still is, the dominant means of communication between literatures worldwide (Heilbron 206). For comparatists, translations are an important source of information for understanding the *rapports de faits* between literatures: what may they reveal about the openness of particular literatures, of their literary preferences?

'Translation' is traditionally understood, first, as an *interlingual* substitutive operation engaging at least two discourse systems. In addition, translation is an *intralingual* substitutive operation manifest in many types of so-called monolingual discourse (rephrasing, code-mixing, etc.). Finally, translation is an *intersemiotic* substitutive operation engaging different media (language and film, music and dance, novel and strips, etc.). These different occurrences of translation may be mixed to a certain extent, as in cases such as the dubbing or subtitling of movies based on novels (think of the international spread of *The Da Vinci Code* to name but one example).

In the following, I will deal more particularly with intralingual and interlingual translation, while taking into account two translation directions: I will distinguish 'intranslation' (from out to in) and 'extranslation' (from in to out). I will also raise the question whether it is sufficient to distinguish translation types and directions on the basis of a linguistic parameter only: since both are part of a larger set of transfer procedures (such as reproduction, plagiarism, hybridization, or adaptation) that are used for the exchange of information, irrespective of whether these procedures take place within a single literature or between different literatures, we probably also need an adapted comparative framework for the study of both these different transfer procedures and of translation proper.

Even if for practical reasons we would prefer to limit our scope to interlingual translation between literatures, it does not make much sense to understand literatures as stable, well-delineated entities, i.e., as autonomous discursive and institutional organizations – as organizations, in other words, that can be adequately labelled by a single epithet: 'Portuguese' literature vs. 'Russian' literature vs. 'Dutch' literature, and so on. The presupposition underlying these labels is of course that literatures exchange only a limited number of products, and that these exchanges have no major effects on their autonomy and internal cohesion: each literature seems to have its own repertoire, its own distribution of genres and of writing techniques, its own institutions, etc., which are not drastically affected by its sharing of forms and concepts with other literatures, or of its taking part in transnational relations, such as literary movements. In fact, this presupposition simply reproduces the 19th century model of so-called national literatures, and no doubt many literary histories, educational systems (including university departments), and other institutions (such as literary criticism) are even today not ready to abandon the idea that literatures are *by definition* national literatures.

Importantly, the appeareance of translations (and of other transfer procedures) makes sense only when we assume there *are* differences between the 'literatures' we can distinguish. Hence our previously mentioned historical approach comes into the picture: it is more fruitful to try to know which European literatures have intranslated more than others during their history; which ones have extranslated more than others; which literatures do not intranslate or extranslate the same types of texts (novels, poetry, essays, etc.); and which literatures extranslate into non-European literatures as well as intranslate from them. Still, it would be naïve to think that the pure accumulation of facts will be sufficient to answer the ensuing 'why' question. In other terms, if we want to advance our understanding of the role of translation within the complex interplay between literatures, we need a model or theory that brings 'when' and 'why' together in an explicit way. In my view, systems theory as developed by the Israeli scholar Itamar Even-Zohar since the late seventies of the 20th century is one of the better candidates for this task. According to systems theory, a literature is to be understood as a complex network of relations that regulates both its internal structure and its relations with other systems. Let me shortly bring to memory these two claims (see also D'hulst, "Intra- and Intersystemic Relations").

The first property of a system is the latent or overt tension between its constituent strata. Each system has a number of central and peripheral strata – 'strata' being general labels for repertoires of different shapes and types (genres, macrostructural and microstructural devices such as topoi, narrative models, character portraits, dialogue structures, or prosody):

> It is the permanent tension between the various strata which constitutes the (dynamic) synchronic state of the system. It is the prevalence of one set of systemic options over another which constitutes the change on the diachronic axis. In this centrifugal vs. centripetal motion, systemic options may be driven from a central position to a marginal one while others may be pushed into the center and prevail. (Even-Zohar, "Polysystem Theory (Revised)" 42)

The main source of tensions, and of resulting changes in positions for the different strata, lies in the unequal status and legitimacy of these strata. Dominant groups tend to canonize specific strata, and, accordingly, to push other ones towards the margins of the system. On the other hand, if the dominant strata resist renewal or change, they may in the longer run lose their position in favor of different, often lower ranked, strata supported by other groups of writers and critics.

The second property of systems, i.e., their relationality, is a direct outcome of the first one, since tensions between strata cover a number of relations between them. Historical analysis shows that a current type of relation depends on a current type of system. More precisely, as long as the idea of a unified literary system prevails, steered by a number of parameters, such as a center-periphery hierarchy, centrally controlled procedures of canonization and of allocation of genres and writing techniques, the prevailing relations between the strata of the system may be called 'intrasystemic relations' – i.e., relations that take place between strata that belong to a single system. More often than not, both the concept of system and the resulting relations are in such cases supported by political and/or institutional factors, which may also link the literary system with other cultural systems that are produced by the same community. Yet, when the system changes, i.e., when the parameters that determine the positions and functions within the system are no longer capable of exerting control over its constituent elements, and notably over the system's peripheries, relations with other systems may very likely expand without, however, necessarily superseding intrasystemic relations. The functions of 'intersystemic relations' are quite comparable to the functions of intrasystemic relations, since, like peripheral strata within a single system, exogenous systems try to challenge the dominant strata within the system in view of a change or replacement of the dominant repertoires.

Translations are traditionally considered to be among the best barometers of the intersystemic relations taking place *between* literatures. Indeed, translators are decision makers by vocation, as they simply *have* to find practical solutions to overcome language and culture barriers, and their solutions, whatever their logic or extent, may reveal strong connections as well as major obstacles between literary systems. But once again, translations are also vehicles of intrasystemic relations between strata belonging to *one system*; their functions are in such cases similar to the functions of translations taking place between systems. Logically, from such a viewpoint, translation should be labeled as either "intrasystemic" or "intersystemic." The only way to understand the complex of available options as well as the constraints, be they linguistic or literary, that influence the translator's behavior, is to carry out actual descriptions of these two types of translation, and understand what they can tell us about intrasystemic and intersystemic relations.

Even if taking into account published translations only, and leaving aside the study of the theories and techniques of particular translators and of the reading and criticism of translations, historians have not been able, so far, to collect even representative samples for all European literatures of all periods, from the massive transfer from Greek culture to Rome in the first centuries till the globalizing trends at the end of the 20th century. Therefore, what follows will be limited to a short presentation with examples of the two translation types.

Intrasystemic translations take place within one system: they are vehicles of the relations established between different strata making use of different languages. In such cases, translation is used in a diglossic or in a multilingual system. Such systems have rarely been studied, and yet they have been the rule rather than the exception in the history of European cultures: think for instance of the opposition between Latin and most vernacular languages, or between dialect and standard language, or between older and newer variants of one language. Translations may unsurprisingly be understood as bridges between these strata. But their functions are much more complex.

Let us consider briefly the case of Belgian literature in the early 19th century: two languages coexist in the national space, each contributing through its own genres and language forms to so-called 'Belgian literature.' Yet, a tension between both languages rapidly develops: French being the language of the cultural elite, it is chosen by this elite as the major vehicle of the national literature in view of its optimal positioning on the international scene. At the same time, the Belgian nation is considered incapable of gaining literary, cultural, and even political autonomy and legitimacy in Europe because it lacks sufficient specificity. In other words, Belgian literature has to develop into a system in which literary language (register, style), genres, writing forms, are up to a certain point different from what is offered by the highly prestigious French repertoire. While it cannot compete with the latter, it may at least try to become an established literature with a certain autonomy instead of being simply assimilated by the periphery of the French literary center.

One major opportunity available to achieve this goal is to enrich the Francophone production with lower genres (such as the ballad, or short narrative forms), macrostructural devices (chronotopes and characters), and microstructural ones (plurilingualism, popular dialogue forms) that are borrowed from Flemish culture and literature. In this process of cultural hybridization, intranslation from Flemish into French plays a possibly important role: it shows Francophone authors how to assimilate Flemish form and content elements into French. But this opportunity is not very successful during most of the 19th century: since French intranslation means selection and manipulation, it becomes also an instrument of intracultural domination within Belgium.

Of course, the respective positions of the strata may gradually change in the course of time. From the viewpoint of the lower strata, such as literature written in Flemish, one may easily imagine that intranslation from French would equally be an alternative in the search for a better positioning of literature written in Flemish within the Belgian system. But this alternative in its turn remains ineffective, mainly because French is largely accessible to the Flemish reading public. As a consequence, the scarcity of translations from French into Flemish has been compensated for (especially in poetry) by translations from other literatures (such as German). In other terms, since the former option does not lead to the recognition of literature written in Flemish within the context of Belgium, other ones are developed, which helps to shape different contents and forms for Flemish poetry, all in view of escaping intrasystemic domination by Francophone literature. Intrasystemic translation may thus be superseded by intersystemic translation and help to establish new cultural communities, which by the way was the case in Belgium during the 20th century, when Flemish literature gradually managed to gain recognition.

Translations taking place within one system have hardly received any attention from comparatists.[1] The reason, once again, has been that literatures were predominantly understood as monolingual 'national' constructs. Time has come to open up new perspectives on the study of intranslation of literary texts (or parts of texts) produced in non-standard languages (such as dialects). It is especially in this respect that the necessary correlation of intrasystemic translation with other transfer procedures becomes conspicuous. One may even argue that in 19th century Belgium, the construction of an

---

1   For a recent example, see Meylaerts.

endogenous repertoire made more intense use of non-translational procedures such as editions and re-writings of ancient narratives (*Thyl Ulenspiegel, Le Roman de Renard*) and of historical chronicles, in addition to amplification techniques applied to anecdotes, fragments, and topoi. From a historical viewpoint, it is far from sure whether it is useful to trace *a priori* border lines between translation and transfer or between intrasystemic and intersystemic relations, and even between intrasystemic and intersystemic translations: it is the particular situation of a given system that explains the intensity and function of its relationality policy.

When different communities have no language in common, *intersystemic translation* becomes an obvious bridge between them. Thousands of such translations between most European literatures have been studied so far. Yet, as I mentioned, it is still not possible to lay bare the main tendencies of translational behavior or even to answer more general questions such as: what have been the size and content of translation flows in Europe? What have been the major functions exercized by translations? Did translations gradually contribute to the genesis of the concept of 'Europe?' It may seem strange, but such questions are still rather new, and attention has been drawn to them by sociologists rather than by literary scholars. For a long time, comparatists have limited themselves to the study of binary relations, as if literatures changed their translation methods and ideologies according to the language pairs and literatures involved, as if translation from, say, French into Spanish had little in common with translation from English into Spanish, from German into Spanish, etc. It is, once again, the work of Even-Zohar that opened up new vistas. In his seminal paper on "The Position of Translated Literature within the Literary Polysystem" (1990), he develops the idea according to which translation may assume either an innovative or a conservative role within its target literature. The former option depends on one of three possible conditions:

> It seems to me that three major cases can be discerned, which are basically various manifestations of the same law: (a) when a polysystem has not yet been crystallized, that is to say, when a literature is 'young,' in the process of being established; (b) when a literature is either 'peripheral' (within a large group of correlated literatures) or 'weak,' or both; and (c) when there are turning points, crises, or literary vacuums in a literature. (48)

The latter (conservatory) role is no less prominent:

> A highly interesting paradox manifests itself here: translation, by which new ideas, items, characteristics can be introduced into a literature, becomes a means to preserve traditional taste. This discrepancy between the original central literature and the translated literature may have evolved in a variety of ways, for instance, when translated literature, after having assumed a central position and inserted new items, soon lost contact with the original home literature which went on changing, and thereby became a factor of preservation of unchanged repertoire. Thus, a literature that might have emerged as a revolutionary type may go on existing as an ossified *système d'antan,* often fanatically guarded by the agents of secondary models against even minor changes. The conditions which enable this second state are of course diametrically opposite to those which give rise to translated literature as a central system: either there are no major changes in the polysystem or these changes are not effected through the intervention of interliterary relations materialized in the form of translations. (50)

More scholars nowadays try to promote international translation research in several directions, and, while it is impossible at this moment to give answers to the general questions just raised, it is useful to show by some examples that research devoted to more than one literature or to more than one pair of literatures may yield original insights. I will briefly, and in a very superficial way, suggest two possible topics: the study of translation figures and of translation flows. The figures at our disposal are based on statistics produced by national agencies, which means of course that they only concern books produced in the national language and within the borders of the state.

As to translation figures in general (literature and other genres), some of the most detailed results available concern translations into Dutch during the 20th century (Heilbron). The main conclusions are as follows: intranslation has increased considerably since the Second World War (nowadays up to 25% of all books published in the Netherlands); these translations are most often based on originals written in English (over 60%); German and French each represent between 10 and 12%. Extranslation from the Dutch is also growing, first in German, then in English and French. These figures should eventually become more detailed as to distribution in genres (literature and other cultural practices) and in literary subgenres in particular (translated popular narratives seem to have become quite successful in recent times).

The European translation market is also growing. In France, for example, intranslation represented 8,5% of the total book production in 1838, and 19% in 1991 (D'hulst, "Traduire"). More generally, it seems, the international position of languages is a major factor determining the exchange rates (De Swaan). As a consequence, there seems to be less intranslation in dominant languages in comparison with intranslation in so-called peripheral cultures. An additional explanation for the low rate of intranslation into English (less than 5%, and approximately 20% for Spanish) could be the dominance of worldwide 'intra-English' literary relations.

On the basis of such figures, it becomes possible to infer the existence of macrosystemic networks of systems that are capable of determining translation flows within Europe as a whole. We all know, for instance, to what extent French culture dominated other cultures for centuries (think of "L'Europe des Lumières" in the 18th century). Translation has very probably played a crucial role in the establishment and dissemination of this dominance. Some years ago, I studied, together with Dirk Delabastita, the continental spread of translations of Shakespeare during the period of his rediscovery at the end of the 18th century. Shakespeare has been channelled into Europe via France and via French translations and translation models. More particularly, French translations of Shakespearean drama were quite successful in large parts of Europe (up to Russia), to the extent that they were preferred not only to the originals, but also to endogenous translations, and that in a number of cases they have even been translated themselves into the endogenous languages. We should understand that translations were not only expressions of literary norms, but that they also became actively involved in literary evolution. As a consequence, during the second half of the 19th century, in Germany, Poland, Russia, Italy, Sweden, and so on, French versions of Shakespeare have seen the competition of new endogeneous versions that became the symbol of a new poetics and often accompanied the emergence of national literatures.[2]

---

2   It would be quite interesting to see what happens transnationally with other major icons of European culture, such as Homer, Virgil, the Bible, Marx, Freud, Foucault, Derrida, etc. Such studies should be able to reveal not only the institutional channels of transmission, but also the influence of interpretive patterns and of translation procedures developed by one culture before being adopted by a chain of other cultures.

It should be clear by now that it does not make sense anymore to approach the issue of translation restrictively, as an activity that is simply initiated by the absence of language knowledge on the side of the receiver of the source text. This is what it, of course, also is, because we do write and read translations whenever there are linguistic and culture barriers. But translations are more than just that. They help to shape national literatures, to regulate power relations between literary communities, to dominate literatures and emancipate others. All in all, the extent to which they have been able to 'construct' Europe is far from clear at this moment; but at least they show we should 're-think' Europe from a set of relational viewpoints.

Turning back to our starting point, this also means that we need adequate methods to integrate the study of translation into comparative literature. For some, like Susan Bassnett (1993) and, more recently, Emily Apter (2006), it means even more, namely that translation should become the heart of comparative literature:

> In attempting to rethink critical paradigms in the humanities after 9/11, with special emphasis on language and war, the problem of creolization and the mapping of languages "in-translation," shifts in the world canon and literary markets, and the impact of enhanced technologies of information translation, I have tried to imagine a program for a new comparative literature using translation as a fulcrum. (Apter 243)

Things may eventually develop the way Apter is imagining, if enough people share such a belief. And of course, the criticism of monolingualism and of nation-states may well be supported by translation, but maybe the question is not whether we should 'use' translation or not, but rather how we should study it and for what purpose. One may wonder how much space a new program for comparative literature is ready to accept for translation studies as a fully established discipline in its own right? From the latter's perspective, at least, research may go on using its techniques for the investigation of the multifarious forms of translation in society. But within a European or a global perspective, a truly interdisciplinary dialogue between comparative literature and translation studies becomes indispensable. Such a dialogue requires vast and detailed research programs, in which the conceptual status of both translation and comparison should not be reduced to any sort of trope.

Works Cited

Apter, Emily. *The Translation Zone: A New Comparative Literature*. Princeton and Oxford: Princeton University Press, 2006.

Bassnett, Susan. *Comparative Literature: A Critical Introduction*. London: Blackwell, 1993.

Delabastita, Dirk and Lieven D'hulst, eds. *Shakespeare Translations in the Romantic Age*. Amsterdam: John Benjamins, 1993.

De Swaan, Abram. "The Evolving European Language System." *International Political Science Review* 14.3 (1993): 241-55.

D'hulst, Lieven. "Traduire l'Europe en France entre 1810 et 1840." *Europe et traduction*. Ed. Michel Ballard. Arras, Ottawa: Artois Presses Université – Les Presses de l'Université d'Ottawa, 1998. 137-57.

——. "Intra- and Intersystemic Relations in the Caribbean: A Research Project." *Caribbean Interfaces*. Ed. Lieven D'hulst e.a. Amsterdam: Rodopi, 2007. 235-45.

Even-Zohar, Itamar. "The Position of Translated Literature within the Literary Polysystem." *Poetics Today* 11.1 (1990): 45-51.

——. "Polysystem Theory (Revised)." *Papers in Culture Research*. Tel Aviv: The Porter Chair of Semiotics, Tel Aviv University, 2005. 38-49.

Heilbron, Johan. "Nederlandse vertalingen wereldwijd: Kleine landen en culturele mondialisering." *Waarin een klein land: Nederlandse cultuur in internationaal verband*. Ed. Johan Heilbron, Wouter de Nooy, and Wilma Tichelaar. Amsterdam: Prometheus, 1995. 206-53.

Meylaerts, Reine. *L'aventure flamande de la Revue Belge: Langues, littératures et cultures dans l'entre-deux-guerres*. New York: Peter Lang, 2004.

Ben van Humbeeck (K.U.Leuven)

The (Im)Possibilities of a European Literary History: The Case of Flanders

With the Balkans as a notable exception to the rule, the greater part of Europe has been living in peace since the armistice that concluded the Second World War. Still, conflicts have been part and parcel of European history throughout the centuries. From even before the Roman period to the great traumas of the First and the Second World War, Europe has suffered a history of conflict and war, and although the weapons may have been silenced, more recent developments show that Europe is still a continent looking for a way to harmonize conflicting interests. Two major tendencies seem to collide: on the one hand, the European Union shows a remarkable tendency towards economic and political expansion and internationalization, demonstrated, most notably, by the accession of fifteen new member states in 2004 and of Bulgaria and Rumania in 2007, while negotiations with Turkey and a number of Balkan states are still under way; on the other hand, a regionalizing tendency can be discerned as well, as in the past and in the present, linguistic, religious, and ethnic dividing lines have defined a significant part of the political agenda in Europe, leading to discussions on and demands for the autonomy of a number of regions.

Both in the fields of literature and politics, these discussions are often dominated by rather vague concepts such as 'national character' and 'national identity.' As the division of the world into sovereign nations seems almost self-evident, these terms are quite familiar to the European citizen. Yet, working in a discipline which – among other things – analyzes and interprets discourses, students of literature and literary scholars alike are equally used to the idea that these concepts are constructs, that nations are man-made and, moreover, of a fairly recent date. Indeed, as Anne-Marie Thiesse reminds us: "nations are a recent creation, barely two centuries old. They were literally invented. And, once invented, they were consolidated by founding myths – and sometimes by bouts of ethnic cleansing." And she adds: "The recent upsurge of nationalism in Europe reflects above all a failure of politics and the difficulty of forging new collective identities based on a genuine political project." While Thiesse's claim that recent nationalist and regionalist movements reflect a failure of politics relies on a conception of politics that I neither want to affirm nor contest here, she does point to an issue that will serve as a central focus of this essay and that could be called 'the paradox of Europe.'

This paradox takes the following form. On the one hand, there is the ideal of a 'United States of Europe,' which is or was the dream of several European statesmen, most notably perhaps Winston Churchill and Paul-Henri Spaak.[1] The theory behind this ideal is simple: the multiplicity of European nations is to be transformed into one unified economic and political entity. After the formation of this European Union, the continent will then – quite naturally – develop a cultural unity as well. This theory may seem overtly naïve, but the success of this dream is nonetheless reflected in the continuous growth of the EU. Although member states are primarily driven by economic motives, their increasing number is also a growing guarantee for peace and prosperity and fuels a growing belief in the European dream. On the other hand, however – and bearing in mind the French and Dutch rejection of the European Constitution – it seems that a European Union modeled after the United States of America is not exactly on the horizon, as the union of Europe is countered by a number of nationalist and regionalist movements. These nationalist sentiments not only arise in notably chauvinistic countries like France, but also in the Netherlands, and even in notably non-chauvinistic countries like Belgium (on which more below). The evident growth of the European Union notwithstanding, the realization of the dream of a true European union is hindered by various nationalist sentiments. This paradox shows the vulnerability of the dream of unification, and suggests the utopian nature of Europe's project of establishing a stable and collective unity. 'Utopian,' in this sense, points to both the ideality and the elusiveness of this goal.

The (literary) situation in the northern part of Belgium (Flanders) in the 1980s and 90s suggests that a comparable conflict between regionalizing and internationalizing tendencies also holds for literary discourse, and more precisely for literary historiography. In this essay, I will use Flanders

---

1   More recently, then Belgian prime minister Guy Verhofstadt has expressed his belief in the possibility of a 'United States of Europe' in his book *De Verenigde Staten van Europa*, published in 2005.

as a case study in order to show how these conflicting tendencies manifest themselves in both politics and literature and to suggest how we can try to deal with their opposition.[2] The paradox mentioned above is apparent in the various ways the northern part of Belgium constructs its relations to its closest neighbor, the Netherlands. Since both regions have united and separated on more than one occasion, the relations between them have always been somewhat ambiguous.[3] While the Netherlands have *de facto* constituted a country since 1585, Flanders is one of the most recently constituted political entities in Europe: it was only 150 years after its secession from the Netherlands that Belgium – in the 1980s and 90s – became a federal state, and that Flanders was created as a political and institutional entity. It goes without saying that this establishment of Flanders as a semi-autonomous region with its own government and institutions had repercussions on its relations with its neighbors: on the one hand, drawing on a long tradition of struggles for emancipation,[4] Flanders tried to chart its own course and to construct its own cultural identity and literature; on the other hand, Flanders seemed to be looking for ways to become part of a larger unit, and it was therefore not at all reluctant to accept external influences.

Following the recognition of its semi-autonomy in the Belgian constitution in 1980,[5] one of the first concrete accomplishments of the newly in-

---

2   Flanders seems to be an especially relevant case in more than one respect. Belgium is one of the founding members of the European Union and has thus been exposed to European internationalization for some decades now. Yet, in the 1980s and 90s the country showed signs of both integration and regionalization. While the EU welcomed six new member states between 1980 and January 1st 1995, Belgium was in the process of federalizing a significant part of its political institutions. Apart from offering an addition to Brems, "Het kritische discours," the research presented here is especially relevant to illustrate the tensions I am describing.
3   At the end of the 16th century, the Northern part of the Low Countries (now the Netherlands) seceded from the Spanish empire, which effectively separated Flanders and the Netherlands. In 1815, after the Napoleonic wars, the Low Countries were re-united in the United Kingdom of the Netherlands, which lasted for fifteen years until Belgium declared independence in 1830.
4   This struggle is known as the Flemish Movement and goes back to the first half of the 19th century; it fought – in a then predominantly francophone Belgium – for the emancipation of the Dutch language, the Flemish citizens (the Flemish laborers in particular), and Flanders in general. See Simons for the historical background.
5   For Flanders, a special law issued on August 8th 1980 decreed the installation of a

stalled Flemish authorities was the joint foundation, together with the Netherlands, of De Nederlandse Taalunie ("The Dutch Language Union"). After Surinam joined the Union in 2004, the institution now has three members. This is how the Union presents itself on its website:

> The Dutch Language Union: three countries united by one language. The Dutch language is spoken in the Netherlands, Belgian Flanders and Surinam. These three areas have been working together on *linguistic issues, language policy, language teaching and literature* for many years. In 1980, the cooperation between the Netherlands and Flanders was confirmed by founding the Taalunie. Surinam has been an associate member of the Taalunie since 2004. Three countries, each with its own history, but with a shared interest: a language that can be used effectively by as many of their inhabitants as possible, both within and outside their language areas. (*The Nederlandse Taalunie*, italics are mine)

Uniting the Netherlands and Flanders in a common concern for "linguistic issues, language policy, language teaching and literature," the Dutch Language Union in the long run intended to integrate the cultural institutions of both regions. Although that goal has not been achieved, Flanders has in the meantime implemented a subsidizing system for literature which was modeled after the Dutch system.

Apart from these institutional evolutions, Flanders' internationalizing tendency since 1980 can also be seen in the development of its literary magazines. An important year in this respect was 1984, which saw the birth of one of Flanders' most ambitious literary magazines. Risen from the ashes of *Nieuw Vlaams Tijdschrift* (or the "New Flemish Magazine" – note the overt regional reference), this magazine was named *Nieuw Wereld Tijdschrift*, (or "New World Magazine"). Although the global aspirations suggested in this title were only half-serious,[6] it is nonetheless symptomatic for a certain change in thinking about Flemish literature and, more generally, literature in Flanders. In one phrase: "Flemish" became "World," and this broader perspective can also be glimpsed from the growing interest in foreign literatures in other literary magazines. The *Nieuw Wereld Tijdschrift*, but also other literary periodicals such as *Yang* and *Dietsche Warande en Belfort*, published an

---

Flemish Parliament ("the Flemish Council") and a Flemish government, determined their powers and responsibilities, and outlined the territorial borders of the Flemish region.
6   Both the editor-in-chief, Herman de Coninck, and one of the editors, Piet Piryns, have admitted this in interviews (see Piryns, "Journalistje," and De Coninck).

increasing amount of articles dedicated to foreign writers and literatures. The *Nieuw Wereld Tijdschrift*, as its name suggests, consistently paid attention to foreign literatures. American (both North and South), African, and English, French, German, but also Polish, Russian, and Czech authors were represented in the magazine, be it with reviews, with translations, or with essays on their work. From 1986 onwards, *Yang* had special issues on, amongst others, Thomas Pynchon, Ernst Jünger, French poetry, and literature from the GDR. Even the oldest Flemish literary magazine, *Dietsche Warande en Belfort*, followed up on these developments and started paying attention to what the editors called the "Europeanizing tendency" (Bousset 3) and started publishing work by foreign authors in translation in 1993. In the years preceding this decision *DWB* had already published annual overviews of German literature and a number of articles on foreign literature, for example on Beckett, Mallarmé, and Calvino. In general, it seems clear that Flemish literary magazines welcomed the influence of other literatures, including other European literatures; they accepted it without much resistance, and even considered it indispensable in order to keep Flemish literature alive and dynamic.

Yet in contrast to this undeniably more international orientation of the literary field, the situation in Flanders seems to reflect the regionalist tendencies in Europe as well. The mere fact that a small country like Belgium lends a considerable form of autonomy to its constituent parts – the Flemish and the Walloon region – by itself already indicates that this regionalist tendency has had a considerable impact. The federalization of Belgium was, in fact, inspired by the Flemish Movement and its demand for more autonomy for Flanders and the Flemish citizens in Belgium. In this respect, however, the question remains in which way (if at all) Flanders has tried to mark out its own literary territory and to develop its own (sub)national literary characteristics. Since Flanders shares its primary language with the Netherlands, this question has special significance in its relation to the Netherlands.

First of all, several works of literary history published in the 1980s and 90s have given rise to the image of two completely separated literary domains, though there are numerous occasions on which Flemish and Dutch literary history have in fact interfered with each other. Three works by the Flemish academics Hugo Brems and Dirk de Geest, for instance, focus exclusively on Flemish poetry, and pay no significant attention to Dutch authors, although they, too, feel compelled to mention several Dutch poets who are then linked to their Flemish colleagues as precursors, as influences, or as 'comrades in arms.' It is striking, however, that this overlap between Flemish and Dutch literature never leads to a problematization of the project of a literary history focusing exclusively on Flemish poetry. Similarly, the short-entry system used in the more recent *Nederlandse literatuur, een geschiedenis* (1993) ("Dutch [or Dutch-Language] Literature, a History"), which is modeled after the well-known multiperspectival *A New History of French Literature* edited by Denis Hollier, results in an almost complete separation of the two stories of Flemish and Dutch literature. The short articles make it virtually impossible to take a broader perspective and to include a comparative analysis of Flemish and Dutch authors. Hence, the different sections can only focus on subjects such as "the classical tradition in Flanders" (chapter 136), "the confrontation between literature and religion" (chapter 137), or "tensions between literature and the public opinion in Flanders" (chapter 138). The most recently published work on modern-day Flemish and Dutch literary history, Hugo Brems's *Altijd weer vogels die nesten beginnen* (or, "Always Again Birds Building Nests") from 2006 seems to take a different perspective. As this work was financed by the Dutch Language Union, Brems explicitly wanted to understand the word "Dutch" in a broad sense, i.e., in such a way that it includes both Flanders and the Netherlands, and he thus set out to write an integrated literary history of these two Dutch-speaking regions, trying to fit the two literatures in one story. Yet at the same time he notes that he "did not simply assume that Flanders and the Netherlands were one homogeneous whole" and that "similarities and differences are not a starting point of the description, but rather the subject of it" (Brems 14).[7] Still, despite this unifying perspective, a quick look at the book's table of contents already shows that the histories of Flemish and Dutch literature in quite a number of cases apparently demanded to be treated separately.

The idea of an integrated literary history of Flanders and the Netherlands is not always put into practice, in Flanders as well as in the Netherlands. In 1990, the Dutch scholar Ton Anbeek published his *Geschiedenis van de Nederlandse literatuur tussen 1885 en 1985* (or, "History of Dutch Literature between 1885 and 1985"), which paid very little attention to Flemish au-

---

7   All translations from the Dutch are the author's.

thors. In this sense, there seem to be signs of a more or less regionalist tendency in the Netherlands as well, at least as far as literature is concerned. Moreover, this regionalist tendency is apparently strong enough to produce an exclusively Dutch literary history, leaving out or ignoring all, or almost all overlap between Flemish and Dutch literature. In contrast to Brems's most recent work, which (at least officially) uses language as its primary criterion, Anbeek explicitly uses national borders as the criterion to select the authors for his literary history. In what seems to be a somewhat paradoxical reaction, given the almost simultaneous and equally insular project of the Flemish scholars Brems and De Geest (whose works on Flemish poetry were published in 1988, 1989, and 1991), Anbeek's literary history (published in 1990) met with much protest and disdain in Flanders. Although this protest was later dismissed as a result of the terminological ambiguity inherent in the phrase "Nederlandse literatuur" (Dutch literature) in Anbeek's title, there might have been another cause for this reaction as well.

The terminological dispute can be summarized as follows. Anbeek describes *Nederlandse literatuur* (Dutch literature) in a strict sense, as literature coming from *Nederland*, the Netherlands, whereas *Nederlandse literatuur* is traditionally understood in a broader sense, as literature written in the Dutch language, or at least as literature from the Netherlands and Flanders (generally leaving out other regions where Dutch is recognized as an official language). In the wake of this discussion, Anbeek revised his book in 1999 and changed its title to *Geschiedenis van de literatuur in Nederland, 1885-1985* (or, "History of Literature in the Netherlands, 1885-1985"), thus regionalizing his title in spite of his effort to include more references to Flemish literature in this revised edition. Yet the Flemish reaction to Anbeek's work can also be interpreted as resulting from a fear of being neglected as a small literature, from a desire to belong to a more prestigious entity, i.e., the domain of literature written in the Dutch language. The Flemish critic Anne Marie Musschoot has remarked that there has been a significant shift in the literary historiography of the Low Countries. Referring to *Het literair klimaat 1970-1985* ("The Literary Climate 1970-1985," published in 1986), another book on literary history in Flanders and the Netherlands edited by three Dutchmen, she notes that in that work "the way of thinking had already changed. Clearly, Flemish literature had been marginalized: it was added to the whole at the very end, included as an appendix as it were" (167). In Anbeek's work, Musschoot notes to her dismay, even this appendix had disappeared.

A more detailed analysis of the general critical practice in Flanders in the 80s and 90s allows us to better understand the opposition between Flanders and the Netherlands. Overall, Flemish literary criticism in this period tries to characterize contemporary Dutch-language literary works by ascribing properties to them that are then supposedly typically Flemish or typically Dutch. As one marked example of this attribution of 'typical' characteristics, consider this sketch of the reception of the Dutch poet Rutger Kopland:

> Particular to Flemish Neo-Realist poetry is that it is said to be more personal, warmer, and more human than the stern objectivity of *The New Style* or the poetry of *Barbarber*. This is why the early Flemish reception of Kopland was situated in Neo-realist circles [...] His "human touch" is highly appreciated by the Flemish neo-realists, whereas in the Netherlands – where the impersonal poetry of *The New Style* and *Barbarber* are at the center of attention – this emphatic emotionality is precisely what is frowned upon. (Evenepoel 725)[8]

The attributed characteristics boil down to a basic opposition between, on the one hand, an experimental, emotional, spontaneous, and 'warm' literature in Flanders, and, on the other, an all too intellectual, cerebral, unexciting, and 'cold' literature in the Netherlands. It is striking, however, that this opposition most often manifests itself *ex negativo*, i.e., it characterizes specific authors as exceptions to the rule. Yet, rather than nuancing the stereotypical opposition between Flemish and Dutch literature, Flemish literary criticism generally treats authors whose example *contradicts* the rule as exceptions that *confirm* the rule, stating that some Dutch authors write "un-Dutch poetry" (Piryns, "Gevoelens" 76) or "rather Flemish" novels (Vlaeminck). Moreover, as the works of literary history that I discussed before suggest, the reasons to separate Flemish and Dutch literature on a number of occasions seem to lie in actual literary and poetical developments. By reiterating the stereotypical opposition I just mentioned and using it to characterize Flemish and Dutch literary movements and trends, works on literary history seem to lend 'objective' grounds to the opposition.

---

8   *De Nieuwe Stijl* (*The New Style*) and *Barbarber* are Dutch literary magazines that advocated an extreme form of (neo-)realism, incorporating ready-mades and *objets trouvés* in poetry.

So what do we make of all this? Earlier research by two comparatists – Hugo Dyserinck, a Fleming, and Joep Leerssen, a Dutchman – offers an interesting perspective on this opposition between the "experimental, emotional, spontaneous, and 'warm'" and the "intellectual, cerebral, unexciting, and 'cold'." Both have demonstrated that this kind of opposition is a recurrent topos in the construction of national identity. This means that this opposition can be used (and often is used) in all possible North-South constellations in Europe:

> The opposition between North and South activates an invariant array of characteristics regardless of the specific countries or nations concerned. Any North-South opposition will ascribe to the northern party a 'cooler' temperament and thus oppose it to its 'warmer' southern counterpart. The oppositional pattern 'cool North/warm South' further involves characteristics such as a more cerebral, individualist, more rugged, less pleasing but more trustworthy and responsible character for the northern party, as opposed to a more sensual, collective, more polished, more pleasing but less trustworthy or responsible character for the southern party. Democracy, egalitarianism, a spirit of business enterprise, a lack of imagination and a more introspective, stolid attitude are northern; aristocracy, hierarchy, fancy, and extrovert spontaneity are characteristic of the South. This opposition will be encountered wherever a European North-South comparison is made. (Leerssen 274-75)

As Leerssen shows, the opposition between Flemish and Dutch literature is not so much the product of essential national characteristics, but rather the product of stereotypical models that are widely deployed in national identity construction. Although the question where these stereotypical models come from is an important one,[9] the crucial thing here is to note that the way in which Flemish and Dutch literary criticism distinguish their own literature from the other is neither original nor limited to the Flemish-Dutch context. In order to develop that last point, Leerssen states that the basic elements in the construction of national identity – elements he calls "imagemes" – are ambivalent and contradictory:

---

9   Likely sources for the opposition are 19th century race theories. These theories divided European peoples into three or five races, each with their own characteristics. Geographically speaking, the theory came down to the supposition that the more northern the race, the greater its ability to rule the other races. The recurring geographical opposition between cerebral and emotional could be seen as a derivation of these views.

> National imagemes are defined by their Janus-faced ambivalence and contradictory nature. They define a polarity within which a given national character is held to move. As a result of their ambivalent polarity, their various manifestations (national images such as we actually encounter them) are highly impervious to historical obsolescence or desuetude. Once the idea that Flemings are sensual, Irish are sentimental, or Germans are efficiently systematic fails to meet with a given audience's concurrence, the effect will be that the opposite pole of the selfsame imageme is activated: that of Flemish mysticism, Irish violence, or German musico-philosophical abstraction, which is considered to complement rather than contradict the stereotype in question. (278)

Although according to Leerssen, this ambivalence helps to keep national stereotypes in place, it also makes clear that the given characteristics are in no way a reflection of essential national characteristics, as they can just as easily be transformed into their opposite.

The situation in Flanders suggests a close interaction between political thinking and literary discourse. In both respects, the case of Flanders makes clear that Europe has to cope with contradicting elements and goals, as it embodies both the possibilities and the impossibilities of Europe and a European literary-historical project. On the one hand, there clearly is a regionalist tendency in Europe: smaller regions are given considerable autonomy and bigger countries are divided into smaller ones. In this sense, nationalist parties have a major impact on European politics, not in the least because they are often critical of the European Union and its project for European integration. To give a Flemish example, the Flemish far-right nationalist party Vlaams Belang ("Flemish Interest") mentions on its website that "[t]he party is very reserved and critical when it comes to the European Union, its bureaucracy, and its compulsion to interfere in domains where the sovereignty of a people should take priority." With this statement, Vlaams Belang advocates a 19th century and ultimately romantic view that sees the people (as an abstract unity) as the undisputed basis for creating a political entity. Yet, on the other hand, the party advocates legal, military, economic, and in some respects even cultural unity on a supranational level; the same Vlaams Belang states in the same paragraph that "[t]he collaboration of the European peoples in a civilizing and cultural community forms a historical opportunity for peace, stability, and prosperity." So while they are in the first place struggling for the political independence of a small region, Vlaams Belang at the same time seeks to be part of a greater, prospering community, which to a certain extent mirrors the developments we discerned in Flemish literature and literary criticism. Note that these tendencies are not restricted to the Belgian situation alone, but can be witnessed in other parts of Europe as well, most recently in Serbia-Montenegro, where the population of Montenegro voted to become an independent state, mainly in order to be able to rapidly become a member state of the European Union. The case study presented here shows parallels with these political developments, in the sense that the literary domain in Flanders strives for more autonomy in relation to its bigger neighbor while trying to mark out its own literary territory. At the same time, however, this young literary community immediately broadens its perspective with the foundation of the Dutch Language Union and, moreover, shows signs of a certain fear of becoming too small and insignificant when it is written out of literary history by the Dutch.[10]

When it comes to re-thinking Europe and European literary studies, I believe it is probably best to look for constructive elements in these contradicting evolutions. All in all, the writing of an explicitly European literary history seems to be a definite theoretical possibility. Using the mechanisms of literary history, and of the construction and invention of – in this case – a European tradition, it seems possible for such a project to affirm and to a certain extent even create a European literary history. Hugo Brems's most recent literary history, for instance, is such an example of a literary history that sets out to unite the stories of literatures that are for a good part separated. There is no reason why a European literary historical project could not venture to do the same, i.e., attempt to unite several of the different literatures that exist in Europe.

Moreover, Brems's book also reflects a canon of Dutch and Flemish authors. Together with other works on modern-day literary history in the Low Countries, Brems's recent work shows that this canon is quite stable, including Louis Paul Boon and Hugo Claus as inevitable Flemish writers and Gerard Reve and Willem Frederik Hermans as their Dutch counterparts. Broadening our perspective to the situation in Europe, we can note that a

---

10   Faced with disdain in the Netherlands for Flemish literature, Flanders has found itself in the role of the underdog on a number of occasions. In this sense, the Flemish reaction to Anbeek's literary history is not an exception. See Billiet and Spilleheen for similar reactions.

stable canon of European authors has *de facto* to a large extent been in place. This canon includes authors such as Baudelaire, Joyce, Brecht, and Cervantes. Teaching courses in European literature for a number of decades, several European universities, including Dutch and Flemish ones, have helped to create and cultivate this canon in the consciousness of European citizens. In an age where political power is shifting from the nation-states to the supranational European Union, it seems possible to focus on a postnational literary history that releases itself from the restrictions of the national traditions of the past centuries. As the example of the Dutch Language Union has shown, the project for a European literary history does not necessarily entail one single monolithic story, although naturally some overlap between national literatures has to be described or created in order to justify such a project. Hugo Dyserinck thinks along the same lines when he writes about the future of imagology:

> Therefore we should conclude that one of the tasks of comparative imagology consists not only in investigating identity problems, to go all the way from former "ethnopsychology" to a new scientifically well-founded "ethno-imagology" in the vein of critical rationalism. But imagology should also investigate the possibility of developing – in literature and its surrounding field – post-national identity models.

According to Dyserinck, these postnational models will reflect "something like an inherent need of collectivity formation and of a sense of belonging and being 'sheltered,'" and will be situated on a supranational level. What I laid out in the preceding paragraphs as Europe's regionalist tendency is in this context then often labelled and neutralized as 'diversity' and seen as a possibly productive asset. In its issue on what it calls "Unprocessed Europe," the Flemish-Dutch editorial board of the *Jaarboek voor literatuurwetenschap* ("Yearbook for Literary Studies"), for instance, summarizes its view as follows:

> What is often forgotten is that the great period of nation formation in the nineteenth century was a radical and sometimes violent process which forced a multiplicity of regional cultures into one monolithic national culture. Chances are slim that the same scenario would be successful for Europe as well. If we are to create a European culture in the twenty-first century, we should make something productive out of the existing diversity. If the concept of Europe has any significance at all, it is polyperspectivism. (6-7)

Echoing Brems's methodological principles, then, a European literary history must not assume that all literatures in Europe form one homogeneous whole. It can, instead, take as its subject the similarities and differences of the literatures at hand.

Writing a proper European literary history incorporating all literary output in Europe would be a difficult task that faces several obstacles. First of all, the body of texts that should be included in such an undertaking is too extensive to be covered in a lifetime. And even if we would agree upon which texts to include and which ones not, it would be hard to come to a conceptualization of a European literary-historical project, since it has been standard practice for centuries to write literary history from a national(ist) or monolingual point of view. University literature departments have traditionally been dedicated to the study of specific literatures separated by linguistic and/or national boundaries. At the same time, literary histories produced by these same departments show that these different literatures are not bound by their national borders or languages and often cite influences from outside the boundaries of the literature in question. Literature, in other words, has always moved across man-made boundaries, and a European literary history may very well be an instrument to counter the regionalist tendencies in Europe and to move towards a more integrated Europe. The case of Flanders suggests that – at least as far as Flanders and Flemish literature are concerned – a distinct tendency towards internationalization definitely exists, and while the regional identities in Europe may perhaps come across as more 'natural,' we must bear in mind that *every* identity is a construction and *never* reflects essential, absolute, and transhistorical regional characteristics. The task facing the European literary historiographer will be to find a way to cope with the tendency toward regionalization and to valorize the various transnational literary connections in Europe.

Works Cited

Anbeek, Ton. *Geschiedenis van de Nederlandse literatuur tussen 1885 en 1985*. Amsterdam: De Arbeiderspers, 1990.

———. *Geschiedenis van de literatuur in Nederland, 1885-1985*. Rev. ed. Amsterdam: De Arbeiderspers, 1999.

Billiet, Daniël. "Gesprek met Eddy van Vliet: 'Nederlanders moet je Vlamingen voeren met mondjesmaat.'" *Poëziekrant* 2 (1978): 1-3.
Bousset, Hugo. "Beste lezers." *Dietsche Warande en Belfort* 138 (1993): 3-4.
Brems, Hugo. "Het kritische discours over Vlaamse literatuur in Nederlandse kranten en weekbladen (1980-1994)." *Nederlandse Letterkunde* 4 (1999): 98-115.
——. *Altijd weer vogels die nesten beginnen*. Amsterdam: Bert Bakker, 2006.
Brems, Hugo and Dirk de Geest, eds. *Wij bloeien, maar bloeien vergeefs: poëzie in Vlaanderen 1945-1955*. Leuven: Acco, 1988.
——. *Barbaar in mijn mond: poëzie in Vlaanderen 1955-1965*. Leuven: Acco, 1989.
——. *Opener dan dicht is toe: poëzie in Vlaanderen 1965-1990*. Leuven: Acco, 1991.
De Coninck, Herman. "Het Nieuw Wereldtijdschrift." *Opener dan dicht is toe*. Ed. Hugo Brems and Dirk de Geest. 228-30.
Dyserinck, Hugo. "Imagology and the Problem of Ethnic Identity." *Intercultural Studies* 1 (2003). August 2007. <http://www.intercultural-studies.org/ICS1/Dyserinck.shtml>.
Evenepoel, Stefaan. "Twintig jaar Kopland in Vlaanderen." *Ons Erfdeel* 32 (1988): 721-31.
Hollier, Denis, ed. *A New History of French Literature*. Cambridge, Ma.: Harvard University Press, 1989.
Leerssen, Joep. "The Rhetoric of National Character: A Programmatic Survey." *Poetics Today* 21.2 (2000): 267-92.
Musschoot, Anne Marie. "Geschiedenis van de Nederlandse letterkunde 1885-1985: Een verhaal zonder Vlaanderen." *Yang* 26 (1990): 167-70.
Onverwerkt Europa: jaarboek voor literatuurwetenschap. Leuven: Peeters, 2001.
Piryns, Piet. "Gevoelens in een jampot." *Knack* 7 Sept. 1994: 76-78.
——. "Journalistje van zijn ziel: la petite histoire van het NWT: een kroniek." *Nieuw wereldtijdschrift* 14 (1997): 24-29.
Schenkeveld–Van der Dussen, M.A, ed. *Nederlandse Literatuur, een geschiedenis*. Amsterdam: Contact, 1993.
Simons, Ludo, ed. *Nieuwe encyclopedie van de Vlaamse Beweging*. Tielt: Lannoo, 1998.

Spillebeen, Willy. "De Nederlandse poëzie volgens Komrij." *De Nieuwe* 28 March 1980.

"The Nederlandse Taalunie." *Taalunieversum*. Nederlandse Taalunie. August 2007. <http://taalunieversum.org/en/>.

Thiesse, Anne-Marie. "Democracy Softens Forces of Change: Inventing National Identity." Trans. Barry Smerin. *Le Monde Diplomatique* 17 June 1999. August 2007. <http://mondediplo.com/1999/06/05thiesse>.

Van Deel, Tom, Nicolaas Matsier, and Cyrille Offermans, eds. *Het literair klimaat 1970-1985*. Amsterdam: De Bezige Bij, 1986.

Verhofstadt, Guy. *De Verenigde Staten van Europa*. Antwerpen: Houtekiet, 2005.

"Waarom Vlaams Belang?" *Vlaams Belang, Nationale webstek*. Vlaams Belang. August 2007. <http://www.vlaamsbelang.org/index.php>.

Vlaeminck, Mark. "Louis Ferron: 'Ik doe het niet bescheiden.'" *De Standaard* 26 May 1990.

PART II

Performing Transnational Identity

Nagihan Haliloğlu (University of Heidelberg)

Re-Thinking Ottoman Empire: East-West Collaboration in Orhan Pamuk's *The White Castle*

April 23 is a day of importance in Turkey, not because it is the birthday of Shakespeare, but because Turks celebrate the anniversary of something that is closer to their hearts: their current Parliament. Among the plethora of Turkish national holidays, April 23 is surrounded with the strongest anti-Ottoman discourse; poems and children's songs composed for the day speak of throwing off the oppressive caliphate, of embracing wondrous new values such as secularism and how the very bad sultan was kicked out of the country. In 2006, however, a couple of days before the celebrated day, Turkish media were following with glee the Istanbul visit of the granddaughter of the last and very bad sultan Vahdettin, who now figures in children's songs, lies buried in Syria, and whose offspring have only very recently been allowed to return to Turkey. The papers and TV channels all exalted the European, ladylike manners of this very well aged 80-year-old woman, who, though the media made no direct reference to it, wore no headscarf, in contrast to the current first-lady of the country.[1]

I start this essay with this news item to point to the unresolved tension that still reigns in discussions concerning the Ottoman Empire in Turkey. Any piece of writing that deals with the Ottoman period is always perceived as partisan, either pro-Ottoman or pro-Republic, and *The White Castle* (1985) can hardly escape such investigation, although, I argue, it proposes a re-thinking which is far more pragmatic. In this essay I will look at the terms through which Orhan Pamuk conceptualizes the East-West collaboration in the context of Ottoman history. I would first like to place Pamuk's writing, especially *The White Castle*, within the current wave of historical novels in Turkey. After looking at some of the reception of his work in the domestic and international arena, I will investigate the narrative modes through which Pamuk conjures up history in *The White Castle*. I will look particularly at his

---

[1] An article in *Referans Gazetesi* follows Neslişah Sultan's wanderings in Istanbul. She is quoted as having said that all that is beautiful in Istanbul has been built by her ancestors, and the journalist tacitly agrees.

use of embedded narrative, especially with respect to its implications of inaccessibility of the past. Lastly, I will suggest a link to a wider field of discussion of how certain modes of remembering the past may serve to forge a lineage in a literary tradition of one's choice.

That the Ottoman Empire can be talked about, publicly, as anything other than an oppressive state from which the Turks were delivered by Atatürk[2] is a relatively new phenomenon, and coincides with the movement towards greater freedom of thought and speech in Turkey, spurred on by the Turkish bid for joining the EU. The usual suspects to appear in such a move to speak about the Ottoman period are, in the first place, the sensationalist novels in which stories of the Harem are told. The second category, I would argue, are the pop-historical novels in which plots that were hatched to bring down the Empire are revealed, with contemporary references to the sorry state that the Balkans and the Middle East are in at the moment. Orhan Pamuk's *The White Castle* makes an appearance in such a literary scene, upsetting both the expectations of pure exoticism and the jingoistic rhetoric.

The White Castle is the doppelganger story of an Italian slave and a Turkish scholar, the Hoja,[3] who, in their efforts to work and invent together, learn each other's way of life well enough to swap places. It is told from the point of view of the Italian slave who has taken on Hoja's identity. I read the novel within the context of a general trend in Turkey of reviving a glorious Ottoman past, a period when Turks consider themselves to have been, if not superior, on a par with Europeans, in terms of military prowess and in propagating value systems. In that respect, I consider *The White Castle* a ritual of remembering, in which a particular period of the Turkish past is both revived and exorcised at the same time, with a view to drawing support for its claim to being part of Europe. I argue that in *The White Castle*, as part of this

---

2   A general in the Ottoman army, Mustafa Kemal Atatürk went on to found the Turkish Republic in 1923, with six new ideological pillars that were to be institutionalized in the new state. Though some look awkward in English translation, they can best be described in the following terms: Republicanism, Statism (Protectionism), Populism, Nationalism, Secularism, and Revolutionism.

3   'Hoja' (the transliteration of the Turkish '*Hoca*') means scholar in Turkish. The name of the Hoja in the novel is never revealed and the narrator always refers to him as 'Hoja,' using it like a proper name. In the English translation, as in this essay, when the Hoja's profession is stressed, the name is used with the definite article.

enterprise, Pamuk evokes Turkish concerns about the forgetting and inaccessibility of the past, along with the question of what kind of Ottoman past is considered appropriate to celebrate.

The novel can be considered an exorcism to the extent that the evil of oppression during Ottoman times is expunged by presenting forces that have always been against reactionism in Turkey: the progressive Turkish intelligentsia. Confessing himself to be of this progressive (read westernizing) intelligentsia almost by birth rather than by choice,[4] when it comes to chronicling the feats of this category, Pamuk is a genealogist to be reckoned with. As James Clifford points out: "Genealogy makes sense in the present by making sense selectively out of the past. Its conclusions and exclusions, its narrative continuities, its judgments of core and periphery are finally legitimated either by convention or by the authority granted to or arrogated by the genealogist" (267). Indeed, Pamuk decides to make sense of the actions of a section of Turkey's society today by making sense of the past selectively, by choosing to tell the story of a character whose adventures may be meaningful for the type whose history he wants to depict and also for the end he wants to achieve.

When we consider what Daniel Cohn-Bendit, the Green European MP, has said in a newspaper article about Pamuk, the authority given to the Turkish writer's genealogy becomes clear. Cohn-Bendit says that Pamuk is "one of the intellectuals who made me understand the importance of Turkey joining the European Union. It is so important for democrats in that country. Orhan is not only one of the most important modern writers in Europe, he is one of the examples of the possible modernity of Turkey" (quoted in Wroe). Just how important Pamuk's actions and character of genealogist are, both domestically and internationally, became clear when Pamuk made a reference to hundreds of thousands of Armenians that were killed during World War One: it resulted in cases of 'defamation against the Turkish nation' being filed against him. It was obvious that those who had filed the cases were aware of Pamuk's aspirations as a historiographer, a chronicler of events who did not follow the preferred line of either the republicans or the conservatives. After a short while Pamuk received the Nobel Prize and while such

---

4 In his recent book *Istanbul*, Pamuk talks at length about his family background and his own very western education. For a description of his family's westernized perception of itself see 165-66.

European support has helped open some people's eyes to Pamuk's work in his home country, it has also helped him earn the title of a 'homebred orientalist,' or as Hilmi Yavuz puts it, "Levantine in his homeland" (57).

Yavuz, a writer very well-read in Ottoman literature and staunchly opposed to an exotization of an Ottoman past which he believes to be ever-present in Turks' daily lives, devotes two chapters of his 2006 anthology of 'eminent Turks' to Pamuk. He states that Pamuk has sacrificed his literary talent to the dictates of his agent in the United States, who wanted Pamuk to write something 'oriental' (54). Yavuz also criticizes Pamuk for confessing to enjoying moments when his viewpoint on his own country converges with that of European writers[5] – read, for Yavuz, 'orientalists' here (57). Whereas for Pamuk this convergence is testimony to the universality of a humanist world view, it is, from Yavuz's perspective, a selling short of a Turkish epistemology which harbors in itself all the tools of the trade and narrative view points that are required for the writing of first class Turkish fiction. Yavuz attributes Pamuk's ambition and determination to represent Ottoman history in his writing to his envy of the acclaim of his brother, the historian Şevket Pamuk (64). These reactions help Pamuk stage himself as the *wunderkind* of Turkish letters, ostracized by the echelons of academia, and his re-thinking of the Ottoman Empire in *The White Castle* accordingly takes the shape of writing the history of alienated intellectuals.

The White Castle opens with a preface by the novel's fictional editor Faruk Darvinoğlu, who claims to have found the story we are about to read in Ottoman-Arabic script in some archive and to have transcribed it for the modern Turkish reader. Faruk is a figure that the Pamuk reader knows from a previous novel, *Sessiz Ev* ("The Quiet House," 1983). Literary critic and eminent professor of English Jale Parla describes *Sessiz Ev* as: "haunted by the memories and actually, the memoirs of [...] one of those Turkish pioneers of westernization [Faruk's encyclopedist grandfather] who believed they

---

5   This is a repeated undertone in Pamuk's work in general. In *Istanbul: Memoirs of a City*, he provides a refined explanation of this view, possibly in response to the orientalist accusations: "For people like me, Istanbullus with one foot in this culture and one in the other, the 'Western traveller' is often not a real person – he can be my own creation, my fantasy, even my own reflection. But being unable to depend on tradition alone as my text, I am grateful to the outsider who can offer me a complementary vision – whether a piece of writing, a painting, a film. So whenever I see the absence of Western eyes, I become my own Westerner" (260).

could single-handedly bring about an epistemological revolution."⁶ Faruk, as revealed in the fictional preface, seems to have similar aspirations as his grandfather and from the very start, the question of whose story we are about to read is blurred: are these the orientalist conjectures of an Italian slave, the chronicles of the scholarly enterprises of the Hoja or the story of Faruk who wants to add an interesting entry to his grandfather's encyclopaedia? Each of these stories vies for centrality, and the whole introduction prepares the ground for a novel which will be presented through embedded narratives.⁷ This is what Faruk has to say concerning his stake in the story: "For a time I told *my story* to everyone I met, as passionately as though I had written it myself rather than discovered it. To make it seem more interesting I talked about its symbolic value, its fundamental relevance to our contemporary realities, how through this tale I had come to understand our own time, etc." (*The White Castle* 3; italics are mine).

Thus Faruk lays a claim on the story by calling it his own, not only because he has found it, but also because in it he recognizes his own predicament. The uneasy relationship between a distrusting public and the Turkish scholar keeps surfacing throughout the novel with the Hoja referring to his pupils and staff repeatedly as fools, and his neighbors spreading rumors about him. At one point of utter despair the Hoja rants away in the presence of the Italian slave: "Was it mere coincidence that so many fools were collected together in one place or was it inevitable? Why were they so stupid?" (94). Thus, Pamuk depicts the forefathers of the westernizing republican intelligentsia who will remain on the defensive and are at the same time defiant concerning any innovation they bring to the 'people.' The Hoja's impatience not only with the backward people but also with the oppressive Sultan makes him the perfect prototype for the republican intellectuals.

But even before we move on to the story, the preface contains yet another representative of the republican intelligentsia, who has the following to say concerning the manuscript Faruk claims to have found and internalized:

> A professor friend, returning the manuscript he'd thumbed through at my insistence, said that in the old wooden houses on the back streets of Istanbul there were thousands of manuscripts filled with stories of this kind. If the simple

---

6   For a fuller description of the novel see Parla.
7   I use this term as expounded by McHale (115).

people living in those houses hadn't mistaken them, with their old Ottoman script, for Arabic Korans and kept them in a place of honor high up on top of their cupboards, they were probably ripping them up page by page to light their stoves. (3)

Both Faruk claiming the story as his own and the professor friend revealing his distance from the 'simple people' are instances where Pamuk sketches the republican Turkish intelligentsia, the forefathers of whom will be introduced in the story itself in the person of Hoja. The passage quoted also points to one in a series of cultural revolutions carried out by Atatürk in a move to distance the new state from all that had been deemed oppressive in the Ottoman Empire: the alphabet reform which had rendered Turks who could read and write illiterate overnight and which is considered to have been the most effective of all republican reforms. By stressing that a whole literature and historiography was lost to generations of postrepublic Turks, Pamuk sketches a Turkish brand of inaccessibility of the past. Thus, we are led to gather that due to this linguistic rupture, those interested in historical facts are left to the mercy of 'savants' such as Faruk, scholarly charlatans, or even worse, to writers of fiction.

Indeed, the way Faruk has transcribed the book leaves much to be desired, and is a pointed critique of historical writing: "My readers will see that I nourished no pretensions to style while revising the book into contemporary Turkish: after reading a couple of sentences from the manuscript I kept on one table, I'd go to another table in the other room where I kept my papers and try to narrate in today's idiom the sense of what remained in my mind" (3). Here the power the intelligentsia have over the written word is made clear, and with this oblique reference to the narrator and translator structure in *Don Quixote*, Pamuk reveals where Turkish novelists, the practitioners of this novel form, take their cue from.

When we move on to the narrative of the Italian slave that follows upon Faruk's preface, we are at once greeted by further salutes to Cervantes. The Italian slave runs into a Spanish slave who has lost an arm and who, encouraged by the feats of a forefather of his who had also lost an arm and gone on to write a novel of chivalry, dreams of writing his own novel. The Italian entertains similar thoughts of writing his life story and has a table made where the Hoja and he can work on whatever text or device the Sultan has requested. They sit at opposite ends, and when not working, they write about their childhoods. The table upon which they write their life stories works as a symbol for the novel genre, introduced by a European, distrusted at first by the Turk, but then adopted and naturalized.[8] The following is the Hoja's reaction to this novelty: "Hoja was not pleased. He likened it to a four-legged funeral bier, said it was inauspicious, but later he grew accustomed both to the chairs and the table; he declared he thought and wrote better this way" (24). Once the Hoja gets going, his appetite for stories proves insatiable and he spurs the Italian to write more and more stories about his childhood, making him resort to his imagination rather than facts.

As I have mentioned above, Pamuk conceives of the relationship between the East and West as a collaboration, and he does not use the word lightly. The suspect partnership between the Hoja and the Italian, which starts with fabricating stories, almanacs and astronomical gadgets for the sultan, turns into a complicity of writing stories about themselves for each other, sometimes willfully confabulating in order to entertain or outwit each other. More often than not, it is the Hoja who succumbs to insecurity concerning the relevance of what he writes: "After scrawling a few sentences he showed them to me with the innocent humility and eagerness of a child: were these things worth writing about, he wondered? Naturally, I gave my approval" (53). Inherent here is Pamuk's identification of orientalism as a complicity, the narrative of the oriental just as instrumental as the imagination of the European in producing exotic stories about the East. It is through writing that the Hoja and the Italian slave learn enough about each others' lives to be able to swap places. This reciprocal writing allows for the mimicry on which the whole plot hinges: their writing and reading makes them "almost the same but not quite" (Bhabha 86), yet similar enough to pass for each other. Thus, *The White Castle* chronicles how East and West collaborate in remembering histories and depicting the other.

However, the physical embodiment of the collaboration comes with the 'war machine' they build for the Sultan, the ultimate product of their hours spent at the table working. Once they build this monstrous cannon-like ma-

---

8   The genre of the novel was introduced into Turkish in the 1860s. For the stages through which the Turkish novel went and for its European influences, see Ahmet Evin's *Origins and Development of the Turkish Novel*.

chine which is to be worked by manpower turning the wheels inside it, they find it difficult to recruit people to operate it. However, they manage to bring it all the way to the battlefield and at the ramparts of a white castle in Poland, the war machine, along with Hoja's world view, is thrown off balance and Turks now face defeat. This is a bitter pill to swallow for Hoja and it is after having realized that they will lose the battle that he at last resolves to change into the clothes of his Italian slave. Apart from his understandable concern to save his head, his total defection, his adoption of a European identity, comes about only after the realization that Europeans can be superior. Becoming someone else, however, in an Ottoman system of values, is equal to defeat. This world view is revealed to us during a conversation the Hoja and the slave have before they launch their ill-fated weapon:

> Did we understand "defeat" to mean that the empire would lose all of its territories one by one? [...] Or did defeat mean that people would change and alter their beliefs without noticing it? We imagined how everyone in Istanbul might rise from their warm beds one morning as changed people; they wouldn't know how to wear their clothes, wouldn't be able to remember what minarets were for. Or perhaps defeat meant to accept the superiority of others and try to emulate them: then he would recount some episode from my life in Venice, and we would imagine how acquaintances of ours here would act out my experiences dressed up with foreign hats on their heads and pants on their legs. (96)

The above is an oblique description of the enterprise of forgetting that is undertaken by the republican elites in the name of the Turkish nation, an enterprise which Pamuk's novel – at a certain level – seems to be working against. The Hoja, by swapping places with his Italian slave and going to Venice in his place, manages to immolate himself in European life altogether – a feat that Turkish republican elites had sought to achieve without having to flee to Europe through a cultural revolution in their homeland. This rising up one morning and not being able to wear one's own clothes is in a way what happened in Turkey due to the aggressive westernizing agenda of the republican elites. Indeed, the whole passage sounds like a republican dream, achieved overnight, but in reality, it would take many public hangings and exiles to realize this dream.[9] The passage reads, then, like a piece of wishful

---

9   Among the hundreds of people who were hanged for not complying with the Hat Revolution, as it is known today, was the religious scholar, İskilipli Atıf Hoca, who had

thinking that could have cut losses and prevented the resentment that had been incurred in conservative sections of society.

However, the *ressentiment* described in the passage is not to be attributed to one section of society in particular, but to the Turkish public at large, because the feeling is the result not only of the transformation but also of having succumbed to this adoption, having accepted the superiority of others. This emulation is bound up with feelings not of progress or collaboration but of defeat, a feeling Pamuk admits he himself likes to indulge in:

> There's an element in me which enjoys the role of victim, wallowing in western orientalism – which I take great ironic delight in – that sense of looking through the eyes of others, seeing one's own culture as an elegant, charming, exquisite failure. All my novels are about the gulfs and complicities between East and West. (Wroe)

This seeing one's own culture as an exquisite failure, I argue, is what informs Pamuk's exercise of drawing from the Ottoman past to speak of today's needs.

The *ressentiment* surrounding discussions about the Ottoman Empire today is foreshadowed by the appearance in the novel of a real Ottoman travel writer known for his apocryphal and fantastical stories, Evliya Çelebi.[10] He visits the Italian slave towards the end of the novel and reads the manuscript of the story that the Italian slave has been narrating to us since the beginning of the novel. Çelebi summarizes the moral of the story, conveniently making a reference to Pamuk's mentor Cervantes. The following passage records what the Italian and Çelebi have discussed, along with the Italian's afterthoughts:

> But we should search for the strange and surprising in the world, not within ourselves! To search within, to think so long and hard about ourselves, would only make us unhappy. This is what had happened to the characters in my story: for this reason heroes could never tolerate being themselves, for this reason they always wanted to be someone else. Let us suppose that what happened in my story were true. Did I believe that those two men who had taken each other's

---

published a pamphlet in 1923 entitled "Aping the Franks and the Hat", which voiced concerns similar to those presented in the passage I have quoted from *The White Castle*. For more information see *Selsus*.

10   Evliya Çelebi was born in 1611 and wrote a ten-volume work called *Seyahatname* ("Book of Travels").

places could be happy in their new lives? I was silent. Later, for some reason or other, he reminded me of one detail in my story: we must not allow ourselves to be led astray by the hopes of a one-armed Spanish slave! If we did, little by little, by writing those kinds of tales, by searching for the strange within ourselves, we, too, would become someone else, and God forbid, our readers would too. (139)

Evliya Çelebi warns against the self-reflexive aspect of writing, against finding what one does not like in one's self, and against the resulting urge to become someone else. This is, as he observes, what has happened to Hoja in particular – the ancestral figure for the republican elites. He has become a slave to "the hopes of a one-armed Spanish slave," to the aspirations of the novel genre. This becoming someone else through reading or writing literature is, however, the humanist philosophy Pamuk abides by. According to the discourse in *The White Castle*, then, the East-West collaboration par excellence is not going to be brought about through technological partnership as in the example of the war machine, but through the means they devise together to tell their stories in order to understand each other.

An Italian writer, recognizably Edmondo de Amici,[11] visits the Italian slave who is now living as Hoja and, in agreement with Evliya Çelebi's warnings concerning the novel form, is full of misgivings about Hoja's practices in his new life as an Italian. Hoja, in his Italian impersonation, now has become the orientalist, and the following description by Amici (mediated of course through the Italian narrator) is almost prophetic for Pamuk himself:

> He was not a true friend of the Turks, He'd written unflattering things about them: He'd written that we were now in decline, described our minds as if they were dirty cupboards filled with old junk. He'd said we could not be reformed, that if we were to survive our only alternative was to submit immediately, and after this we would not be able to do anything for centuries but imitate those to whom we had surrounded. (143)

This regular description of an orientalist is, then, the last station of Pamuk's genealogy of the Turkish intelligentsia. The Turk who has collaborated with Europe can now look at the world through European eyes and wallow not in a western, but in quite a homebred Orientalism. This then, is what re-

---

11   Born in 1846, Edmondo de Amici was an Italian writer who visited Istanbul in 1874 and wrote a memoir, *Constantinopoli* (1883).

thinking the Ottoman Empire gravitates towards: a sort of orientalism, or exotization of the past, occasioned, as Pamuk seems to suggest in his novel, by its inaccessibility.

Looking for Ottoman forefathers that help position Turks as equal partners to Europeans, Pamuk evokes Turkish traditions of story-telling, scholarship and remembering, and reveals how these traditions are intervened by European ones, resulting in a not too easy partnership. Making Hoja his prototype, Pamuk sketches the forefathers of the republican elites whose adoption of western forms should – but does not – earn them or their countrymen a place as Europeans. Skirting the issue of side taking, *The White Castle* remains a ritual of remembering that traces not so much what the Turks forgot, but the origins of critical self-reflection in the Turkish intelligentsia. Proving to be of this bloodline, Pamuk engages in much rumination on the origins of westernization and the adoption of the novel genre: he feels obliged to salute the founding fathers of the novel form, so blatantly that at points *The White Castle* chokes on its self-reflexivity.

Harold Bloom famously holds that the reason students of literature become 'amateur political scientists' and 'overdetermined cultural historians' is because "they resent literature or are ashamed of it" (25). In the context of Turkey's accession to the EU, reading or re-thinking the Ottoman history involves a resentment which turns the ordinary reader or writer into a political scientist: it is the resentment concerning the failure of the republic's westernization project to put Turkey on the European map, although it may have succeeded in cutting ties with the Ottoman history. It is in an attempt to understand and critically assess the extent and cause of this failure that in *The White Castle* Pamuk sets out to draw a genealogy of the westernizing Turkish intelligentsia. The way that the Hoja and the Italian resort to making up stories when telling their own histories calls our attention once again to the limits of historiography, and to how orientalism can be conceptualized as a complicity.

As Faruk makes us aware, in Turkey, these limits are very constricting indeed, due to the change of alphabet and the state policy that encourages the forgetting of Ottoman history. Pamuk seemingly goes against this project by remembering a particular sort of subject in Ottoman history, which helps him re-write the Turkish intellectual into the European world of letters. On the cover blurb, the Observer lauds *The White Castle* with "Up there with the best of Calvino, Eco, Borges and Marquez." When one considers the last two names in this statement, Pamuk's re-writing of Turkish culture into the European one, both through invoking traditional forms and laying bare European interventions, can be seen as operating in a wider field of cultures ex-centric to Europe that claim a space within it. Thus, I argue, the novel opens up a further discussion about the ways in which non-European literatures seek a place within that tradition.

Works Cited

Bhabha, H.K. *The Location of Culture*. London: Routledge, 1994.
Bloom, Harold. *The Western Canon*. New York: Harcourt Brace, 1994.
Clifford, James. *The Predicament of Culture: Twentieth-Century Ethnography, Literature, and Art*. Cambridge, Ma.: Harvard University Press, 1988.
Evin, Ahmet. *Origins and Development of the Turkish Novel*. Minneapolis: Bibliotheca Islamica, 1983.
McHale, Brian. *Postmodernist Fiction*. New York: Methuen, 1987.
Pamuk, Orhan. *The White Castle*. Trans. Victoria Holbrook. London: Faber and Faber, 2001.
——. *Istanbul: Memoirs of a City*. Trans. Maureen Freely. London: Faber and Faber, 2005.
Parla, Jale. "Why *The Black Book* is Black." *Worldandi*. 20 February 2007. <http://www.worldandi.com/specialreport/1991/june/Sa19296.htm>.
Referans Gazetesi. 22 May 2006. <http://www.referansgazetesi.com/haber.aspx?HBR_KOD=34031>.
Selsus. 20 May 2006. <http://www.selsus.com/modules.php?name=Kitap&c_op=Ekbilgi&ekbilgino=172540&kisino=62900>.
Wroe, Nicholas. "Occidental Hero." 8 May 2004. *Guardian Unlimited*. 20 May 2006. <http://books.guardian.co.uk/review/story/0,12084,1211183,00.html>.
Yavuz, Hilmi. *Yüzler İzler*. İstanbul: Aşina Kitaplar, 2006.

Mary Stevens (University College London)

Kader Attia's *Arabesque*: Inscribing Islam in a Provincialized Europe

> Shortly before his death Frantz Fanon launched this appeal: "Come on comrades, the European game is over for good, it is time to find something new, to position ourselves according to another way of thinking, a perhaps unprecedented way of thinking difference" […]. But which "European game" did he mean? Or rather, do we not need first to postulate that Europe is still an issue that shakes us to the core of our being? To make this observation marks the start of an investigation, an inevitable event [that] forms the basis of a responsibility still to be shouldered that goes beyond feelings of resentment or our troubled consciences. The desire to rebel will not suffice to gain access to the beyond: it depends on a work of self-analysis, a constant labour to transform our suffering, humiliation and depression in the relation to the other and to others. (Khatibi 11)[1]

In the exhortation cited by Khatibi, Fanon sets an agenda for postcolonial thought: it is time to turn away from Europe and from its seductive narratives of cultural superiority and progress that disguise their dependence on practices of domination. Whilst admiring Fanon's motivation Khatibi calls his petition into question. For Khatibi it is a delusion to believe that after the lengthy and fraught encounter of colonialism it is possible just to turn the page. The idea of Europe continues to shape the mentality of formerly colonized peoples, even down to the "core of our being," and it is this continuity, the inextricability of colonizer and colonized that needs to be explored. Occupying a position between two cultures is a complex, awkward and often anguished experience; Khatibi does not deny this, but at the same time he sees it as an opportunity ("a responsibility still to be shouldered"). The legacy of colonialism requires a serious engagement both with the past and with the self ("a work of self-analysis, a constant labour to transform our suffering") and even though it is always imposed, never chosen, this engagement should still be seen as potentially productive. Moreover, a "work of self-analysis" necessarily initiates a similar work of re-evaluation on the part of the other, since the self and the other exist in a strict relation. Both par-

---

1   All translations from the French are the author's unless otherwise stated.

ties, the formerly colonized and the former colonizer, are transformed and both move forward from this new position to a renewed interrogation. For Khatibi, unlike for Fanon, 'Europe' is not a given that can be either accepted or rejected; it is a variable to be re-worked precisely through the re-working of the self. The process of postcolonial reinvention is thus a cycle, a work always in progress, never complete. Whilst Khatibi was writing about the Maghreb, his reflection is even more pertinent when applied to Europe itself, and particularly to the descendants of formerly colonized peoples who today live in the continent's towns and cities, and who are obliged to engage with the "European game" in its various forms each and every day. If we follow Khatibi's argument through, within Europe the presence of postcolonial 'others' could be said to represent an opportunity for change and progress, through mutual re-thinkings. And whilst all who bear the legacy of colonialism are engaged in questioning the self and their relation to society, it is artists who take this process into the public sphere and whose productions – be they musical, literary or visual – catalyze the shifts "in the relation to the other and to others."

This essay will discuss the work of a particular contemporary artist working in France, Kader Attia, who, in questioning the relations of power that regulate French society, is profoundly engaged in this process of re-thinking Europe, not so much in its indeterminate and internally variegated geographical sense but rather as the reified figure of the imagination described by Dipesh Chakrabarty that has dominated thought in the social sciences and which constitutes one half of the Europe-Orient binary first put on the critical agenda by Edward Said (Chakrabarty 27). It is interesting to note that whilst they come from very different backgrounds and write about very different contexts – India and Morocco – both Chakrabarty and Khatibi start from an observation of the same antinomy. In Chakrabarty's terms this is the idea that "European thought is at once both indispensable and inadequate in helping us to think about the experiences of political modernity in non-Western nations" and therefore that the goal of "provincializing Europe" (perhaps this corresponds to what Khatibi refers to as the "responsibility still to be shouldered") becomes "the task of exploring how this thought – which is now everybody's heritage and which affects us all – may be renewed from and for the margins" (Chakrabarty 16).

Before discussing Attia's work I wish first to introduce the ways in which museums and galleries have been instrumental in shaping both a sense of national identity and, through the promotion of a shared canon, an idea of 'Europeanness.' Bakhtin's work on the European novel will then be used to consider the ways in which artists can subvert this function. Traditionally, galleries and museums have been key sites for the making of collective identity. Ever since the opening of the Louvre as the first national public gallery in 1793 they have been intimately connected with the nation, as manifestations of its power, as reflections of its values and as sites for the forging of citizens (Hooper-Greenhill, *Shaping*; Duncan; Bennett). Later on, as Benedict Anderson reminds us, the museum functioned as a key technology of colonialism. Thus museums and galleries can be understood as key sites of 'reterritorialization,' defined as a process of mapping, in which a certain set of values – aesthetic, social, cultural – are made to overlay a certain geographic territory, notably the space of the nation. Such institutions are spaces where communities are 'imagined' and where borders are established, that is, they 'reterritorialize' a given community on the space of the nation (Macdonald; Coombes). It should also be noted that a great 'national' collection is above all, in Europe and North America at least, one that contains not just works from that country but also a significant quotient of masterpieces of European art. This enables the state to position itself in an international cultural hierarchy; the national grandeur embodied in a museum is both absolute and relative.[2]

However, in response to challenges to authority from various underrepresented communities, museums are increasingly called upon to provide a forum for diversity and a space for debate, questioning their reified presentation of European culture. If today, "museums have the power to remap cultural territories, and to reshape the geographies of knowledge" (Hooper-Greenhill, *Interpretation* 21), this function is often now geared not so much towards 'reterritorialization' as to '*de*territorialization,' understood as the

---

2   The project for a Museum of Europe in Brussels is a sign that in the future museums may transcend the national dimension. The correspondence between the territory of the museum and the space of sovereignty is maintained; the project (which, like several aspects of the construction of the European Union, is currently on hold) is indicative not of a revised conception of the function of the museum but rather of a changing balance of power within Europe. For a more detailed discussion see Pomian.

probing and potential undoing of the boundaries of, in particular, national belonging. This is not to suggest that the idea of the nation or the community has been entirely abandoned, rather that museums are increasingly becoming sites that propose the deconstruction of the narrower and more exclusive identity categories. For as forums, "[m]useums may be seen as cultural borderlands, where a range of practices are possible [...] and where diverse groups and sub-groups, cultures and subcultures may push against and permeate the allegedly unproblematic and homogeneous borders of dominant cultural practices" (Hooper-Greenhill, *Interpretation* 140). No longer radiating a fixed vision from the center, some museums have themselves 'deterritorialized' and, in situating themselves in the borderlands, have the potential to establish a real dialogue with dominant discourses.

This shift towards 'deterritorialization' could be seen as replaying the move Bakhtin identifies in *The Dialogic Imagination* between the epic and the novel, wherein a space of polyglossia succeeds the hierarchical categories of an earlier official narrative. Clear parallels exist between the galleries and museums of the 19th century and the Bakhtinian 'epic': both were engaged in the elaboration of a national tradition and both were concerned to present this tradition as eternal, immutable, and untouchable by the listener/visitor (Bakhtin 13-20). In contrast, Bakhtin saw the novel as establishing "a zone of contact with the present in all its open-endedness" (7), something to which most museums and galleries today aspire (Carbonell 8).[3] For Bakhtin, the creation of the "zone of open-endedness" was linked to the opening up of Europe to different cultures. In the era of European political union, globalization, and migratory flux Europe is more open to a "multi-languaged consciousness" (11) than he probably ever imagined. One consequence of this

---

3 In the wake of the 'new museology' (Vergo), Bakhtin has become an increasingly popular reference in museum theory. Different authors use his work in different ways. For example, Pascal Gielen uses the concept of the chronotope to model the various options available to museums in presenting historical narrative, that is, structuring time, within the three-dimensional space of the exhibition. James Clifford also draws on the idea of the chronotope but in a rather different way; for Clifford, museums increasingly constitute 'contact zones' in which a power struggle between center and periphery takes place. Whilst still understanding the chronotope as the spatialized time of museum display, in Clifford's work the space is now doubled since it is simultaneously both central – a locus of power – and displaced – on the cultural frontier (Clifford, *Predicament* 236; Clifford, *Routes* 192).

diversification is that the "zone of open-endedness" is more dispersed; it is no longer limited to a single cultural form (that of the novel). However, given the competing pulls of hegemonic and pluralistic discourse in the museum – or the processes of *re-* and *de*territorialization as described above – it is perhaps here that this "open-endedness" is most often problematic and therefore, paradoxically, most visible.

Bakhtin's ideas about the discourse of the novel are also useful in thinking about the meanings generated by exhibitions. In the essay "Discourse in the Novel" Bakhtin develops his ideas in relation to hybridity. He distinguishes between "organic" or "unintentional" and "intentional" hybridity; whereas the former describes the fact that an utterance may "belong simultaneously to two languages" (305) the latter exploits this polysemic dimension of language to "set [two points of view] against each other dialogically" (360). The idea of "intentional" hybridity is developed further in Robert Young's deconstructivist reading:

> Hybridity [...] involves an antithetical movement of coalescence and antagonism, with the unconscious set against the divisive, the generative against the undermining. [...] For Bakhtin himself, the crucial effect of hybridization comes with the latter, political category, the moment where, within a single discourse, one voice is able to unmask the other. This is the point where authoritative discourse is undone. (22)

Both unintentional and intentional hybridity can be observed in the museum. Unintentional hybridity could be understood as the consequence of the museum's intrinsic material heterogeneity; the proliferation of objects, texts and interpreters inevitably generates an infinite proliferation of meaning (Hetherington).[4] Intentional hybridity occurs when an exhibit or artwork deliberately seeks to undermine the institution's authority.

Young's description of the oscillating movement of hybridity makes it a concept particularly well suited to an exhibition where the works displayed can be seen as working to reinforce the authority of the gallery (since its status depends very heavily on the reputation and standing of the artists it displays) whilst simultaneously seeking to undermine its authoritative discourse, espe-

---

4   In addition to being a structural feature of any collection of objects, heterogeneity was particularly characteristic of the 'baroque' or classical *Wunderkammer* or 'cabinet of curiosities' (Foucault; Hooper-Greenhill, *Shaping*).

cially in the case of a state-funded institution. Attia's work does not escape this ambivalent logic. However, his installation *Arabesque* can legitimately be read primarily as an act of 'intentional hybridization' that sought to pull the exhibition "Notre histoire ..." firmly towards the pole of contestation in diversity. Moreover, his antagonism will be shown to be grounded in an engagement with the legacy of French colonialism. For if, as Bhabha observes, hybridization is also an inevitable effect of colonial power, then "the ambivalence at the source of traditional discourses on authority enables a form of subversion, founded on the undecidability that turns the discursive conditions of dominance into the grounds of intervention" (*Location* 160). In the case of the museum this statement can be read literally; through the work of artists such as Attia its traditionally authoritarian spaces physically become the grounds of their subversive interventions. Or, to return to the terms used above, through the tactic of intentional hybridization, Attia's work seeks to destabilize a dominant understanding of collective identity fostered by galleries and museums and can therefore be understood as engaged in a process of 'deterritorialization.'

The work discussed in this essay was created for an exhibition entitled "Notre histoire ..." that ran from January to May 2006 at the Palais de Tokyo, the major public contemporary art space in Paris. Whilst there are many possible interpretations of the phrase "Notre histoire ..." the curators clearly sought to position the exhibition in a national context: "'Notre histoire ...' aims to gather together all the different forces making art in France today," a point underscored by the exhibition's subtitle, "an emerging French art scene" (Bourriaud and Sans). The national ambitions of the exhibition were endorsed in the exhibition's first week by the visit of the Prime Minister, Dominique de Villepin, whose concerns about the status of French contemporary art in the international arena, and therefore the perception of France as a modern, innovating nation, are well known.[5]

---

5   From 10 May to 25 June 2006 an exhibition entitled "La force de l'art" ('The Power of Art') was held at the Grand Palais in Paris, reportedly in response to a direct demand from Prime Minister de Villepin, who was said to be concerned about the low status of French contemporary art on the international art scene. The exhibition was rapidly nick-named "l'expo Villepin." The Minister of Culture, Renaud Donnedieu de Vabrès, denied the government was trying to promote an official art, whilst acknowledging that the Prime Minister is "crazy about contemporary art" ("'La force de l'art' inaugurée à Paris").

Far from looking backwards then, "Notre histoire ..." was resolutely focused on the future; its intention was to create a "memory for tomorrow" (Palais de Tokyo). It thus invited contemporary artists to reflect on the present and to consider what they would like to communicate to future generations. It is this aspect above all that allows us to read the exhibition as profoundly engaged in a work of collective identity formation. The exhibition did not particularly foreground the dilemmas of multiculturalism; however, the figure of the marginalized 'other' haunts its rhetoric particularly in the collective pronoun of the title that clearly stimulates a reflection on what it means and what it takes to belong. Attia's work takes up this challenge by exploring some of the most complex and pressing issues in contemporary French (if not indeed European) politics: the place of Islam and the impact of the marginalization of certain elements of the Muslim community.[6]

Kader Attia, *Arabesque*.
© Palais de Tokyo/Kleinefenn, 2006.

Attia's piece for the exhibition was entitled *Arabesque*. The term "arabesque" has two meanings. As an adjective in common usage it often designates anything that conforms to an exoticized image of Islamic design. The

---

6   In some ways this is the same question posed by Khatibi in the opening quotation, only in reverse. Where Khatibi considers the impossibility of excising a European heritage in the postcolonial context of North Africa, Attia's work for "Notre histoire ..." foregrounds the impossibility and undesirability of distinguishing between a European 'us' and a Muslim 'them' in the heart of Europe.

OED gives the following definitions for the adjective: "1. Arabian, Arabic. 2. esp. Arabian or Moorish in ornamental design; carved or painted in arabesque. 3. fig. Strangely mixed, fantastic." As a noun, however, it has a more technical meaning: it is a decorative form, originally found in architecture, that operates within fixed margins and that fills the whole of the space assigned (Marçais quoted in Khatibi and Sijelmassi 183). Attia's work engages with both these meanings; the reference to Islamic architectural traditions can be read as part of a strategy to undermine orientalist stereotypes.

The particular force of Attia's *Arabesque* comes from his choice of materials: it is composed of four hundred riot police batons or *matraques*. The morning after a night of violence in November 2005 Attia picked up two *matraques* in the street in his Parisian suburb. He became fascinated by the object, its physical quality, its weight. By sending out an appeal on the internet he was able to acquire several more. In the end, however, he purchased four hundred batons from a police supplier to make the work (Attia). Whilst the batons used in the installation no longer possess the aura of the real – unlike for example the guns used in Cristóvão Estevão Canhavato's *Throne of Weapons* commissioned in 2002 by the British Museum – there is nevertheless still a clear line of filiation between the original baton found on the street and its memory-less, identical successors.

Attia was born in France of Algerian parents and much of his work addresses issues connected with multiculturalism and hybrid identities. It is my argument that *Arabesque* can be considered an 'intentional hybrid,' determined to disrupt the discourse of the Parisian elite, particularly in relation to young 'Arab' men. In France, young 'Arab' men are often stigmatized as violent and 'un-integratable' on account of their religious beliefs (Silverstein; Deltombe and Rigouste; Guénif-Souilamas). Media coverage of the violence of November 2005 contributed to reinforcing this impression (Hargreaves). In bringing this violence into the museum, Attia confronts the state and the Parisian elite with the stereotype they have produced. In particular the accumulation of the *matraques* draws attention to the asymmetrical relations between the forces of the state and the residents of the suburbs. As Max Weber famously remarked, the state is that which claims for itself the monopoly of legitimate physical violence (310). Displayed in cold, mechanical form on the wall of the gallery, the legitimacy of this violence is called into doubt, not least because Attia's installation, in using the batons to signify the troubled suburbs, also underlines the absence in all other respects of the residents of these areas from the privileged space of the gallery.

One of the consequences of the stigmatization of young 'Arab' men is the closing down of possibilities for positive self-expression; art is not something they are supposed to be interested in (Attia). Perhaps in reaction to this, Attia's work exists in a dialogue with both the European and Islamic traditions. The geometric and chromatic simplicity of *Arabesque* evokes Mondrian or Sol Le Witt, for example. Yet where Mondrian's precision establishes clear boundaries in space, Attia's re-working underlines the violence of these divisions, of the lines that separate inside from out, insider from outsider. There is something particularly potent about undermining geometric divisions in the Parisian context where the influence of Le Corbusier has left the city space scarred by radical postwar experiments in urban planning, the unintended consequences of which include a near-impermeable boundary between the city center and the neglected peripheries and the relegation of the poor to the long, thin multi-storey blocks known as the *grandes barres*, whose angular design is echoed in *Arabesque* (*barre* in this instance means a 'block,' but can also be translated as 'rod' or 'baton').[7] In *Arabesque*, Attia carves out his space in the canon of western art, disrupting its certainties through the irruption of a 'double,' or 'unintentionally hybrid' violence: the violence inherent in the codes of aesthetic modernism also conveys the violence of the state against its citizens. In looking at *Arabesque* we are acutely aware of Bachelard's observation in *The Poetics of Space*: "simple geometrical opposition becomes tinged with aggressivity. Formal opposition is incapable of remaining calm" (212).

Arabesque does not just belong in the European tradition, it also engages with the history of Islamic art and architecture, as discussed above. Whereas in European art geometric abstraction is a relatively recent development, in Islamic culture to move towards abstraction is to return to some of the earliest forms of Arabic script. 'Archaic' kufic script, characterized by the lack of vocalization and its paired-down style, was the dominant form of writing from the beginning of the Islamic era until approximately the 10th century

---

7   For a discussion of urban planning practices and their implications for the exclusion of minority ethnic groups, in particular Algerians, see Silverstein 76-120.

(C.E.) (Khatibi and Sijelmassi 78). The coming together of these two visual temporalities in *Arabesque* – the kufic and the modernist – works to comprise what Edward Said has described as "another time of *writing* that will be able to inscribe the ambivalent and chiasmatic intersections of time and place that constitute the problematic 'modern' experience of the western nation" (quoted in Bhabha, "DissemiNation" 293).[8] As the Palais de Tokyo website says in reference to Attia's film *Correspondances* (2002-2003), in which the Paris-based artist exchanges still and moving images with his family in Algeria, "[Attia] inscribes himself (*s'inscrit*) as a messenger between two worlds that had ceased to communicate" (Palais de Tokyo). This idea of the artist as envoy ties in with Said's search for a medium to express the ambivalence of the postcolonial experience. Moreover, given the hybrid meanings of *s'inscire* in French – it means 'to write,' 'to register,' including in the sense of 'registering support' or 'standing up for something' and also 'to belong to' (a group or community) – the statement is perhaps even more true of *Arabesque*.

To write a sacred text publicly in Arabic is to express membership of a broad Muslim community. According to Attia, the batons spell out the text of the prayer "El Hamdoullah" ("Praise be to God"), the very first text that children learn at Qur'anic school. Khatibi and Sijelmassi ground the experience of learning to read the Qur'an firmly in the collective: "The child learns not a convention, but to vibrate in the voice of the divine" (31). This formula could equally be applied to *Arabesque* since, although Attia is clearly expressing solidarity, he does so through the mobilization of his unique perspective as an artist, just as the child who "vibrates" becomes part of the whole without entirely losing her/his sense of self. Similarly, the implication of Attia's work is that there are as many ways to participate in the Islamic community as there are Muslims. Since, as Silverstein reminds us, "one of the constants of the alarmist accounts from the mid-1990s [...] was the portrayal of *banlieue* Islam as a mass movement [...] whereby the individual believer loses his identity to the group" (133-34), this message of artistic freedom within the collectivity is both pertinent and necessary.

---

8   Attia is not the only artist to have explored the interface between Islamic and modernist geometric abstraction. His work can interestingly be compared to that of the calligrapher Boullata (Khatibi and Sijelmassi 230-33).

However, in making of himself a writer Attia also underscores the ambiguity of his position between communities and between worlds. Iain Chambers has described the process of writing as "a constant journeying across the threshold between event and narration, between authority and dispersal, between repression and representation, between the powerless and the powerful, between the anonymous pre-text and the accredited textual inscription" (11). Chambers is drawing attention to writing's inherent ambivalence; it is both that which fixes and imprisons our thoughts and ideas and that which enables us to communicate with the world and possibly even to have those ideas in the first place. This is true of language generally, but doubly so of a form of writing where the idea of the trace and of the irrevocability of the inscription weights the scales towards "authority" and "repression," to use Chambers's terms. Thus Attia is not just a "messenger" between two worlds or two communities; he is also shuttling back and forth between the textual inscription, "accredited" by the art world and the "anonymous pre-text," the sum of experiences recovered from life in the suburbs. Moreover, given the privilege of being granted a platform in the Palais de Tokyo, Attia's position between "the powerless" (the rioters whose only voice is violence) and "the powerful" (the curators, the art buyers, even the Prime Minister) is particularly delicate. His work reflects all the dilemmas of speaking 'for' or 'on behalf of' the subaltern other, but his solution is original; the hybrid nature of his installation, between text and sculpture, enables him to give voice to the "powerless" but in the words with which many, as Muslims, would also be familiar and which they would claim as their own. Whilst Attia's voice vibrates "in the voice of the divine," the voices of the voiceless vibrate in the lines and spaces of his object/text. In other words, the physical hybridity of the art object facilitates the undoing of authoritative discourse characteristic of Bakhtinian intentional hybridity.

Furthermore, the use of Qur'anic Arabic in the form of the installation could be seen as a technique of "becoming-minor," to use Deleuze and Guattari's terms. As the pair note, "even when major" – and few languages can be so "major" (that is, authoritative) as classical Arabic, whose purity is the measure of its capacity to convey absolute truth – "a language is open to an intensive utilization that makes it take flight along creative lines of escape which […] can now form an absolute deterritorialization" (Deleuze and Guattari

26). To "become minor" is, in this sense, to shift a discourse from a position of dominance to one of subversion; the subversive act takes the form of a "deterritorialization," an uncoupling of language from its domain of control. Attia's usage is perhaps not quite what Deleuze and Guattari had in mind but nevertheless it cannot be denied that he succeeds in rendering the text strange through an "intensive usage." For Deleuze and Guattari an "intensive usage" is anything that contributes to expressing "the internal tensions of a language" (22) and hence to a "becoming minor." According to Khatibi and Sijelmassi, the primary tension in Arabic writing is between meaning and form: "calligraphy reveals the plastic scenography of a text" (6). Thus in accentuating the "plastic scenography" by rendering it in three dimensions, Attia indeed operates a calligraphic "intensive usage." And in this act of deterritorialization the artist not only pulls at the restrictions imposed on the speakers of classical Arabic, he also intervenes in the struggle between re- and deterritorialization inherent in the museum, as described above. All the borders are called into question.

According to Jean Borreil, artists have a particular role to play in the rethinking of communities: "The becoming-strange of the artist shows that an undoing may be tragic, but that it may also be 'happy' and that there is sense in unraveling consensus and communities. Because it is in the unraveling of communities that the incompleteness of all communities, be they natural or national, may emerge [...]" (95-96). In this essay I have attempted to show how the idea of the "becoming-strange" – which might also be a "becoming-minor" – is at the heart of Kader Attia's creative practice, and how this "work of self-analysis" (to pick up Khatibi's terms) becomes, in the encounter with the public, a work "in the relation to the other and to others," leading, as Borreil suggests, to the unraveling of fixed communities: the French, the Muslim, the 'Arab,' the European. In its celebration of the loosening of the bonds of community, Borreil's work, like others in a certain poststructuralist tradition, risks advocating their complete dissolution, producing a fragmented society of radically 'other' atomistic individuals. In Europe, the determined persistence and even strengthening of ethnic and religious bonds since the end of the Cold War (in the former Yugoslavia for example) has made this postmodern utopia seem at best naïve. As Pnina Werbner argues provocatively, "the real voices from the margins want no truck with hybridity. The reality is one of fragmentation and ghettoization, or ethnic primordialism in the face of a weakened nation-state" (12). Recent controversies, such as the furore over the publication of cartoons of the Prophet Mohammed by the Danish newspaper *Jyllands-Posten*, regrettably seem to confirm this analysis.

Yet the success of Attia's work derives, I suggest, from his desire to explore ways to accommodate these two positions: 'identity' as fluid, hybrid, and malleable or as geographically and ethnically determined. For in Attia's installation, personal identity is experienced not as a radical separateness in which, in Kristeva's terms, we are all strangers both to others and to ourselves, but rather as a vibration "in the voice of the divine," a metaphor that combines both the uniqueness of the individual and overall harmony through group identification. This strategy corresponds to what Abdellali Hajjat has described as the "opening-up retrenchment" (*"repli d'ouverture"*) that he has identified in the politics and poetics of certain French hip-hop groups (88). Superficially paradoxical, this attitude is an approach to hybridity that refuses assimilation and the dissolution of cultural specificity whilst at the same time seeking to expand the bounds of belonging in order to make space for greater cultural diversity within the national community. It operates at the point of transition from 'difference' to 'diversity,' where 'difference' denotes a deviation from an assumed 'norm' and 'diversity' the proliferation of 'differences' that results in the dissolution of the 'norm.' The *"repli d'ouverture"* is therefore a way of asserting specificity (a "retrenchment" or *"repli"*) – which, in a departure from the poststructuralist line, may indeed be defined in group terms – that not only does not refuse participation in a broader collective but rather makes of this assertion the very condition of participation ("opening-up" or *"ouverture"*). Above all, in an echo of the quotation from Khatibi with which this essay began, *"le repli d'ouverture* is a form of resistance in that it requires an effort at self-analysis" (*"travail sur soi"*) (Hajjat 87), a work in which the artist is continually engaged.

Could this hybrid position, as explored in *Arabesque*, provide a model for national (or indeed supranational) belonging for European Muslims? Perhaps, but Attia is an artist, not a politician in search of practical solutions. In his dizzying labyrinth his aim is neither to dissolve the boundaries between 'us' and 'them,' nor to displace them, but rather to set them in motion so that they must be constantly negotiated, never assumed, as we struggle to locate the "third space" of a "heterogeneous public sphere," somewhere between the two poles of cohesive communities and atomistic individuals (Carter, Donald, and Squires xiv). And whilst it is important to acknowledge the gallery's capacity to neutralize radical messages, be they aesthetic or political (Fraser), Attia's "intentional hybrid" in the Bakhtinian sense does indeed turn "the discursive conditions of dominance into the grounds of intervention" (Bhabha, *Location* 160) through, as Khatibi advocates, the translation of his "sufferings, humiliation and depression" – in this instance the very specific suffering caused by the riots of November 2005 – into a reflective art practice. In so doing, he inscribes alternative forms of belonging in an increasingly hybrid, "provincialized" and thereby maybe – we can all but hope – renewed Europe.

Works Cited

Anderson, Benedict. *Imagined Communities*. 2nd ed. London: Verso, 1991.

Attia, Kader. "Tokyoclip: Kader Attia." 2006. Palais de Tokyo. 17 May 2006. <http://palaisdetokyo.com/notrehistoire/medias/tokyoclip.php?id_doc=1323>.

Bachelard, Gaston. *The Poetics of Space*. New York: Orion Press, 1964.

Bakhtin, Mikhail M. *The Dialogical Imagination: Four Essays*. Ed. Michael Holquist. Austin, Texas: University of Austin Press, 1981.

——. "Discourse in the Novel." *The Dialogical Imagination: Four Essays*. Ed. Michael Holquist. 259-422.

Bennett, Tony. *The Birth of the Museum: History, Theory, Politics*. London: Routledge, 1995.

Bhabha, Homi. "DissemiNation: Time, Narrative and the Margins of the Modern Nation." *Nation and Narration*. Ed. Homi Bhabha. London: Routledge, 1990. 291-322.

——. *The Location of Culture*. London: Routledge, 1994.

Borreil, Jean. *La raison nomade*. Paris: Payot and Rivages, 1993.

Bourriaud, Nicolas and Jérôme Sans. "L'édito des directeurs." 2006. Palais de Tokyo. 17 May 2006. <http://palaisdetokyo.com/notrehistoire/exposition/presentation.htm>.

Carbonell, Bettina Messias. "Introduction: Museum/Studies and the 'Eccentric Space' of an Anthology." *Museum Studies: An Anthology of Contexts*.

Ed. Bettina Messias Carbonell. Oxford: Blackwell, 2004. 1-13.

Carter, Erica, James Donald, and Judith Squires. "Introduction." *Space and Place: Theories of Identity and Location*. Ed. Erica Carter, James Donald, and Judith Squires. London: Lawrence and Wishart, 1993. vii-xv.

Chakrabarty, Dipesh. *Provincializing Europe: Postcolonial Thought and Historical Difference*. Princeton, N.J.: Princeton University Press, 2000.

Chambers, Iain. *Migrancy, Culture, Identity*. London: Routledge, 1994.

Clifford, James. *The Predicament of Culture: Twentieth-Century Ethnography, Literature, and Art*. Cambridge, Ma. and London: Harvard University Press, 1988.

——. *Routes: Travel and Translation in the Late Twentieth Century*. Cambridge, Ma. and London: Harvard University Press, 1999.

Coombes, Annie. "Museums and the Formation of National and Cultural Identities." *Oxford Art Journal* 13.2 (1990): 70-84.

Deleuze, Gilles and Félix Guattari. "What Is a Minor Literature?" *Kafka: Toward a Minor Literature*. Minnesota: University of Minneapolis Press, 1986. 16-27.

Deltombe, Thomas and Mathieu Rigouste. "L'ennemi intérieur: la construction médiatique de la figure de 'l'Arabe.'" *La fracture coloniale: la société française au prisme de son héritage colonial*. Ed. Pascal Blanchard, Nicolas Bancel, and Sandrine Lemaire. Paris: La Découverte, 2005. 191-98.

Duncan, Carol. *Civilizing Rituals Inside Public Art Museums*. London: Routledge, 1995.

Foucault, Michel. *The Order of Things*. London: Routledge, 1989.

Fraser, Andrea. *Museum Highlights: The Writings of Andrea Fraser*. Ed. Alexander Alberro. Cambridge, Ma. and London: MIT Press, 2005.

Gielen, Pascal. "Museumchronotopics: On the Representation of the Past in Museums." *Museum and Society* 2.3 (2004): 147-60.

Guénif-Souilamas, Nacira. "La Française voilée, la beurette, le garçon arabe et le musulman laïc: Les figures assignées du racisme vertueux." *La république mise à nu par son immigration*. Ed. Nacira Guénif-Souilamas. Paris: La Fabrique, 2006. 109-32.

Hajjat, Abdellali. *L'immigration postcoloniale et mémoire*. Paris: L'Harmattan, 2005.

Hargreaves, Alec G. "An Emperor with No Clothes?" 28 November 2005.

The Social Science Research Council. 27 February 2006. <http://riotsfrance.ssrc.org/Hargreaves>.

Hetherington, Kevin. "From Blindness to Blindness: Museums, Heterogeneity and the Subject." *Actor Network Theory and After.* Ed. John Law and John Hassard. Oxford: Blackwell, 1999. 51-73.

Hooper-Greenhill, Eilean. *Museums and the Shaping of Knowledge.* London: Routledge, 1992.

———. *Museums and the Interpretation of Visual Culture.* London: Routledge, 2000.

Khatibi, Abdelkébir. *Le Maghreb pluriel.* Paris: Denoël, 1983.

Khatibi, Abdelkébir and Mohammed Sijelmassi. *The Splendour of Islamic Calligraphy.* New York and London: Thames and Hudson, 1996.

Kristeva, Julia. *Strangers to Ourselves.* New York and London: Harvester Wheatsheaf, 1991.

"'La force de l'art' inaugurée à Paris." *Le Nouvel Observateur* 10 May 2006.

Macdonald, Sharon. "Museums, National, Postnational and Transcultural Identities." *Museum and Society* 1.1 (2003): 1-16.

Palais de Tokyo. "Présentation." 2006. Palais de Tokyo. 17 May 2006. <http://palaisdetokyo.com/notrehistoire/exposition/presentation.htm>.

Pomian, Krzysztof. "Le musée de l'Europe face à la question des migrations." *Hommes et migrations.* 1255 (2005): 63-71.

Said, Edward. *Orientalism.* 2nd ed. London: Penguin, 1999.

Silverstein, Paul A. *Algeria in France: Transpolitics, Race, and Nation.* Bloomington: Indiana University Press, 2004.

Vergo, Peter, ed. *The New Museology.* London: Reaktion, 1989.

Weber, Max. "Profession and Vocation of Politics." *Weber: Political Writings.* Ed. Peter Lassman and Ronald Speirs. Cambridge: Cambridge University Press, 1994. 309-60.

Werbner, Pnina. "Introduction: The Dialectics of Cultural Hybridity." *Debating Cultural Hybridity: Multi-Cultural Identities and the Politics of Anti-Racism.* Ed. Pnina Werbner and Tariq Modood. London: Zed Books, 1997. 1-26.

Young, Robert. *Colonial Desire: Hybridity in Theory, Culture and Race.* London: Routledge, 1995.

Reindert Dhondt (K.U.Leuven)

The Old World through a Baroque Mirror: Europe in the Work of Alejo Carpentier

For centuries, Latin American artists have taken hold of European developments in literature and in the arts and used them in order to revise their own cultural traditions. This idiosyncratic appropriation of imported artistic expressions becomes deliberately counter-hegemonic when indigenous artists or *tlacuilos* try to undermine the function of the original models or tend to subvert the Western literary myths of their continent presented as a paradisiacal blank page or a political Utopia. Even by simply repeating features of occidental art, autochthonous writers and painters make a critical commentary on it and simultaneously present 'alterity' as an inherent aspect of their own identity. The hybrid New World Baroque or Neobaroque is, in this sense, a striking example of Latin America's self-conscious transculturation – the Brazilian critic Oswald de Andrade called this process "cannibalization" – of something of which the origins were mainly European. This decolonizing poetics and postcolonial ideology has played a key role in articulating the continent's unique position within a global culture: countless Latin American writers, from Severo Sarduy to Carlos Fuentes, ironically revived the colonial aesthetic in order to make their particular reality understood.

A similar remark applies to another phenomenon that is closely associated with the continent's international fame: magical realism, a literary mode that was initially developed from European avant-garde sources and that crossed the Atlantic Ocean in the opposite direction as quintessentially Latin American. Europe and its imagery of the New World have, in other words, more than once been used in Latin America's search for its own, composite (Indo-Afro-Ibero-American) identity. It was not unusual that cultural expressions of Latin American artists, after having incorporated Western influences, were exported to other parts of the world – including to the initial place of 'origin' in the Old World, from where they corroded the mostly ideologically motivated constructions of Latin America. From this angle, the translation of 'otherness' into selfhood and the process of "returning Europe's gaze," to quote the subtitle of a book by Peter Beardsell (2000), can be seen as a strategy for contesting the pre-eminence of the European view of the world. Or to put it differently, the boomerang effect as an inevitable consequence of the 'invention of America' obliges us to reverse the persistent Eurocentric view of the Other and to reconsider the interaction between the two continents.

One of the major figures in this complex assimilation of European culture in Latin America is, without any doubt, Alejo Carpentier (1904-1980), a Cuban-born author of eclectic education and background. Although he vehemently underscored the 'Americanness' of his literary enterprise, Carpentier frequently acted as a Janus-like go-between for the rationalist, reflective Western civilization (*el allá*) and the multicultural Latin American society (*el acá*), where marvels and prodigies are supposedly still alive. Being the son of well-to-do Franco-Russian immigrants, and having learned Spanish from his mulatto playmates in a popular Havana neighborhood, his adult life was in many ways a never-ending struggle to synthesize European culture and the (Afro-)American world of his childhood. As has been pointed out by the Latin Americanist Klaus Müller-Bergh, who once described Carpentier as "cubano por nacimiento, esencialmente europeo por educación y profundamente hispanoamericano por inclinación" ("Cuban by birth, essentially European by education and profoundly Spanish-American by inclination") (2),[1] both worlds seem to converge in his personality and literary enterprise.

Like so many other fellow artists of his generation, Carpentier used Western civilization as a vantage point from which he saw his own culture in a new perspective: apart from a few exceptions, the main characters in his novels are systematically Europeanized native Americans. Throughout most of his writings Carpentier subtly presents a New World/Old World dichotomy, a cultural bifurcation he became aware of in Europe during the 1930s, when he earned his living as a correspondent for different Cuban magazines. Curiously, it was in the cosmopolitan Paris of the interbellum period, which was the artistic and intellectual capital of Spanish America at that time, that he voraciously read all the books about American history and culture he could find, training himself in a sense for the role he would

---

1 Apart from the quotations from *Concierto barroco*, all translations from the Spanish are the author's.

play in America. Like the main character in *Concierto barroco* (1974), who is constantly comparing the European sights and sounds with their American counterparts, Carpentier feels out of place in Europe. Nevertheless, he sorely needs the distance in order to appreciate his own continent better: "*A veces es necesario alejarse de las cosas,* poner un mar de por medio, *para ver las cosas de cerca*" (76) ("*It is sometimes necessary to distance yourself from things,* to put an ocean in between, *in order to get a close look at them*") (110-11). In fact, during his entire life Carpentier would spend so much time in his father's homeland that Pablo Neruda once cynically referred to the highly erudite and even academic author as "un escritor francés" ("a French writer") (González Echevarría 38). But Carpentier, although constantly searching for an image of himself in a European mirror, has always stubbornly insisted on his 'Cubanhood.'

As a two-way translator, his writing encloses numerous styles and techniques. Although he shared with the so-called "novels of the earth" an interest in the lush settings and exotic cultures of the *mestizo* continent,[2] which he considered as the chosen homeland of the baroque, he repeatedly criticized every tendency towards a literary 'nativism' that has no universal aspirations. Even in the works in which he primarily adopts an Afro-Antillean perspective, the Old World, and more precisely "la tradición hispano-greco-mediterránea," inevitably turns up (Fernández Ariza 17-18). But in his origin-obsessed fiction, Carpentier does not only emphasize the impact of European thought on the Spanish colonies – in *El reino de este mundo* (1949) for instance, the massive slave uprising in Haiti in the 1790s appears as an echo of the French Revolution, while his last novel, *El arpa y la sombra* (1979), centers on Christopher Columbus's discovery of America – he also portrays the impact of the natural and mythological lushness of the New World on the European sensibility.

In his historically based novels, which are all haunted by an ardent desire to express the Latin American world, he never fails to emphasize the dubious value of European influence. The Old Continent, whenever the narrative impinges upon it, is shown as degrading and degraded. Only the alternative

---

2   The so-called *novelas de la tierra* or "telluric novels" describe local realities through rural life and nature. These regional novels played an important role in defining the continent's cultural modernity.

culture of Latin America seems to be able to offer new hope. Although he had been an advocate of the European avant-garde in the 1920s, in the following decade Carpentier writes a rather surprising series of articles for the Cuban review *Carteles* in which he formulates an acrimonious critique of the state of Europe. In contrast with most of his early journalistic and fictional work, which reflects his conviction that Western civilization is in an irremediable state of decline, in later works such as *Concierto barroco* Carpentier focuses his attention primarily on the productive encounter of both traditions, where the minor, peripheral culture influences the major one. This paradigmatic expression of Carpentier's baroque style undeniably inverts the *topos* of the conquest of America when an unnamed Mexican landowner (*el Amo*) and his black servant travel to Spain and Italy where they contaminate European civilization with their own culture, creating a new culture of multiple origins. By advocating a syncretic approach and by reversing the point of view of the colonizer, Carpentier constantly questions the one-sidedness of traditional historiography and obliges the reader to reconsider or 're-think' Europe's (cultural) hegemony.

In his 1982 study *La conquête de l'Amérique*, the literary theorist Tzvetan Todorov writes that we are all direct descendants of Columbus and that the otherness of Latin America prefigures our present-day identity (13). Carpentier, however, turns this point of view around when he treats Latin America as subject and Europe as "ancestral Other" (Kadir 8). But he, surprisingly perhaps, does not confine himself to what Peter Beardsell has called – by analogy with Edward Said's notion of Orientalism – "New Worldism" (21); he also embraces a discourse of sameness that emphasizes the mutual transformation without hierarchy and the continuity between both cultures. Eager to assume the marvelous American reality as an attribute that would distinguish his own peripheral culture from an anemic Western civilization, Carpentier in many of his essays written between the 1920s and 1940s establishes an opposition between the faith in the magical American reality and the decadent reflectivity of occidental thought. There is no doubt that the question of Europe's status in the world as a model of civilization was under discussion during the first decades of the 20th century. Influenced by the Spenglerian model of Fall and Redemption, Carpentier diagnoses the loss of European centrality and conceives the New World as a place for rebirth, as a reservoir of meaning for a decaying Western culture whose capacity for creating prodigies seems to be – at least momentarily – exhausted. According to the Cuban author, the Second World War corroborates Spengler's persuasive prophecies about the decline of the "Apollonian" Western culture, which provides him with the philosophical ground for affirming the autonomy of the "Faustic" Latin American world (González Echevarría 55-56). The unprecedented hecatomb of citizens during World War II and especially the Holocaust seem to provide confirmation of the spiritual bankruptcy of the West and the transfer of the focus of universal history to America, as had been forecast by *Der Untergang des Abendlandes* (1918-22). The apparent irreversibility of Europe's imminent demise is confirmed by the newly arrived immigrants in America.

In line with the negative assessments of European culture as expounded by the surrealist movement, Carpentier predicts in his 1931 essay "América ante la joven literatura europea" that American culture will surpass the metropolitan center because of its vitality and its creative assimilation of a broad spectrum of traditions. He significantly punctuates his text by some jocular remarks about the twilight of the Old World that he borrowed from, among others, the German author Walther Mehring: "¿Cómo serán los últimos europeos? ¿No los exhibirán de la misma manera, algún día, en un museo de Montevideo?" ("What will happen to the last Europeans? Won't they be exhibited, some day, in a museum of Montevideo?") (54). The New World is thus the site where the moribund occidental model will be preserved. But Carpentier's attitude towards Europe is more ambivalent than one might think at first glance. In his view, there is no need whatsoever to deny the filial relation of Latin America to Europe or to throw the baby out with the bathwater by wiping out the European heritage: "Todo arte necesita de una tradición de oficio" ("Every art needs a tradition of professions") ("América" 57). Ten years later, Carpentier publishes a series of programmatic articles in the review *Carteles*, entitled "El ocaso de Europa" ("The Dusk of Europe" 1941), that reveal a strong confidence in the young culture of Latin America and a rejection of contemporary European art, in particular surrealism. Carpentier thus revises his opinion and argues that Latin America, not afflicted with the sense of exhaustion that characterizes contemporary Western art, has everything it needs to create a great culture.

In line with Spengler's ideas on degeneration, Carpentier in his novels also criticizes the relative poverty of Western traditions, to which he opposes younger, more spontaneous, less intellectualized cultures and art forms. In the famous prologue-epilogue to *El reino de este mundo*, which launched the concept of the "marvelous reality of America," Carpentier outlines the directions of his own work and tries to recuperate a lost origin destroyed by the violent invasion of the Spanish conquistadors. But just like those New World intellectuals who choose a stylistic period of post-Renaissance European art, namely the Baroque from the period of Absolutism and the Counter-Reformation, to express the American colonial difference, Carpentier paradoxically adopts a Western perspective in order to discover the marvelous everyday reality of his own continent (Steenmeijer). His vision is also European because it is undoubtedly part of a turn towards primitivism and the unconscious initiated by modernism. In order to highlight the differences between Latin American and European culture, Carpentier contrasts the marvelous with the fantastic, the authentic American reality with the artificial and cold "maravilloso europeo" that allegedly consists in "el encuentro fortuito de un paraguas y de una máquina de coser sobre una mesa de disección" ("the fortuitous meeting of a sewing machine and an umbrella on a dissection table") (*El reino* 6). Once again he urges the Spanish American artists to have faith in their own culture and to overcome their inferiority complex with regard to Europe.

In *El reino de este mundo*, the refined world of the European upper class and the rationalism of 18th century French Enlightenment collide with the instinctive natural impulses of a magical, esoteric African culture as a first step towards a genuine America-in-the-making. The multiple geographical voyages of the main characters at a symbolic level constitute the passage between freedom and slavery, between culture and barbarism, between nationalism and cosmopolitism – all twin concepts that remind us of the key debates in the Latin American intellectual tradition from Domingo Faustino Sarmiento to Roberto Fernández Retamar. But instead of reaffirming Latin America's subordinate status with regard to former centers of empire, the Cuban novelist tries to reformulate the question of the relationship of the (ex-)colony to the metropolis by focusing on the continent's cultural autonomy and, to a lesser extent, its contribution to the emergence of modern Western civilization. Even for characters who repeat all the typical features of the proto-capitalist settler-tyrant in the Americas, such as the plantation owner Lenormand de Mézy in *El reino de este mundo*, the New World never represents a pale imitation of Western modernity, on the contrary; the continent of temporary residence even becomes the real home of the rich colonist who is alienated from the Parisian *beau monde*.

Esteban, the central character in *El siglo de las luces* (1962), undergoes a similar experience when he returns to his homeland and is highly disenchanted with the outcome of the French Revolution. Whereas as an adolescent he had cherished illusions about the literary gatherings of the Parisian intelligentsia, the art galleries and the Collège de France, he is now confronted with the hypocrisy of the Jacobin extremists, the reign of terror, the violation of human rights, and a widespread anti-intellectual climate. Post-revolutionary France is, in Esteban's view, anything but a blueprint for a Brave New World. Most revealing of all, to his understanding, is the fact that "el Gran Vértigo" ("the Great Frenzy") has broken out in the home base of the *philosophes*, "[...] precisamente donde parec[ía] que la civilización hub[ía] hallado su equilibrio supremo" ("exactly there where civilization had found its supreme equilibrium") (329). Recognizing that the so-called Age of Enlightenment has ended with one of the bloodiest periods in Western history, the hero states on his return in Cuba: "Vengo de vivir entre los bárbaros" ("I have lived between barbarians") (319). But by making clear that the pre-Colombian Caribbean has never been an Arcadia either, Carpentier corrects the tendency to absolutize the distinction between civilization and barbarism, between the unshakeable belief in progress and the stagnation caused by the caudillismo-system.[3] Esteban's account of an American exodus called "la Gran Migración" ("the Great Migration") reminds us that the Europeans were as much a conquering tribe as were the original inhabitants of the continent. In the end, the main character concludes that the Promised Land only lies within the Self.

The protagonist of *El recurso del método* (1976) follows a similar trajectory in his critical awakening to the sanctimony and doubleness of European

---

3   Related to the phenomenon of personalism, *caudillismo* refers to the government of dictatorial local leaders or *caudillos*. The "little chiefs" were ubiquitous in the early decades of independence and remained a common feature of Latin American states until well into the 20th century.

culture. This profoundly comic novel deals with a frenchified benevolent despot, a cultural-historical caricature, who rules the fictitious Nueva Córdoba from his splendid Parisian *hôtel particulier* in the rue de Tilsitt and who returns periodically to the tropical "país de salvajes" ("land of the savages") in order to temper revolutionary outbreaks. Once again the major focus is on the mixture of elements from different cultural traditions, a kind of baroque *summa* of art forms. By rejecting his own indigenous identity, the tragicomic figure of the illustrious tyrant aims to appear refined and elegant in the sophisticated circles of the Parisian upper ten. And just like his son Ariel, whose name evokes a number of polemical readings of the continent's position within the global order, this archetypal exponent of the Latin American dictator epitomizes the world-weary intellectualist who submits to foreign idols. In order to achieve respectability, he imports styles and street names, however ludicrous their application may be. His own education was dominated by school books in which more space was occupied by the Crusades and the Soissons Vase than by the conquest of Peru or the battle of Carabobo (67). The First Magistrate is vainly seeking "over there" an illusory lost origin. Whenever the occasion arises, he praises the vigor of the Gallic cockerel to the skies.

Whereas the accomplishments of French art defy all description, the Spanish ex-colonizers are depicted as innate Philistines. Just as in *El siglo de las luces*, the cultural gap with the backward Iberian Peninsula is inevitably deepening with the passage of time – hence the recurrence of the old French adage "L'Afrique commence aux Pyrénées" ("Africa begins at the Pyrenees") to which the oppressor subscribes. In spite of the frequent eulogies on the virtues of Latinity, on the Cartesian spirit, and on Belle Époque culture, the narrator does not refrain from satirizing some "horrid French customs" and mindsets by means of a Distinguished Academician (*el Ilustre Académico*) who clearly undercuts Old World culture. Slowly but surely, the head of state himself begins to see through the varnish of

> [...] la Europa agonizante, agotada, ya sin savia ni genio – y bueno sería que acabáramos de librarnos de su ya inútil magisterio –, cuya decadencia irremediable había proclamado, no hacía mucho, el filósofo alemán Oswaldo Spengler.
> ([...] the agonizing Europe, without vitality nor genius – it is highly necessary to get rid of its superfluous teaching –, whose irremediable decadency the German philosopher Oswald Spengler had only recently proclaimed.) (320)

This time, the New World seems to be, rather than the privileged territory of the marvelous, a tasteless caricature of the European culture whose "eje de gravitación – era tiempo ya de proclamarlo – se había desplazado hacia América [...] Europa era el mundo del pasado" ("center of gravity – it was high time to proclaim it once and for all – had been displaced towards America [...] Europe was the world of the past") (214). Eventually it turns out that the unscrupulous dictator is incapable of breaking with his roots. The hammock that hangs in his Parisian mansion and the local dishes prepared by his mulatto concubine symbolize how Latin America does not lend itself to Europeanization. By his final return to the City of Light, the overthrown tyrant's eyes are opened and he rediscovers his Latin American identity in exile.

In all the previously mentioned novels, Latin America is considered as a worthy, rejuvenated alternative for a decaying Western culture characterized by a self-sufficient lethargy and a complete lack of inventiveness. Only the positive alternative culture of "el Continente-de-poca-Historia" ("the Continent-of-little-History"), which Carpentier systematically opposes to effete Western culture, seems to be able to offer new hope. Nevertheless, Europe is not always regarded as the Manichean counterpart of Latin America. The reverse transculturation between the Old and New World recurs as a predominant theme in *Concierto barroco*, a novella that carries the dateline "La Habana-París, 1974." Instead of describing a voyage to the West Indies with its implications of bringing Western civilization to the New Continent, Carpentier relates, in this stylistically complex novel, the coming to consciousness of an upper-class Mexican connoisseur of music by means of a "viaje a la semilla" or a come-back to the native soil of his ancestors. Opposite to a narrative of immigration that begins in Europe, the work once more situates the moment of return from a reverse perspective, when the westernized native returns – not to his own indigenous culture, but to the Old World in order to find a new perspective upon his identity and the history of his own culture.

The protagonist, the grandson of Spaniards born in Castilla-La Mancha, acquires wealth and decides to set out on a long journey with his black servant Filomeno. In his quixotical *recorrido* through the Old Continent the Mexican miner finds the Madrid of Philip V's reign and even the brightly-colored city of Venice in carnival time sleepy and drab in comparison with the baroque opulence of his homeland. During his stay in Spain and Italy, the *indiano* perceives Western music and performing arts as an expression of a *Weltanschauung* that has exhausted itself so completely that it must infuse itself with elements of the New World. The novel principally underscores America's contribution to Western music: without the wealth supplied by America, Carpentier suggests, European culture would be squalid.

The anti-colonial twist is obvious in this inversion of cultural power. The Mexican *nouveau riche* and his *criado* succeed in revitalizing European culture by providing new musical techniques such as jazzy improvisation and by suggesting new, properly American themes. In a century in which the representation of the Americas is determined by the 'noble savages' that populated the writings of Montesquieu, Rousseau, and Bernardin de Saint-Pierre, convincing *el Fraile Pelirrojo,* in whom we recognize the baroque composer Antonio Vivaldi, to stage an opera based on the life of Montezuma appears to be an unprecedented *tour de force*. The play marks the beginning of an increased tendency in European art to use America as a foundational metaphor or merely as an exotic and phantasmagoric setting. Carpentier demonstrates that without this kind of spectacle, the reality of the New World could not exist for the European. The performance of *Motezuma* (1733), an outstanding example of a Eurocentric re-writing of the Conquest, revives the dormant nationalistic feelings of the Creole protagonist and ignites his resistance to colonialism. His sympathies are not with Cortés but with his antagonist:

> [...] mientras más iba corriendo la música de Vivaldi y me dejaba llevar por las peripecias de la acción que la ilustraba, más era mi deseo de que triunfaran los mexicanos [...]. (75) (The longer I listened to Vivaldi's music and the more I became caught up in the twists and turns of the action that illustrated it, the more I wanted the Mexicans to win [...]) (109).

The performance introduces a profound schism within his cultural identification and he finds himself somewhere in between the Old and the New World.

As said before, the relation between both cultures is anything but black-and-white in *Concierto barroco*. The history of the New World, even though repeatedly scorned because of its lack of tradition, is able to convert itself into a subject matter suitable for opera goers tired of the repertoire based on classical antiquity: "¡Cuántos Orfeos, cuántos Apolos, cuántas Ifigenias, Didos y Galateas!" (50) ("All the Orpheuses, all the Apollos, the Iphigenias, Didos, and Galateas!") (81). The anachronistic character of the jazz trumpeter Louis Armstrong is in command of this Lezamian 'counter-conquest' of the supposed cradle of civilization. During the concluding jam session in the Venetian Ospedale della Pietà, the baroqueness reaches a delirious climax: the diverse musical traditions of southern Europe combine with the Afro-American rhythms in a synthesis that is full of the promise of cultural renewal. The text of the novel, which contains numerous references to Cervantes's *Don Quijote*, Ariosto's *Orlando Furioso*, Shakespeare's *Hamlet*, and Silvestre de Balboa's *Espejo de paciencia*, partakes of this cultural intermingling.

Carpentier makes clear that the purveyors of culture traveled as much from America to Europe as they did from Europe to America and that the impact of both cultural areas has been fundamentally a two-way traffic. Moreover, the idea of 'returning Europe's gaze' does not suffice to articulate a syncretic culture on the confluence of Hispanic, African, and pre-Columbian traditions. Instead of simply throwing light on the importance of Latin America for the development of European arts, the Cuban writer subverts the binaries of domination and subordination by asserting that the capricious baroque of Latin America and the harmonies of Europe do not neutralize each other, but rather enrich each other mutually: only a cultural cross-fertilization between both continents – whatever their historically embedded differences may be – is able to bring forth 'the kingdom of this world.'

Works Cited

Beardsell, Peter. *Europe and Latin America: Returning the Gaze*. Manchester and New York: Manchester University Press, 2000.
Carpentier, Alejo. *Concierto barroco*. México: Siglo XXI Editores, 1974.
——. *El recurso del método*. México: Siglo XXI Editores, 1976.
——. *El arpa y la sombra*. México: Siglo XXI Editores, 1979.
——. "América ante la joven literatura europea." *La novela latinoamericana en vísperas de un nuevo siglo y otros ensayos*. Madrid: Siglo XXI Editores, 1981. 51-57.
——. *El siglo de las luces*. Madrid: Cátedra, 1985.
——. *Baroque Concerto*. Trans. Asa Zatz. London: André Deutsch, 1991.

———. *El reino de este mundo*. Barcelona: Seix Barral, 2005.
Fernández Ariza, Guadalupe. *Alejo Carpentier: Ante el espejo del Barroco*. Roma: Bulzoni, 1997.
González Echevarría, Roberto. *Alejo Carpentier: The Pilgrim at Home*. Austin: University of Texas Press, 1990.
Kadir, Djelal. *The Other Writing: Postcolonial Essays in Latin America's Writing Culture*. West Lafayette: Purdue University Press, 1993.
Müller-Bergh, Klaus. *Alejo Carpentier: Estudio biográfico-crítico*. New York: Las Américas, 1972.
Steenmeijer, Maarten. "Identificación ideológica e ironización discursiva: Focalización y narración en *El reino de este mundo*." *Aleph* 13 (1998): 61-74.
Todorov, Tzvetan. *La conquête de l'Amérique: la question de l'autre*. Paris: Editions du Seuil, 1982.

Silvana Mandolessi (K.U.Leuven)

Cultural Hierarchies, Secondary Nations: The Tension between Europe and "Minor" Cultures in Witold Gombrowicz and Jorge Luis Borges

Jorge Luis Borges and Witold Gombrowicz share the biographical circumstance of having lived in Argentina most of their lives. Despite this coincidence, critics do not tend to highlight common features of their work: their origins – Argentina in the case of Borges, and Poland for Gombrowicz – lead to an interpretation within the national contexts to which they belong. These contexts are so dissimilar that they seem to discourage any possible dialogue. Moreover, even though both Gombrowicz and Borges belong, according to Gilles Deleuze, "to the most interesting avant-garde writers transforming the legacy of the Baroque into experimental modern writing" (81), the way they develop their experimental writing places them in opposite ends of that realm. Nevertheless, in this article I would like to show that, in spite of their dissimilar trajectories, they deal with one common issue: both Gombrowicz and Borges reflect on the meaning of belonging to a secondary culture (Poland and Argentina respectively), a locus of enunciation that initially appears to be lacking or is even inexistent, insufficient, and weak. In this sense, belonging to 'secondary' countries is closely related to the permanent tension that the idea of 'Europe' represents for these 'minor' cultures.

Before taking a closer look at the way they articulate minority and the idea of Europe, I will briefly refer to the idea of the Old World that their works evoke. From an external point of view, Europe has often been perceived as a unity: it represents the common tradition, certain humanist values that are believed to constitute the essence of the West. However, this utopian unity falls apart when Europe stops being synonymous with 'the Western tradition' or 'universal culture.' Juan José Saer wonders if, among all the attributes that can be applied to European literature, that of 'European' might be the most erroneous or improper: to talk about European writers in this sense implies from their perspective that their work harmoniously falls within the context of the European tradition. But this bucolic image is denied in the work of several writers who have perceived European culture or European society as a hostile force against which it is necessary to fight, as a superficial or oppressive realm, or even as evil itself. In this sense, Saer points out that "various authors responded to that adversity in different ways: with a disdainful silence (Beckett), insult (Baudelaire), escape (Rimbaud), madness (Nietzsche), confinement (Proust and Kafka), suicide (Pavese or Celan)" (92).[1] Gombrowicz can be added to this list. He considered his withdrawal from Europe and subsequent voluntary exile in Latin America as a necessary condition for his work, making the slogan "write against Europe" a program for Polish literature. According to him, Polish literature suffers from an excessive concern about the cultural and political position of Poland in relation to other European countries. He argues that in order to write, the author needs to distance himself from this tension. In this sense, Gombrowicz's exile constitutes a metaphor of this required external perspective. Therefore, rather than representing a linear and homogeneous tradition in which Gombrowicz would inscribe himself, the term 'Europe' evokes an obstacle to be overcome.

Borges's oeuvre, for its part, quite obviously celebrates European culture as a whole, but he also acknowledges that 'European culture' is a superficial way to refer to a multiplicity of traditions. In his texts this multiplicity does not take the form of a conflict but is expressed as a source of limitless possibilities. For Borges, European culture is a personal choice among this wide variety, as his personal vindication of English literature – even including obscure writers – illustrates, whereas he barely mentions Proust or even claims that Rimbaud is an artist "in search of experiences he did not qualify for" (Saer 34). The willfulness with which Borges judges European literature points out his distance towards it, characteristic of an external position and similar to that of Gombrowicz, although different in tone and sense. Both also agree on the idea that every work of art implies a paradox regarding its origin: every work displays marks of its context of production, while at the same time necessarily exceeding this context. In accordance with this conception, Saer declares that "the less Europeanness it possesses, the more artistic European art becomes" (93). This relates to the fact that, for Gombrowicz and Borges, the labels 'Argentinean' and 'Polish' were constantly thought of as random attributes from which to distance themselves, rather than essential traits of their writing. As Gombrowicz argues,

---

1   All translations are the author's unless otherwise stated.

The writer, the artist, or anyone who attaches importance to his spiritual development, must feel no more than a resident in Poland or the Argentine, and it is his duty to regard Poland or the Argentine as an obstacle, almost as an enemy. That is the only way to feel *really* free. And only those people for whom their country is an obstacle rather than an advantage will have a chance of becoming truly free spiritually, and, in the case of Europe, truly European. (57)

In what follows, I will closely analyze the ways in which Gombrowicz and Borges state the tension between Europe, as a synonym for the Western tradition, and the so-called secondary, minor, or peripheral countries.[2]

From Gombrowicz's point of view, 'Europe' appears to contain at least two 'Europes': one rendered by culturally 'mature' and politically central countries that have well-defined forms, forms of expressions that have been developed for centuries, such as France, Germany, and England, the other by the so-called 'secondary European cultures' that are historically situated in a place of inferiority, the so-called 'countries of weakened form' (of which Poland would be an example). Being a minor nation like Poland means being at the edge of Europe, in constant tension with a strong desire to fortify a national identity that is perceived as weak or insufficient in relation to other strong nations. As a result, Poland, although belonging to Europe, appears to be in a peripheral position, similar to that of Argentina. Thus, despite their multiple geographical, historical, and cultural differences, both Argentina and Poland are linked by their peripheral nature. But what exactly constitutes this secondary character? Which problems does it imply? The duality between mature and immature cultures, which Gombrowicz introduces, cannot be understood without referring to a central notion in his poetics: the notion of Form, or "the conflict between man and Form." Although he uses this notion as a social, cultural, and political category, at the root of the concept lies a particular definition of subjectivity.

---

2   In the context of Gombrowicz's work, the terms 'secondary', 'minor', or 'peripheral' are somehow equivalent. They refer to cultures situated in a position of inferiority (that is, cultures that have not developed perfect, mature forms) when compared to 'universal' West European tradition. Borges also refers to a peripheral position as a general way of describing Argentina as a country whose tradition and culture appear to be less important than their European model. Therefore, although these metaphors might have different connotations, they are used here interchangeably to describe the tension between the centrality of Europe and the marginality of other countries.

According to the traditional Western understanding of the self, the individual is conceived of as a separate, unique, and integrated motivational and cognitive universe, a dynamic center of emotion, reasoning, and action organized as a totality. Conversely, Gombrowicz highlights that the *desire* to be a coherent whole – in Gombrowicz's terms, the desire of Form – is what characterizes subjectivity. At the core of this conception is the idea that the subject is made out of parts, and even though they may try to achieve coherence, every integration will be precarious and there will always be some remainder of incoherence. This incoherence is essentially inexpressible. The self can only express itself and be perceived by others in a well-defined form. Thus, the individual identifies himself with an external form, such as social roles or national forms, and other models of subjectivity that allow him to be part of a community. The organization of this community, based on the mechanical repetition of rituals and fixed forms, is judged by Gombrowicz as absurd and false. It is true that the self manifests a continuous tendency to give and acquire a Form, but, as Valérie Deshoulières mentions, Gombrowicz "acknowledges that the principle of identity is the main condition of logic and he is not unaware of the fact that, beyond pure a priori, life would be impossible if the relationships of which it is woven were not intelligible and transmitted in a univocal manner" (53). Yet, it is not less true that every definite identity betrays what is essential in the individual, namely its constitutive heterogeneity: those disparate, anarchic, irrational, 'immature' elements that persist under the surface of our official, socialized, cultivated 'selves' – immature components that, when coming to the surface, expose the lack of authenticity of established customs, ideologies and culture:

> The drama of human Form, as the ferocious battle between man and his own Form (that is to say his battle against his way of being, feeling, thinking, talking, acting, against his culture, his ideas and his ideologies, his convictions, his creeds [...] against everything by which he appears to the outer world [...]). (Gombrowicz 51)

Importantly, as Ewa Ziarek points out, "despite his relentless emphasis on the exteriority and artifice of linguistic expression, Gombrowicz refuses to see Form merely as an obstacle inhibiting a more authentic or 'true' inner self." The misleading desire for authenticity or unmasking could lead, therefore, only to a tragic de-facement, to a loss of one's constitution. The struggle with

Form is expressed as "the conflict of two contradictory desires, the desire for order and expression on the one hand, and on the other an equally strong, although experienced as illegitimate, desire for the unfinished and the chaotic, for the state symbolized as the always already lost immaturity" (12).

This conception of subjectivity may lose much of its subversive impact in the light of our familiarity with the idea of an opaque and off-centered self and with poststructuralist theories regarding the performative aspects of existence. It is therefore important to stress that, in his texts, Gombrowicz does not offer a coherent philosophy or a finished theory of subjectivity, but, well, literature. His novels and plays are absurd and grotesque texts that recover the subversive tradition of humor. In this sense, Gombrowicz's texts persuade us of immature and anarchic elements inside us, being themselves anarchic and 'immature' texts, offering, along with a cultural critique that could be called 'serious,' a celebration of the pleasure of banality, of decomposition and nonsense. Gombrowicz's texts thus give us a liberating experience of our own anarchic hybridity, instead of a coherent and rational explanation of subjectivity.

Yet, as Marzena Grzegorczyk points out, Form does not only interest Gombrowicz as an aesthetic, psychological, and social category, but also as essentially related to the nation. As this Polish critic states, if, in *Imagined Communities,* Benedict Anderson stresses the importance of invention in the process of nation formation, Gombrowicz chooses to focus on the pitfalls of this process:

> In the national sphere Gombrowicz is fascinated by the same basic rules of the workings of form that take place in the interpersonal realm: its fundamental, albeit denied, instability and its tendency to produce hierarchies. In criticizing the "national longing of form," to use Timothy Brennan's phrase, Gombrowicz underscores the fact that nationalism bases itself on a false return to pure uncontested origin. While doing this it erases all that threatens a notion of integrity and purity. (138)

In Gombrowicz's view, 'mature,' culturally central nations (France being the icon here) are characterized by their having developed and brought to perfection a precise *form,* an identity, resulting from its long cultural tradition. The affirmative certainty with which a Frenchman declares himself French is therefore clearly different from the uncertainty experienced by an individual coming from a minor nation.

> A Frenchman or an Englishman never experiences such lack of harmony – at least not to this extent. Whatever a Frenchman or an Englishman might feel individually, even if he is profoundly torn within himself, he will always seek refuge in a certain national, English or French, form, which has been elaborated over the centuries.
> I was polish. (Gombrowicz 53)

The literary history of Poland is, in Gombrowicz's view, a tragic one in which literature has been trying to achieve a well-defined form, a cultural maturity that could elevate Poland to the level of mature nations. Gombrowicz refers to his native culture by pointing out the following contradiction: while wanting to protect their authenticity and independence, the Poles are constantly competing against other nations. Trying to join the 'universal' world, the nation becomes infected with a self-imposed rigidity, sacrificing in this way its authenticity. Thus, Gombrowicz believed that his compatriots had more reason than the French or the English not to identify themselves with the national form.

Poland is defined by Gombrowicz as a "country between the East and the West, where Europe starts to draw to an end, a border country where the East and the West soften into each other" (53). The territory of a minor nation is an accidental one, in which no definition can be absolute. The program formulated by Gombrowicz suggests that instead of considering this immaturity a deficiency, the Poles (or the Argentines) should consider it a virtue. We encounter an inverted symmetry here: the larger the degree of national maturity and power, the less individuality, and vice versa. Therefore, immature nations such as Poland or Argentina are able to allow individuals to make contact with their more authentic components. Immature nations bring individuals nearer to their own immaturity, releasing them from the weight of an excessive cultural tradition. Gombrowicz insists on the potential that is released by occupying a 'minor' position: 'immaturity', as well as its irreverence regarding tradition, can only be held by minor countries. It would be the patrimony, the symbolic capital and the main strategy of a minor culture, a position from which the characteristic maturity of European culture is regarded as an artificial imposition built on the repression of its chaotic and low elements. As Gombrowicz points out,

> [...] Throughout my life, during twenty-three years of the Argentinian pampas or anywhere else, I never lost the certainty that I was European, more European,

perhaps, than the Europeans of Rome or Paris. I was virtually sure that the revision of European Form could only be undertaken from an extra-European position, from where it is slacker and less perfect. The profound conviction that the imperfect is superior to the perfect (because it is more constructive) was one of the basic intuitions in *Ferdydurke*. (63)

Gombrowicz's notion of 'Europeanness' appears thus as a paradox. Being Polish defines him as European, but at the same time he is not truly European since he belongs to a country that is perceived as inferior by 'European' standards. Nevertheless, becoming 'truly' European does not necessarily imply an identification with what is commonly understood as European, but a precarious positioning of the self suspended between West and East.

In his well known essay "The Argentine Writer and Tradition," Jorge Luis Borges formulates a comparable thesis. His point of departure is nationalism: a conception of literature, inherited from the 19th century, that asks from writers a loyalty to national values and traditions: a writer born in Argentina *must* be an Argentine writer, just as a Polish author *must* translate the Polish Nation into his literature. This duty, which is one of the main problems in Gombrowicz's poetics, is for Borges not even a problem at all:

> Creo que nos enfrenta a un tema retórico, apto para desarrollos patéticos; más que de una verdadera dificultad mental entiendo que se trata de una apariencia, de un simulacro, de un seudoproblema. (267) (I believe we are faced with a mere rhetorical topic which lends itself to pathetic elaborations; rather than with a true mental difficulty, I take it we are dealing with an appearance, a simulacrum, a pseudo-problem.) (211)

In the first place, Borges refuses to accept that Argentine literature is to be founded in the 'gauchesque' literature.[3] According to this line of thought, the contemporary writer should be guided by the vocabulary, devices, and themes of gauchesque poetry, which is said to be directly derived from the spontaneous poetry of the *gauchos* – a continuation or enlargement of the poetry of the *payadores*. This would be, then, the spontaneous expression of the Argentine self. Against this position, Borges stresses that the refined and

---

3   *Gauchesque* or *Gaucho literature* is a Latin American poetical genre that imitates the *payadas* ('ballads') traditionally sung to guitar accompaniment by the wandering gaucho minstrels of Argentina and Uruguay. By extension, the term includes the body of Latin American literature that treats the way of life and philosophy of the itinerant gauchos.

cultivated poetry that constitutes the gauchesque tradition is based on imitation, and is not a mere continuation of popular poetry. *Gauchescos* poets, that is, *deliberately* cultivate a popular language; gauchesque poetry is thus a literary genre, as artificial as any other: "La idea de que la poesía argentina debe abundar en rasgos diferenciales argentinos y en color local argentino me parece una equivocación" (269) ("The idea that Argentine poetry should abound in differential Argentine traits and Argentine local colour seems to me a mistake") (214). Moreover, Borges adds, the idea that a literature must define itself in terms of its national traits is a relatively new concept. Undoubtedly Shakespeare would have been amazed if people had tried to limit him to English themes; if they had told him that, as an Englishman, he had no right to write *Hamlet*, the theme of which is Scandinavian, or *Macbeth*, which has a Scottish theme. In order to underline the irony involved in the claims of those who think national literature must address autochthonous themes, Borges writes: "El culto argentino del color local es un reciente culto europeo que los nacionalistas deberían rechazar por foráneo" (270) ("The Argentine cult of local colour is a recent European cult which nationalists ought to reject as foreign") (215). And in order to stress this point, he invokes Edward Gibbons' claim that no camels appear in the Qur'an. Mohammed did not perceive camels as something characteristic of Arabia, since they were part of his daily reality, "en cambio un falsario, un turista, un nacionalista árabe, lo primero que hubiera hecho es prodigar camellos, caravanas de camellos en cada página" (270) ("on the other hand, the first thing a falsifier, a tourist, and Arab nationalist would do is have a surfeit of camels, caravans of camels, on every page") (215).

Nationalist writers invoke some fundamental books of the Argentine tradition as examples of authenticity. Among those books, *Don Segundo Sombra,* a text which belongs to the gauchesque tradition, is a paradigmatic one. However, from Borges's point of view, the book is hardly nurtured by national tradition, since the mythical *gaucho* image it proposes is based on Kipling, Mark Twain, and Montmartre:

> *Don Segundo Sombra* abunda en metáforas de un tipo que nada tiene que ver con el habla de la campaña y sí con las metáforas de los cenáculos contemporáneos de Montmartre. En cuanto a la fábula, a la historia, es fácil comprobar en ella el influjo del *Kim* de Kipling, cuya acción está en la India y que fue escrito, a su vez, bajo el influjo del *Huckleberry Finn* de Mark Twain, epopeya del Misisipí.

(271) (*Don Segundo Sombra* abounds in metaphors of a kind having nothing to do with country speech but a great deal to do with the metaphors of the then current literary circles of Montmartre. As for the fable, the story, it is easy to find in it the influence of Kipling's *Kim,* whose action is set in India and which was, in turn, written under the influence of Mark Twain's *Huckleberry Finn,* the epic of the Mississippi.) (216)

For nationalists, it is also necessary to reject European devices and themes in order to write a valuable literature. Nationalist writers devise a binary opposition and solve the tension between these two poles by rejecting one of them outright. To Borges, on the contrary, and in a way similar to the approach of Gombrowicz, it is precisely the double, ambivalent position of being at the same time outside and inside the Western tradition, of being linked to Europe without in fact being European, that constitutes a value. "What is our Argentine tradition?" Borges wonders,

> [c]reo que podemos contestar fácilmente y que no hay problema en esta pregunta. Creo que nuestra tradición es toda la cultura occidental, y creo también que tenemos derecho a esta tradición, mayor que el que pueden tener los habitantes de una u otra nación occidental. (272) (I believe we can answer this question easily and that there is no problem here. I believe our tradition is all of Western culture, and I also believe we have a right to this tradition, greater than that which the inhabitants of one or another Western nation might have.) (218)

According to Thorstein Veblen, if Jews have been able to innovate many aspects of Western culture, then this fact is not due to supposed racial differences, but to their being at the same time inside and outside this culture: it would always be easier for a Jew to innovate it. Borges also compares the relation between Argentine literature and the West with the peripheral position of Irish literature in relation to England:

> [...] les bastó el hecho de sentirse irlandeses, distintos, para innovar en la cultura inglesa. Creo que los argentinos, los sudamericanos en general, estamos en una situación análoga; podemos manejar todos los temas europeos, manejarlos sin supersticiones, con una irreverencia que puede tener, y ya tiene, consecuencias afortunadas. (273) ([...] it was sufficient for them to feel Irish, to feel different, in order to be innovators in English culture. I believe that we Argentines, we South Americans in general, are in an analogous situation; we can handle all European themes, handle them without superstition, with an irreverence which can have, and already does have, fortunate consequences.) (218)

Minor cultures then have as their patrimony not the narrow limits of a national tradition but the whole Universe, "For either being Argentine is an inescapable act of fate – and in that case we shall be so in all events – or being Argentine is a mere affectation, a mask" (219).

Following a different path than Gombrowicz, Borges's essay arrives at the same point: the national self again appears as an affectation, as a mask, and we again find the vindication of an ambiguous space as the site of potential creativity. But once again, these similarities do not mean that their points of departure are identical. First, significant differences exist in the way both of them conceive of 'tradition,' which is the center of reflection or contention. As Pablo Gasparini points out, Borges, in line with Eric Hobsbawm, Raymond Williams, or even Latin American intellectuals like Octavio Paz, considers cultural tradition to be a continuous state of renovation or invention (180). Tradition is a highly dynamic means and insofar as it is invented, it can unceasingly be recreated. Gombrowicz, on the contrary, seems to conceive of tradition as something inevitably located in the past that only asserts itself in the present as an oppressive force. Opposed to the desired outright dismissal of the cultural tradition, Borges forges a literature based on the appreciation and re-writing of the greater symbols of the Western tradition.

It is important to realize that the origin of their dissimilar strategies can be found in the way in which 'Europe' functions for them both. If, at the beginning, we underlined that Poland and Argentina are equivalent in that they occupy a peripheral position in relation to Western Europe, this cannot hide the fact that Gombrowicz is situated inside Europe. For Gombrowicz, Europe becomes the burden of a legacy that must be forgotten; its inheritance is a damned legacy because it always takes the form of an excess from which it is necessary to distance oneself – something that Gombrowicz did in his long exile of twenty-four years in Argentina. Gombrowicz's belligerent gesture is translated into the importance he gives to the problem of Form in relation to the nation: the pages of his *Diaries*, which he once and again devotes to persuading the Poles to put aside their inherited identity, clearly reflect the extent of the problem of 'national' writing. Borges, on the contrary, seems to underestimate the problem, calling it "a mere rhetorical topic which lends itself to pathetic elaboration," even though his own essay in part contradicts this claim. For Borges it does not seem necessary to deepen the distance with Europe, only to be aware of the possibility that arises from this ambiguous position: a privileged use of tradition is possible, one which includes perversion, arbitrariness, mixture, and hybridity as creative tools.

Nevertheless, apart from all their differences, the links between different secondary cultures are clearly stressed in Gombrowicz's work. Moreover, he emphasizes that this topic also concerns "the heirs of superior culture":

> The passages in my diary where I mention 'Polishness' have only been read very superficially by western readers. I was almost told: "You'd better cut all that. What has that got to do with us?" It is high time that the heirs of superior cultures stopped turning up their noses. Instead of 'Poland' put the Argentine, Canada, Roumania and so on, and you'll see that my allusions (and my sufferings) can be applied to most of the globe. They concern all secondary European cultures. Look at them still closer: you'll see that they constitute a poison which may affect *you* too. (53)

But beyond these arguments, both writers contributed the renegotiation of hierarchies that separate 'mature' from 'immature' cultures, peripheral from central: we could state that the idea of Europe (and consequently the rigid cultural hierarchies it implies) dissolves as the result of contaminations, hybridities, and borrowings that appear throughout their work. In Borges's games, in which Brutus's words are repeated by a *gaucho* in the 19th century, or in Gombrowicz's work, where a theory of insurrection – that is also valid for Europe and Latin America – is developed, or in the way they both contribute to the discussion of the stereotypes of Latin American or European writers, the contours of Europe are blurred and the boundaries become fuzzy, fusing territories that once seemed strangely remote.

Works Cited

Borges, Jorge Luis. "The Argentine Writer and Tradition." *Labyrinths: Selected Stories and Other Writings*. Ed. Donald A. Yates and James E. Irby. Harmondsworth: Penguin, 1972. 211-19.

——. "El escritor argentino y la tradición." *Obras completas I, 1923–1949*. Barcelona: Emecé, 1996. 267-74.

Deleuze, Gilles. *The Fold: Leibniz and the Baroque*. Minneapolis: University of Minnesota Press, 1993.

Deshoulières, Valérie. "Witold Gombrowicz: Toward a Romantic Theory of Incompleteness." *Gombrowicz's Grimaces*. Ed. Ewa Płonowska Ziarek. 51-64.

Gasparini, Pablo. *El Exilio Procaz: Gombrowicz por la Argentina*. Rosario: Beatriz Viterbo, 2007.

Gombrowicz, Witold. *A Kind of Testament*. Ed. Dominique de Roux and Alastair Hamilton. Philadelphia: Temple University Press, 1973.

Grzegorczyk, Marzena. "Formed Lives, Formless Traditions: The Argentinean Legacy of Witold Gombrowicz." *Gombrowicz's Grimaces*. Ed. Ewa Płonowska Ziarek. 135-56.

Saer, Juan José. *El Concepto de Ficción*. Buenos Aires: Ariel, 1997.

Veblen, Thorstein. *The Theory of the Leisure Class: An Economic Study of Institutions*. New York: Random House, 1934 [1899].

Ziarek, Ewa Płonowska, ed. *Gombrowicz's Grimaces: Modernism, Gender, Nationality*. New York: SUNY Press, 1998.

Kari van Dijk (Radboud University Nijmegen)

Arriving in Eurasia: Yoko Tawada Re-Writing Europe

In the spring of 2006, the Kunsthistorisches Museum in Vienna ran an exhibition organized by the Austrian government (which at that time held the European presidency) under the title "Europa ohne Grenzen" ("Europe without Frontiers"). This exhibition was announced all over the city by means of a picture that showed the abduction of Europe by Zeus. In his 2004 book *Europe: An Unfinished Adventure*, Zygmunt Bauman also used this image and read it as an emblem of what he believes to be a specific characteristic of Europe and/or Europeans: "But the outcome is that we, the Europeans, are perhaps the sole people who (as historical subjects and actors of culture) have *no identity* – fixed identity, or an identity deemed and believed to be fixed: 'we do not know who we are,' and even less do we know what we can yet become and what we can yet learn that we are" (12). Since Europe went away, we have been looking for her – and thereby trying to find ourselves. This difficulty to define who we (as Europeans) 'are' also extends to a geographical level: as Bauman states, "it has been difficult at all times to decide where Europe begins and where it ends – geographically, culturally or ethnically. Nothing has changed in this respect now" (6).

The Japanese-German writer Yoko Tawada, who has been living and writing (in two languages) in Germany since 1982 and who is the winner of numerous literary prizes, both in Japan and in Germany, has also pointed to this rather idiosyncratic aspect of the (Eurasian) continent: her first German text *Wo Europa anfängt* ("Where Europe Begins," from 1991) is to a large extent an *Auseinandersetzung* with the question as to where Europe begins and ends geographically. This attention to Europe and European culture characterizes many of Tawada's German texts;[1] still, as I will show in this essay, this interest in Europe by no means manifests itself in a merely uncritical way. I will highlight one aspect of Tawada's writing in which a critical reconsideration of Europe and its culture makes itself felt, namely the thematics of 'arrival'

---

1   As Anthonya Visser has remarked, when Tawada's texts speak of Europe, they seldom refer to countries other than Germany: "Germany is more or less Europe" (Visser 116-17). All translations from the German and Dutch are the author's.

such as it presents itself on different levels in Tawada's prose. In struggling to connect the interlingual – i.e., in her case, also intrasubjective – 'shores' of Europe and Asia, Tawada's texts enact a critique of a particular aspect of European culture that appears to endanger the process of 'arriving' at *one* Eurasian voice. As one of Tawada's more recent texts describes how the elimination of precisely this (European) aspect must be seen as a condition for the possibility of achieving *one* Eurasian voice, it implicitly enacts a critical *re-writing of Europe* when it actually 'arrives' at this voice. Moreover, as this textual, Eurasian 'arrival' also implies both a *relativization* and an *enrichment* of Europe, in the sense that Tawada's texts bear the traces of an equally important poetical and linguistic source that is not European, Tawada's work can be seen as an invitation to *re-think Europe*, to 'arrive' at new conceptions of what Europe is or should be.

Yet in order to approach the thematics of 'arrival' in Tawada's prose, a return to her early text *Wo Europa anfängt* is necessary. If this text seems to confirm Bauman's statement about the difficulty to decide where Europe begins and where it ends, this text also underlines that, as Tawada formulates it in *Verwandlungen* (2001), definitions are always in a sense fictitious (55): as everything – humans, books, trees, children, lamps, etc. – is connected by sharing the same "Muttererde," the same "mother earth," from which everything comes and to which everything must return (*Talisman* 103), then the "Muttererde" of the Eurasian continent seems even less able to provide us with a ground for assuming a clear and unquestionable division between Europe and Asia. The signpost planted in the midst of Siberia then seems to become a rather ridiculous attempt to mark a frontier between Europe and Asia, an attempt to which the seemingly endless Siberian "Muttererde" not very surprisingly stays utterly indifferent (*Wo Europa anfängt* 82-83). In this way, *Wo Europa anfängt* illustrates what Tawada in both *Talisman* (1996) and in *Verwandlungen* states about signs and language: it is language that divides, that produces differences, whereas Tawada's concept of "Muttererde" marks a dimension in which a silent, underlying connection indiscriminately binds together things as different as a pear, a cat, and an American woman (*Talisman* 103).

If *Wo Europa anfängt*, in so far as it questions the (absolute) dividing line between Europe and Asia, thus proves itself to be a small-scale deconstruction (in the sense that the beginning and the end of either Europe or Asia cannot be unequivocally determined), this same text neverthelesss also tells the tale of an *arrival* in Europe – which presupposes that somehow, notwithstanding Europe's elusiveness, her contours can yet be sensed. For when the train by which the first-person narrator travels reaches Moscow (87), it is said to have arrived in the "middle of Europe"; and also on a much deeper level, Tawada's text shows itself to have 'arrived' in Europe by pointing to an aspect of European culture that prominent thinkers such as Nietzsche and Sloterdijk have identified as "movement," "unrest," or "speed" (Kimmerle 119; Nietzsche 185; Sloterdijk 10). In fact, Bauman's reading of the image of Europe's abduction as a symbol of an ever ongoing European search for itself already implicitly points to this factor of movement: for Europe seems to be about being on the move, endlessly, restlessly, in order to reach that which nevertheless, *necessarily*, will always be eluding us and veiling itself (Irigaray 92) – a drama that has characterized European metaphysics for centuries. Thus Bauman: "The urge to *know* and/or *become* what we are never subsides, and neither is the suspicion ever dispelled about what we may yet become following that urge. Europe's culture is one that knows no rest; it is a culture that feeds on questioning the order of things – and on questioning the fashion of questioning it" (Bauman 12).[2] In *Wo Europa anfängt*, Tawada seems to have this aspect of European culture in mind when she cites Chekhov's 1901 play *The Three Sisters*, in which Irina speaks "the famous words 'To Moscow, to Moscow, to Moscow ...'" (75). As these words accompany the narrator's journey, they seem to express the I's desire to reach Moscow; but as Tawada's text also associates these words with the impossibility of a definite arrival (76), Irina's words become a subtle reference to the "fact" that Europe begins where one is already "unterwegs" (82), on the way, in constant transit – without having a chance of ever really arriving. If, however, arrival after all does seem possible in Tawada's text, one could begin to suspect that Tawada is not just 'citing' an ever moving, restless Europe, but is instead already moving

---

2 The fact that Bauman attributes a lack of identity solely to a restless Europe seems problematic. By opposing 'searching' for an identity to 'resting' within an identity, and 'active' to 'passive,' Bauman is in danger of repeating the hierarchical way in which Europe has traditionally defined itself in relation to its 'others.' As I will show, Tawada's work offers one way to reconsider this binary.

beyond it – a possibility that will be taken into account when the concept of 'arriving' will come to name a critique of Europe at the end of this essay.

For now, another form of arrival should be mentioned, which concerns the person of Yoko Tawada herself – a sense of arrival that can be related to the problematics of bilinguality that, as will be shown, underlie the desire to arrive at *one* Eurasian voice. In 1979, Tawada traveled to Europe by Trans-siberian Express, a journey that *Wo Europa anfängt* somehow seems to mirror, since the narrator of the story, traveling from the East-Siberian port of Nachodka to Moscow, chooses this same means of transportation. The first-person narrator's arrival in the "middle of Europe," in Moscow, furthermore, is paralleled by an autobiographical passage in Tawada's *Überseezungen*, a collection of literary essays that was published in 2002:

> Einige wichtige japanische Schriftsteller schrieben in ihren Büchern über diese Hafenstadt [Marseille], die für sie den Eingang zu Europa bedeutete. In meinem Fall war die erste europäische Stadt Moskau. Europa sieht ganz unterschiedlich aus, je nachdem, durch welchen Eingang man hineinkommt. (Several famous Japanese authors wrote about this port [Marseille] in their books, which to them marked the entrance to Europe. In my case, the first European city was Moscow. Europe looks very different, depending through which gate one enters.) (*Überseezungen* 39)

In view of the above, then, the thematics of arrival in *Wo Europa anfängt* apparently also point to Tawada's own arrival in Europe,[3] an arrival that would prove to be of extraordinary significance for the development of her (bilingual) writing.[4] Yet before this bilingual situation could become a fertile soil for Tawada's writing (Hoffman 50), she went through rather disconcerting experiences many bilingual writers have shared with her. In an essay written

---

3   Of course, by growing up in Japan, Tawada in a sense already had 'arrived' in Europe. See, for example, a passage in *Talisman*: "Japan existiert nicht in Europa, aber außerhalb Europas findet man Japan auch nicht" ("Japan doesn't exist in Europe, but outside of Europe Japan isn't to be found either") (50). In his book *Inventing Japan 1853-1964*, Ian Buruma shows how modern Japan has to a large extent been modeled after Western values and ideas.

4   Of course, there can be "many reasons for being bi- (or multi-)lingual – the word itself can be defined in many ways, though it always involves some sort of continuum – and varying historical and individual contexts color each experience" (De Courtivron 4). In this essay, the focus lies on the "continuum," on the kind of bilingual, existential problematics Tawada's prose shares with other writers.

in Japanese, for example, Tawada recalls having nearly lost her mother tongue after she arrived in Germany, because her Japanese vocabulary seemed unable to render her state of mind any longer; and as she did not master the German language either, she had to live without any language whatsoever for some time (Matsunaga 532). When Tawada's native language gradually began to surface again, it had been transformed and appeared to be no longer identical to the "internal language" (Hoffman 48) she had once self-evidently dwelled in. Bilingual writer Eva Hoffman, to whose famous book *Lost in Translation* Tawada refers in *Überseezungen* (134), also recalls having been "without language" after she emigrated from Poland to the U.S. This experience not only made her aware of "the enormous importance of language and of culture" in the constitution of human identity, it also confronted her with the alienating consequences that losing one's "internal language" can have: "For a while, like so many emigrants, I was in effect without language, and from the bleakness of that condition, I understood how much our inner existence, our sense of self, depends on having a living speech within us. To lose an internal language is to subside into an inarticulate darkness in which we become alien to ourselves [...]" (48).

Now, if language can, to a certain extent, be said to condition all of us, in the sense that it produces differences through and by which our human condition seems at best able to generate a *desire* for identity, unity, and coherence (as, for example, a philosophical concept like Derrida's *différance* suggests), a bilingual situation such as Hoffman's and Tawada's seems destined to intensify the human experience of being irrevocably torn apart. As Isabelle De Courtivron writes:

> We have all lost our childhood paradises, even if this did not happen because we left behind our mother tongue. We all struggle to understand the self as well as to reach out and communicate with others. Bilingual beings have no particular claim to these more universal themes. But perhaps [...] they experience them more acutely as they navigate between words and between worlds [...]." (7-8)

Tawada's (bilingual) prose seems to confirm this observation, since several passages in various of her texts establish a relationship between speaking and bleeding. In *Überseezungen*, we find a bleeding tongue (41); in *Opium für Ovid* (2000), a piece of labial tissue has been severed from the lips and this causes them to bleed (10); and finally, in *Das nackte Auge* (2004), the first-person narrator imagines biting a piece of duck tongue in two: "Es würde blutbitter schmecken" ("It would taste bloodbitter") (23). Inasmuch as this last passage appears to establish a more or less explicit connection between bi-*lingua*-lity[5] and suffering, Tawada's prose seems again and again to speak of a (bilingually conditioned) existential fragmentation, of being cut in half between an *alienated* language (Japanese) and an *alienating* language (German), and of being thereby dislocated and disoriented somewhere between Europe and Asia, between East and West.[6] If, as Isabelle De Courtivron points out, "the anxiety about fragmentation and the search for existential coherence remain primordial human responses" (2), this human need could be expected to appear even more acutely in bilingual contexts. As Eva Hoffman has characterized her own earlier bilingual situation as a world "riven into two parts, divided by an uncrossable barrier" (46), the question is whether or not, as far as Tawada is concerned, the gap between "'hier' und 'drüben,'" between here and there, would prove itself to be "unbridgeable" (Tawada, *Das nackte Auge* 30).

"The rift between the other and me is irreducible," Irigaray states in her 2002 book *The Way of Love*; to a certain extent, Irigaray's observation of irreducible, mainly inter-subjective difference could also be said to apply to the bilingual situations such as Tawada paints them in various of her texts. There, intra-subjective fragmentation is the outcome of an alienating incision that the co-existence of such "radically different" (De Courtivron 7) languages as Japanese and German have brought about, a bleeding incision that no one seems to be able to heal. Two worlds, then, seem to be in conflict (Matsunaga 540) – yet *bridging* does not seem to be a desirable strategy: "Es geht nicht darum, eine bestimmte Grenze zu überschreiten, sondern darum, von einer Grenze zu einer anderen zu wandern" ("It is not about crossing a certain boundary, but about wandering from one boundary to another") (*Talisman* 123-24). How, then, should this borderland-existence be thought? And since a border, as was already shown with regard to *Wo Europa anfängt*, primarily *divides*, should one already at this point have to conclude that Tawada's texts decide to stick with the incision, with the bleeding wound caused by the clash of two radically diverging worlds?

---

5   In Latin, of course, *lingua* means 'tongue' as well as 'language.'
6   In *Wo Europa anfängt*, Tawada points to the fact that the notions of 'east' and 'west' are relative, depending on the point from which one starts to orient oneself (81).

In *Das nackte Auge*, two interrelated scenes could provide a platform from where an answer to these questions could be articulated. In this story, Tawada refers to, among other films, Régis Wargnier's *Indochine* (1992), in which the relationship between a French plantation owner (Elaine, played by Cathérine Deneuve) and a Vietnamese girl (Camille, played by Linh Dan Pham) plays an important role.[7] 'Citing' a scene in which Elaine and Camille dance a tango together, Tawada presents them as lovers who are connected by a "süßlich schwankende Melodie" ("a sweetly wavering melody") (85), stressing the reciprocity of their movements (85). This passage is 'repeated' later on in the story, when two women sit in a bath tub and the capacity of the "sweetly wavering melody" to connect two bodies is now assumed by the water: "Die beiden Körper berühren sich nicht mehr, aber sie sind verbunden durch das Element Wasser" ("The two bodies aren't touching each other any more, but they are connected through the element water") (141). In both situations, a present or past reciprocity between two bodies is being suggested (in German, "sich berühren" presupposes a mutual relationship if the verb concerns more than one subject); and in both situations, two bodies are being connected, either by water, or by something that reminds one very strongly of water (the "süßlich schwankende Melodie").[8] Both scenes, then, seem to stress the possibility of a connection; and as in one of the scenes a (fluid) connection between Europe and Asia is being enacted, one preliminary answer to the question of the open incision would seem to be that, apparently, the intrasubjective cut between Europe and Asia is not just taken as irrevocable: for in view of the problematics of bilingual fragmentation in many of Tawada's texts, the textual stagings of reciprocal tactile contacts between Europe and Asia seem to point to a possible strategy that would be able to counter the intrasubjective fragmentation.

Interestingly, the image of two bodies connected by water points back to Tawada's essay collection *Überseezungen*. There, in a section entitled "Euroasiatische Zungen" ("Eurasian tongues") (7), both the image of a poem trav-

---

7   In *Das nackte Auge*, Tawada deals explicitly with postcolonial problematics. The scene between Elaine and Camille could in this respect be read as a disruption of the repressive, colonial relationship between Europe and Asia.

8   Water plays a considerable role in Tawada's texts, as Andrea Krauß also points out (55). For confirmation, see the rest of this essay.

eling to the bank of another language, and a passage in which the I imagines herself and her interlocutor as two banks divided by a river show a structural likeness to the scenes in *Das nackte Auge* (40, 54). Still, whereas *Das nackte Auge* presents water explicitly as a *binding* factor, *Überseezungen* seems, in contrast, often to ascribe *divisive* characteristics to the water: "Zwischen uns lag ein Fluß" ("Between us a river lay") (54). A first, if preliminary "explanation" for this difference might lie in the fact that the scenes in *Überseezungen* explicitly concern language, and as language divides and produces differences, as Tawada states in *Talisman* and in *Verwandlungen*, the level of connection presented in *Das nackte Auge*, where apparently nothing *needs* to be said and language is thus not a determining force, seems altogether impossible on the level of language. But should language's work of fragmentation lead us to conclude that a Eurasian connection between a German and a Japanese *lingua* should as such be taken to be impossible? Would it be futile to look for interlingual, intrasubjective 'arrivals' between the banks of Europe and Asia? In this respect, a possible answer is provided by the concept of *Überseezung*.

The Tawadian neologism *Überseezung* points to the German word *Übersetzung*,[9] which has three different meanings in German, depending on which syllable is stressed: if the emphasis is on the first syllable, '*ü*bersetzen' means 'to carry or transport something from one bank to another,' 'to pass over'; if, in contrast, the emphasis falls on the third syllable, 'über*se*tzen' can either mean 'to translate' or 'to change,' 'to transform.' As remains to be shown, all three meanings have been gathered in Tawada's concept of *Überseezung*, and hereby a dynamic, transformative process between two banks[10] is being indicated that might take place on different levels: between the two banks of a poem and its translation, for example, or between the two banks of an inter-

---

9   As Tawada's (bilingual) texts explicitly deal with the problematics of translation, they could be called "translational literature" in the sense that Waïl Hassan has recently given to this term: "In the space between translators and translated, there are texts that straddle two languages, at once foregrounding, performing, and problematizing the act of translation [...] I call such texts translational literature. While all bilingual and multilingual discourse dramatizes the interaction of languages, the texts in question lay special emphasis on translation as an essential component of cross-cultural contact" (754).
10   The typography on the cover of *Überseezungen* shows the word as "Über*see*zungen," thereby referring to the image of two banks (*über* and *zungen*) being divided/connected by water (*see*).

subjective dialogue. Since, however, the image of the two banks also seems to echo the image of a tongue cut in half, divided by a seemingly unbridgeable gap, it becomes possible to see the concept of *Überseezung* also at work in the void dividing the two 'banks' of a fragmented, bilingual subjectivity. Interestingly, the movement of carrying something from one (linguistic) bank to another, which is implied in the concept of *Überseezung*, seems to suggest that Tawada is indicating that, despite the fact that language primarily divides, an interlingual connection is still somehow possible. But what could it mean to generate an *Überseezung*, and, most of all, what could it look like on the level of the text?

Clearly, even if Yoko Tawada, as a bilingual writer, is searching for *one* Eurasian voice, she writes in German as wel as in Japanese. Thus, she has at least two voices, and by only considering one language, German, I am painting a rather one-sided picture of an author who has, as she writes in *Überseezungen*, "many souls and many tongues" at her disposal: "Ich habe viele Seelen und viele Zungen" (70). This limitation notwithstanding, the two banks of Asia and Europe make themselves felt *within* Tawada's German texts as well. In one passage in *Überseezungen*, for example, two ideograms are presented, which, as the narrator states, are pronounced as *Shonen* in Japanese. By immediately making a connection between the pronunciation of the two Japanese ideograms and the German word *schonen* (which means 'to be careful with,' 'to take care of'), the text enacts a not yet meaningful *Überseezung* all across a 'sea' separating Japanese from German (the syllable *see* in *Überseezung* means 'lake' or 'sea'). Another *Überseezung* follows, going from the German meaning of the word *schonen* to the meaning of the Japanese ideogram that is pronounced as *Shonen*: 'boy,' *Knabe*. After these two *Überseezungen*, a textual synthesis is achieved, in which both levels are combined and something new has been created: "Ja, Knaben vergesse ich nie. Ich liebe sie. Wenn ich einen auf der Straße sehe, möchte ich ihn am liebsten sofort umarmen und liebkosen, aber man muß behutsam mit ihnen umgehen" ("Yes, I never forget boys. I love them. When I see one on the street, I would most of all like to embrace and caress him instantly, but one should handle them carefully") (49). This, then, is one example of many in Tawada's oeuvre in which a dynamic, transformative relation is being established between German and Japanese, between Europe and Asia. By constantly moving between the two shores of Europe and Asia, the various *Überseezungen* in Tawada's work suggest an undulating movement by means of which a textual water is created that at once divides *and* connects:[11] to the extent that the contours of Europe and Asia are still visible,[12] this interlingual (and intrasubjective) Eurasian encounter is still marked by division; yet to the extent that both languages are so closely intertwined that they somehow seem to touch, a connection has been achieved that supplements this division. Thus, this intrasubjective water-boundary[13] between Europe and Asia marks a fluctuating borderland, in which Tawada's *Seezunge*, her "lake-" or "sea-tongue," could begin to swim like a 'sole' (the normal English equivalent of the German word *Seezunge*), thereby not just *repeating* Europe in Europe, but also, and most importantly, *re-writing* and *enriching* Europe.

If it now seems legitimate once again to speak of an 'arrival,' in the sense that Tawada's German texts bear witness to the fact that gradually *one* (Eurasian) voice has been found in which nevertheless *two* worlds are speaking almost simultaneously (*Talisman* 118), this 'arrival' seems to be connected to the thematics of arrival such as it was presented in the discussion of *Wo Europa anfängt* at the beginning of this essay. There, I suggested the possibility of a twofold 'arrival' in Europe that would imply a subdued critique of European restlessness. That there might be something to this view seems to be confirmed by the fact that in the process of 'arriving' at a Eurasian voice, such as I presented it, this critique is being continued. In Tawada's 2005 libretto

---

11   In *Verwandlungen*, Tawada stresses the fact that a clear division between earth and water is not possible, "da in Gewässern immer etwas Erde enthalten ist und umgekehrt" ("since there is always a little bit of earth contained in water, and vice versa") (55). If, then, water divides the shores of Europe and Asia, it is at the same time also the element in which these shores can be connected.

12   By insisting on a difference between Europe and Asia, Tawada is moving beyond the dream of Europe and Asia melting together, a dream Heinz Kimmerle for example detects in Nietzsche (see Kimmerle 119).

13   The conception of two shores being divided/connected through water could be an intertextual reference to the Austrian writer Ingeborg Bachmann's story *Undine geht*, in which the mermaid Undine speaks of a "wet boundary between me and me" (254). The parallel consists mainly in the fact that in both cases, a fluid, intrasubjective boundary is imagined. As *Überseezungen* mentions a mermaid (36), and Tawada's libretto *Was ändert der Regen an unserem Leben?* also mentions an "Undine" (16), the intertextual connection seems to become even more plausible.

Was ändert der Regen an unserem Leben?, the two banks of Europe and Asia have been transformed into the protagonists "Josef" and "Yukika,"[14] who in the course of the text are both revealed to be writers. Josef, who is connected to Europe, tells the Japanese Yukika that he has cut off his second head, because, he informs us, it forced him to drive on and on and on (72). The head ordering Josef to drive on endlessly seems to point to an ever searching, questioning, and desiring Europe that knows of no movement other than a vertical movement, aiming at the highest height, and therefore never really arriving anywhere. Significantly, the writing-relation between Josef and Yukika is only established in the text after the restless second head has been cut off. And as there is also mention of a river whose water is polluted by the head that has been thrown in it (76), Tawada's text seems to suggest that *Überseezungen*, which make up an 'impure,' Eurasian water between the shores of Europe and Asia, between Josef and Yukika, can only come into being when Europe gives up its restlessness and starts looking around instead of looking up to the skies. Within the process of *Überseezung*, the constant undulations between the shores of Europe and Asia rather suggest a *Seitenbeweglichkeit*, a "sideward movement" (Sloterdijk 11), in whose reciprocal dynamics a critique of European linear thinking patterns is always implied.

By arriving in Eurasia, then, "non-vertical dimensions" are opened up, "spaces of which the curves, the loops can provide places in which to take shelter. Not of course in a definitive manner but the time of a pause – for repose, for thought, for inward gathering" (Irigaray 149-50). Tawada's texts, in continually staging *Überseezungen*, are re-writing Europe both in the sense that a prominent aspect of European culture is being subjected to critique *and* in the sense that *two* worlds are made to speak simultaneously in Tawada's European (or, more properly, Eurasian) borderland. The presence of this 'other' world in Tawada's (German) language is thereby not only constantly reminding Europe of the fact that it is not alone, that it represents only one *part* of a vastness of global dimensions (Kimmerle 196); by staging reciprocal, equivalent dances between (for example) Europe and Asia, her work is creating the space for a re-writing of Europe in which Europe's eurocen-

---

14   Once again, Tawada seems to refer to a work by Ingeborg Bachmann, namely to Bachmanns *Der gute Gott von Manhattan*, in which the main characters are named "Jan" and "Jennifer". Tawada's libretto can be said to 'repeat' the alliteration between the names.

trism[15] can begin to make way for a more ethically aware, for a more just attitude towards that which is deemed to be 'other.' Luce Irigaray has asked the question of how we will "respond, or correspond, to the challenges of globalization, if not through the invention of another language [...] Which allows creating little by little a language of exchange between cultures, traditions, sexes, generations" (Irigaray 42). I take Tawada's work to offer a valuable way to "respond, or correspond" to this urgent question.

Works Cited

Bachmann, Ingeborg. "Undine geht." *Werke II: Erzählungen*. Ed. Christine Koschel, Inge von Weidenbaum, and Clemens Münster. München: Piper, 1993. 253-63.

Bauman, Zygmunt. *Europe: An Unfinished Adventure*. Cambridge: Polity Press, 2004.

Buruma, Ian. *Inventing Japan 1853-1964*. New York: Modern Library, 2003.

De Courtivron, Isabelle. "Introduction." *Lives in Translation: Bilingual Writers on Identity and Creativity*. Ed. Isabelle de Courtivron. Basingstoke: Palgrave Macmillan, 2003. 1-9.

Hassan, Waïl S. "Agency and Translational Literature: Ahdaf Soueif's *The Map of Love*." *PMLA* 121.3 (2006): 753-68.

Hoffman, Eva. "The New Nomads." *Letters of Transit: Reflections on Exile, Identity, Language, and Loss*. Ed. André Aciman. New York: The New Press, 1999. 35-63.

Indochine. Dir. Régis Wargnier. Perf. Catherine Deneuve, Vincent Perez, Linh Dan Phan, Jean Yanne, Dominique Blanc. Bac Films, 1992. DVD. Arrow Films, 2001.

Irigaray, Luce. *The Way of Love*. Trans. Heidi Bostic and Stephen Pluháček. London: Continuum, 2002.

Kimmerle, Heinz. *Philosophien der Differenz: Eine Einführung*. Würzburg: Königshausen & Neumann, 2000.

Krauß, Andrea. "'Talisman' – 'Tawadische Sprachtheorie'." *Migration und*

---

15 In *Talisman*, Tawada stresses the fact that the problem of eurocentrism could be said to apply to Japan as well (49). See note 3 for this.

Interkulturalität in neueren literarischen Texten. Ed. Aglaia Blioumi. München: Iudicium, 2002. 55-77.

Matsunaga, Miho. "'Schreiben als Übersetzung': Die Dimension der Übersetzung in den Werken von Yoko Tawada." *Zeitschrift für Germanistik* 12.3 (2002): 532-46.

Nietzsche, Friedrich. *Morgenröthe: Gedanken über die moralischen Vorurtheile. Werke: Kritische Gesamtausgabe.* Ed. Girogio Colli and Mazzino Montinari. Berlin: De Gruyter, 1971. 1-335.

Sloterdijk, Peter. *Eurotaoismus: Zur Kritik der politischen Kinetik.* Frankfurt am Main: Suhrkamp, 1989.

Tawada, Yoko. *Wo Europa anfängt.* Tübingen: Konkursbuchverlag Claudia Gehrke, 1991.

———. *Talisman.* Tübingen: Konkursbuchverlag Claudia Gehrke, 1996.

———. *Opium für Ovid: Ein Kopfkissenbuch von 22 Frauen.* Tübingen: Konkursbuchverlag Claudia Gehrke, 2000.

———. *Verwandlungen: Tübinger Poetik-Vorlesungen.* Tübingen: Konkursbuchverlag Claudia Gehrke, 2001.

———. *Überseezungen.* Tübingen: Konkursbuchverlag Claudia Gehrke, 2002.

———. *Das nackte Auge.* Tübingen: Konkursbuchverlag Claudia Gehrke, 2004.

———. *Was ändert der Regen an unserem Leben?* Tübingen: Konkursbuchverlag Claudia Gehrke, 2005.

Visser, Anthonya. "Met andere ogen: De grensoverschrijdingen van Yoko Tawada." *Armada* 19 (2000): 113-20.

PART III

Conjuring the Past, Imagining Europe

Iannis Goerlandt (University of Ghent)

Staging a European Republic of Letters: (Supra-)National Concepts of Literature in Arno Schmidt's Early Prose

In 1956, the German author Arno Schmidt wrote *Das schönere Europa* ("The Fairer Europe"), a newspaper essay "In Remembrance," as the subtitle puts it, "of the First Major Common Achievement of Our Continent."[1] In his lifetime, it was reprinted six times and turned into a radio dialogue for the *Hessischer Rundfunk* in 1958.[2] Its subject was the observation of the transit of Venus on June 3, 1769. Such transits are the rarest of all predictable astronomical phenomena: they normally occur in pairs, eight years apart, separated by long gaps of approximately 120 years. The phenomenon was eagerly looked forward to, because measurements of the transit could be used to approximate the mean distance between the Earth and the Sun more correctly, as the famous British astronomer Edmond Halley had pointed out in 1677.[3] The Astronomical Unit (AU), as this mean distance is called, is the

---

1   All translations from the German are the author's, with the parenthetical page numbers referring to the German originals, except in the case of *Die Gelehrtenrepublik*, which was translated in 1979 as *The Egghead Republic* and retranslated in 1994 by John E. Woods as *Republica Intelligentsia*. The double references pertain to the German original and the latter translation respectively.

2   Data gathered from Müther 325, 330, 349, 352, 360, 367, 382, 859. Often, the text was reprinted with (slightly) different, telling titles, e.g., *Einigkeit durch Sternenkunde* ("Unity through Astronomy," 1958) or *Das größere Europa der Gelehrten: Im Juni des Jahres 1769 fanden sich die Völker zur ersten wissenschaftlichen Gemeinschaftsarbeit zusammen* ("The Greater Europe of Letters: In June 1769 the Peoples United for the First Common Scientific Endeavor," 1958). In 1978, the essay was reprinted as *Europas Gelehrte hielten zusammen* ("Europe's Men of Letters Stuck Together") in Harold Theile's collection *Europa ist jung* ("Europe Is Young"), which shows there was a strong interest in Schmidt's ideas on Europe. For a similar discussion see Stefan Troebst's remarks, who quotes the essay as an example of how science can advance the European ideal.

3   Schmidt refers to a letter Halley wrote to Jonas Moore some weeks after having observed the Mercury transit of November 7, 1677 (313). On September 23, 1691, Halley read a paper concerning the possibilities of observing transits of planets across the solar disk before the Royal Society of London, which was not published in the Society's *Philosophical Transactions* until 1716.

key parameter to establish the size of the solar system and to predict the orbit of the Moon, which is essential in naval navigation.

At the time of the previous transit in 1761, the world, again, had stood in flames: "Again," Schmidt writes, "there was war in Europe and the world" (314). Apart from the practical difficulties many of the famous astronomers encountered, it was this war, more precisely the Seven Years' War (1756-63), that prevented the observations of the 1761 mission from yielding any conclusive results. Because of its "unprecedented geographical range," with military action on four continents – Winston Churchill once remarked that this war should properly be deemed "the 'first world war'" (Bowen 7) – it was "[m]ore like a Transit of Mars," with the astronomers "going 'cross *its* Face," as Thomas Pynchon writes in *Mason & Dixon* (40).[4] It should come as no surprise, then, that for the next transit too, scientists had but gloomy prospects.

"[A]fter 1763," however, "after diplomats and soldiers [...] again were salubriously tired, there was time for things more valuable, much grander things," namely, in Schmidt's view, "the incomparably honorable and humanly entrancing event of the first global common-European achievement." Unfortunately, the best places to observe the transit of 1769 were some of the remotest corners of the Earth ("the most northern regions of Europe, in the whole of North Siberia, in the largest part of the Pacific as well as in the western half of North America"), so the undertaking was expensive, bold and hazardous. Moreover, Schmidt adds, "back then, one could not fly in 4 hours across the Atlantic in a jet bomber!" (314):

> As early as one year beforehand, many of the scientists had to sally forth, in the nutshells that were the sailers of those days. Pioneered over 2000 kilometers through howling Indian tribes, through humid=cold or =hot virgin forests, over icy wild rivers, made their way with sleds through the Siberian tundras, toiled round Tierra del Fuego – and most of them weren't in their prime anymore; many of those in service to Urania flowing beards turned gray. (315)

---

4   A famous example of the war's impact is Charles Mason's and Jeremiah Dixon's forced stay at the Cape of Good Hope, though their primary observation site was at Bencoolen in the island of Sumatra. Their ship, the H.M.S. Seahorse, had been compelled to turn back after an attack from the French frigate Le Grand on January 11, 1761. For a fictionalized account of this attack see Pynchon 35-41.

Of course, in such an undertaking there were many disappointments, the worst of which being simply bad weather: "After many months of adventurous travel they stood dejected, as if stupefied, under the hostile=thick heaven: in India, in Lapland; in many places it was 'only partially clouded' – then, with a quick hand, the sparse minutes were used; perhaps some notes would turn out useful after all" (315).[5] But on the whole, enough data could be sampled to compute a new, more correct distance between our planet and our Sun. *The Fairer Europe* ends on a thoughtful note about these scientists briefly united into a kind of "europäische[...] Gelehrtenrepublik" (314), a European *respublica eruditorum*: "Six years before, they had not pointed telescopes at one other, but cannons, these Russians, Prussians, English, Austrian, French (and soon afterwards, again, they started the old bloody play, on and on, until now!). But once, at the least, they had been, and most exaltedly, one: in 1769. On June 3!" (316).

These observations on *The Fairer Europe* can serve as an introduction to some of the major themes and problems of Schmidt's oeuvre. The first feature is Schmidt's strong interest in astronomy, geography, mathematics, and scientific subjects in general (see Willer), the second, his penchant for encyclopedic, often quite 'eccentric' knowledge (Schweikert). A third aspect is his interest in the age of Enlightenment, both in its political significance as well as in the many literary projects and responses generated in that age (Albrecht; Höppner 277-97). Another key issue is Schmidt's experience of World War II, as he was one of thousands of Silesian Germans who had to flee Poland after the War (Manthey 135-43; Fischer; Joachimsthaler). This

---

5   Schmidt tacitly refers to the tragic story of the French astronomer Guillaume Le Gentil. After having been forced to observe the 1761 transit aboard a ship – in January 1761, the British had captured the French outpost in Pondicherry, his destination, and consequently prevented him from disembarking (Sawyer Hogg 40-41) – , Le Gentil was unable to observe the 1769 transit due to the cloudy Pondicherry weather. "That is the fate which often awaits astronomers," Le Gentil writes in his 1782 account *Voyage dans les mers de l'Inde fait par ordre du roi, à l'occasion du passage de Vénus sur le disque du soleil le 6 juin 1761, & le 3 du même mois 1769* (quoted here in translation from Sawyer Hogg 132): "I had gone more than ten thousand leagues; it seemed that I had crossed such a great expanse of seas, exiling myself from my native land, only to be the spectator of a fatal cloud which came to place itself before the sun at the precise moment of my observation, to carry off from me the fruits of my pains and of my fatigues."

trauma, combined with his concern over the Cold War, shaped both his political views and his prose (Reemtsma, "Krieg und Nachkrieg"). The two most important characteristics, however, are Schmidt's strong distrust of politics and his interest in Europe, as a concept, as a past and present opportunity or impossibility, and as a literary background (see Lowsky). In Schmidt's view, politicians can neither be relied upon to establish conciliation and enduring peace, nor to advance *Völkerverständigung*, a resolving dialogue between different nations. It is no coincidence that, even though he admits at the essay's very beginning that "the impulse [for the observation of the transit] came from no less than the politicians" (313), Schmidt points out that in German 'Soldaten' and 'Diplomaten' "rhyme as well" (313), referring to the traditional connective force of rhyming also as regards content, or that later on in Schmidt's argument, the real impetus of the undertaking shifts to the European scientists: "[b]ut because of their joint efforts the European scientific community [...] succeeded in gaining the support of the governments or of wealthy private persons" (314). Typically discrediting the politicians' motives, Schmidt furthermore sharply distinguishes between the theoretical, 'pure' knowledge the astronomers were seeking and the more practical, "vulgar sublunary interests" (313) with which they had to canvass the governments for support (314; see also Willer 228-31).

All these notions were already combined in one of Schmidt's earliest texts, namely the unpublished play *Massenbach: Historische Revue* (1949). The *Historical Revue* deals with the Napoleonic Wars (1799–1815) hinted at in the last line of *The Fairer Europe* (316). Christian von Massenbach, the protagonist, was a colonel in the Prussian army, yet strongly in favor of a union with Napoleon's forces to face Russia's power together.[6] The play starts with a brief prelude with a problematical conversation between the characters Arno and Heinz, a name referring to Schmidt's school friend Heinz Jerowsky:

> ARNO: Really : Tariff unions, economic relief, Benelux and all that – perhaps that's manageable. But not *that* anymore, Heinz, which most of us imagine when they say 'Europe': a large closed entity that could, if need be, be sturdy

---

6   See Massenbach's embellished autobiography *Historische Denkwürdigkeiten zur Geschichte des Verfalls des preußischen Staats seit dem Jahre 1794* ("Historical Memoirs on the History of the Decline of the Prussian State Since the Year 1794"); for commentaries on the relationship between Massenbach and Schmidt, see Engels 803-36; Finke.

and victorious, also, of course, against the superpowers in the East and the West ... [...].
HEINZ: [...] – – But hey, listen, is it perhaps *not* good to finally take Europe seriously? What so many centuries have squandered, we have to catch up with: I do not understand why it should be too late for that. [...].
ARNO: *(fiercely)* No, Heinz: that is impossible! That should have happened one hundred and fifty years ago: when [Benjamin] Franklin still had to collect sympathies for the young America with his round hat. And [general Alexander] Suvorov had not had the opportunity to test how Russia's armies could play a decisive part in any situation: at that time, a united Europe from the Garonne to the Vistula, from North Cape to Lampedusa – then to have used the technical and cultural lead, then to have melted the chains of feudalism with the spirit of 1789: at that time, a unification coming from the west could have been possible still. No, not *still* possible! It was the *only* moment for that in all millennia; because: only in precisely these years 1790–1810 there was a combination of: the fiery breeze of freedom, which could have inspired the *spirits*; the practical man, who could have *enforced* unity; and most of all: Americans and Russians still inferior. – If nowadays [Arnold J.] Toynbee and [Victor] Gollancz write: Save Europe first!, then that is perhaps meant well, but it can only be hot air and mirage. – To say nothing of the Council of Europe. (10-11)

This regret over the 'belatedness' of the European idea and the missed opportunities is a familiar theme in European literature. What is disturbing in this context, however, are the military overtones – the connection Hitler-Napoleon haunting this 'what-if'-history – and the obvious dangers of trying to compare nations in terms of their inferiority (Manthey 129-35; Reemtsma, "Nachkriegsdeutschland" 104-7). Schmidt must have been aware of this problem. It is no coincidence that he never published *Massenbach*. He seems to have been taken aback by his earlier too blatantly *political*, almost militaristic longing for a stronger Europe, which Jürgen Manthey calls the "Machtphantasien der frühen Texte" ("the phantasies of power in the early prose") (135).[7]

Nevertheless, these earlier texts would serve as modes of reflection in Schmidt's later dystopian/utopian novel *Die Gelehrtenrepublik: Ein Kurzro-*

---

7   A reintegration of the Massenbach complex was planned for Schmidt's project *Lilienthal 1801, oder die Astronomen* ("Lilienthal 1801, or the Astronomers") which promised a balanced connection between Enlightenment, European politics and astronomy. However, although Schmidt would return to it several times, *Lilienthal 1801* always remained "das übernächste Buch," "the next but one novel" (Rauschenbach).

man aus den Roßbreiten (1957). The somewhat enigmatic title was translated in English by Michael Horovitz as *The Egghead Republic* in 1979, but this title is too evaluative and wittily negative. John E. Woods's better translation, with the somewhat improved title *Republica Intelligentsia*, was published in 1994. *Die Gelehrtenrepublik* is the fictional travelogue of a distant family member of Arno Schmidt, the American journalist Charles Henry Winer, who in the year 2008 gets permission to visit the International Republic for Artists and Scientists. IRAS, founded after World War III as a safe haven for scientists and artists, is located on a huge ship that by international decree has to be kept safe from the destruction of any new war, and which follows a course through calm, international waters.[8] Before Winer actually reaches IRAS he travels on foot through a so-called "Hominid Sector" (236/317), a vast, enclosed, sealed area in the west of the USA, where as a result of extremely high radiation from atomic bombs humanoid mutations of the human race have developed.

Three kinds of hominids exist, and all of those have – in some way or another – essentially European features. There are "Centies" (229/311, centaurs), so-called 'flying heads,' a mutation and cross-breed with butterflies, and "Never=Nevers," gargantuan monster spiders with a "soft, toxic=grey body about half a yard in diameter," "[u]p front a human head (with all sorts of new knobby organs: ocelli for instance, whereas the ears had been eliminated); with proboscises for sucking" (237/319). These "Never=Nevers" are "scorpion people" with "nasty European face[s]: the eyes small; hanging vertically, long feeler whiskers; all of it specialized for a nocturnal=erinnic life. The mouth a puckerable proboscis, perfect for lethal sucking. On the forestilts, the venomed claws, long as your finger and hooked like buzzards' beaks: revolting!" (244/326).

Here, both translators misrepresent the German original "für nächtlich=parzisches Leben" (Horovitz has "for a night-fury's career" (16)), as the mythological reference pertains not to the Erinyes (with whom they

---

8   The *Horse Latitudes* in the title refer to, amongst other things, the subtropical regions between 30° and 35° latitude in the Northern and Southern hemispheres. These calm waters characterized by light winds and hot, dry weather in which navigation presumably is easy are said to have been dangerous in the past, however, when travelers between New England and the West Indies often got stranded there and were forced to kill their horses in order to preserve precious water supplies or for their meat and blood (Miller).

are sometimes confused ("Moira" 1110b; Preller, vol. 1, 415)), but to the Moirai (*Μοῖραι*) who in German are called the *Parzen*, after their Roman name *Parcae*. Schmidt draws on the traditional representation of the three goddesses as spinsters (*Κλῶθες* in Homer's *Odyssey* (see Preller, vol. 1, 413)). The "Never=Nevers" are a combination of Clotho, "the spinning fate," Lachesis, "the one who assigns to man his fate," and Atropos, "the fate that cannot be avoided" ("Moira" 1110b), which Schmidt, in the tradition of Hesiod, regards as "daughters of the night" ("Moira" 1110a). The "European faces" of these *Parcae*-spiders evoke a grim vision of the destructive power of Europe, prolonged in the dystopian future. From these creatures, the artist has to beg for enough time to finish his poem, in the tradition of Friedrich Hölderlin's famous poem *An die Parzen* (*To the Fates*), which is quoted in the final line of the novella ("Once I lived as did the gods" [349/429]; compare Wolf 63-65).

At one point in the narrative Winer teams up with a group of centaurs and enjoys a brief romance with one of them, the centauress Thalia. Supposedly, her name is pronounced as "*Ssáld*scha" (235) in American English, "with an initial semi-lisped American 'th' and medial double-consonantal 'dzh'" (235/317). This obviously is a reference to Thalia, the muse of comedy, but also to the 'I-*told-you*-so' of the dystopian past future tense.[9]

In both interconnected 'parts' of *Die Gelehrtenrepublik* it soon becomes obvious that the idyll in reality is a mere gloss. The strip of hominids is a "Research Zone" (260/341) where experiments are being conducted: the bucolic way of life of the centaurs in reality is being manipulated by rangers (234/316) and scientists. IRAS, too, does not function as it should. First, the so-called 'republic' is by no means independent or politically neutral, as is illustrated in the map drawn by Schmidt and added to the novel (351/302; compare Höppner 240-44 and Goerlandt, chapter 8.4): the ship consists of two halves, starboard and larboard, East and West, that are being controlled by the USA and the USSR respectively. Moreover, the scientists

---

9   Although pronunciation variations exist (see for instance *Dictionary of Greek and Roman Biography and Mythology* vol. 3, 1019a), Thalia, both in German and English, normally is stressed on the second syllable (/θəˈlaɪə/ in standard English), as Schmidt could have known from his beloved Muret-Sanders dictionary (vol. 1, 913b; vol. 2, 955b). This adds to the impression that Stadion's (see below) knowledge of Classical mythology is actually very limited, notwithstanding appearances (262/344), and it makes the quibble possible.

conduct atrocious experiments on the artists. The Russians, on the one hand, keep themselves busy with brain transplants, also between men and animals, whereas the Americans have succeeded in hibernating whole bodies – both techniques are also used to steal each other's artists. *Die Gelehrtenrepublik* ends in a stalemate, a deadlock, as the Russians let their propellor turn full speed ahead, the Americans theirs full speed backwards.

Furthermore, to make things more complex still, the novel is presented as a translation with explanatory footnotes. Because of its juiciness (for instance in the evocation of the sexual romance between Thalia and Winer) and possibly also because of the feared political impact, the fictional travelogue could only be published in German and not in English, as a legal note informs us at the outset (222/303; compare Helmes 222 and Goerlandt, chapter 4.4.1). German, however, in 2008, is a nearly-extinct language. Chr. M. Stadion, the translator, is a "vestigial German, 1 of 124 remaining!" (260/341), who lives in a colony in South America (a reference to the German war criminals' ratline to Argentina – compare Ringmayr 54), since Europe has been completely destroyed in the war and is now the "Hominid Research Zone" of the Russians.

In my forthcoming monograph *Schulen zur Allegorie* on national images in Schmidt's utopian novels I have studied the peculiar East-West-oppositions and many of the intertextual references abounding in this story. The topic I want to address here is the antagonism between Winer, the narrator, an American-with-German-roots, and Chr. M. Stadion, the translator. This narrator-translator-constellation simulates an old, famous *Literaturstreit*, a literary battle, which raises important questions about the interconnections between European national literatures and the notion of a European literature in general.

An indication of this *Literaturstreit* in *Die Gelehrtenrepublik* are some 'French' elements in the characterization of Winer. By that, I do not mean some kind of 'national character,' but his use of certain French words and his knowledge of French texts and authors. A telling example is the mentioning an old French *conte de fées*, a fairy tale, namely the now obscure *Voyages de Zulma dans le pays des Fées* by Abbé Augustin Nadal from 1735, which was reprinted in the famous collection *Le Cabinet des Fées* from 1785. This reference is not original, as more extensive research shows (Goerlandt, chapter 4.2), but is very likely being quoted from the fictional footnotes of a German work, namely *Der neue Amadis* (1771, "The New Amadis") by Christoph Martin Wieland. This unfortunately now lesser-known champion of German Enlightenment was famous for his use of many French texts, especially this kind of *contes de fées*, not as models, but as materials with which to compose his own, often satirical, fiction (Mayer). A typical example is his meta-fairy tale in the spirit of Cervantes *Der Sieg der Natur über die Schwärmerey, oder Die Abentheuer des Don Sylvio von Rosalva* (1764, "The Victory of Nature over Zealotry or The Adventures of Don Sylvio of Rosalva") which, in a French translation, was the last volume of the aforementioned *Cabinet des Fées*.

The influence of French literature on German literature was, of course, very extensive in this era; the case of the French fairy tales, in vogue all over Europe, is but one example. At that time, foreign influences, and French influence in particular, however, were decried very strongly as well. An interesting case is Friedrich Gottlieb Klopstock's novelistic 'essay' (Kohl, "Gelehrtenrepublik") *Die deutsche Gelehrtenrepublik* (1774, "The German Republic of Letters"), which describes, in legal terms, in political transcripts as well as in mock-historical documents, a utopian body politic of German poets and scientists that is both culturally protectionist and expansionist (Kohl, *Klopstock* 110).[10] The Germans are urged to compete with and overclass foreign science and literatures and to venture into yet-to-be-discovered areas, so that people later will say "*Here, there have been Germans!*" (Klopstock 229). There is even a portrait of a particular type of artist which can be read as a parody and criticism of Wieland:

> Once upon a time there was a man who read lots of foreign books, and who wrote books himself. He walked on the crutches of foreigners, rode their steeds, rode their nags, plowed with their calves, walked on their tightropes. Many of his good-hearted and not well-read countrymen deemed him a real wizard. But some of them did not fail to see what the deal with this man's works really was: they could not, however, disclose everything. But how could they have? It is impossible to go in each of the foreigners' calf stables. (86-87)

One could argue that Klopstock's vision of cultural colonialism and expansionism has to be interpreted in the context of the emerging *Sturm und Drang* and the surge of national sentiment, or one could refer to the fact that

---

10   For an interesting contextualization of Klopstock's project in the larger tradition of European *republicae litterariae* see Eskildsen, esp. 430-32.

Klopstock condemned any bloody-real *real* expansionist war (Kohl, *Klopstock* 108-14). But even so, critics have stated that the rhetoric of this kind of *agonal stance* in and towards literature has become discredited once and for all in the face of the wars that set the 20th century aflame (Japp 271-72; Müller 120-22). This especially holds true as in the exact center of Schmidt's novel, Winer witnesses a staging of *Massenbach*, the *political* message of which (see above) is discredited by the way it is constructed in the whole system of intertextual references.

In Schmidt's novel, it is Stadion who introduces the term 'Gelehrtenrepublik' as a translation of IRAS, "as a way of memorializing the popular – at least it was at one time – work of the great Klopstock" (270/351). This clear indication of his cultural chauvinism is not only long overdue (with 124 Germans left), but also fails to label IRAS correctly, in Klopstock's sense. Klopstock would not have been 'honored' or pleased by the idea of naming an *international* republic after his work. What has been designated as Stadion's "crypto-fascism" (Ringmayr 54), present in the unspecified time reference (it could mean both the 18th and the 20th century), also shows in the way he fails to comment on the mentioning of foreign texts, his very selective appraisal and misreading of German texts, and his problems with Winer's travelogue. At times, for instance, he does not understand Winer's erotic innuendo, which is constructed intertextually (250/332) with reference to Laurence Sterne's *Tristam Shandy* ("the lambent pupilability of slow, low, dry chat" (IV.1, 197)), which greatly influenced Wieland as well. It is very ironic, then, that Chr. M. Stadion shares his initials with Chr. M. Wieland, an author he does not fancy at all, for reasons that should have become clear.

Why, however, all this trouble of simulating the old *Literaturstreit* between protectionist and 'open' systems of literature? The answer to this question, I suggest, lies in the expectations the genre of the novel carries with it.

At first glance, *Die Gelehrtenrepublik* seems a very bleak political dystopia, mainly beause of its political parody of the Cold War and the fact that nationalism seems to have survived, not only among the last speakers of German, but also between the superpowers. The stealing of brains and bodies indeed is but a continuation of the agon of national literatures by scientific means. However, if we dig deeper, it becomes clear that it is not only the muse of comedy, Thalia, who makes this novel a good, rewarding read.

Die Gelehrtenrepublik is so remarkable, in my view, because it not only deploys Klopstock for its intertextual construction; equally important is the fact that the whole outline of the ship-as-island divided in two halves and between opposing forces, which eventually is literally torn apart because of this rivalry, is to be found in a *French* novel, namely Jules Verne's *L'Île à Hélice* (1895, "Propellor Island"). In this way, Schmidt's novel not only points out a real problem of European literature, namely the nationalist outlook of some of its constituents and their at times deprecatory stance towards other literatures. *Die Gelehrtenrepublik*, in its intertextuality, also succeeds in truly becoming an *international*, European novel, its cultural politics being inter- and perhaps supranational, and a genuine act of literary diplomacy.[11] This, I think, is one of the most important aspects of the utopian dimension of Schmidt's text.[12]

Should Schmidt, then, on the basis of these comments, be hailed as a champion of the European ideal and June 3 (which, coincidentally, also is the day on which Schmidt died) be celebrated as a European holiday? On this, I would like to make some final remarks. Though I am convinced that the novel's awareness of the possibilities of its own performance is part of Schmidt's literary program, also because his later utopian/dystopian texts show a similar dynamic, there is the question of elitism, which we have encountered in *The Fairer Europe* as well. Therefore, it remains questionable whether a European ideal can be constructed in a meaningful way if its means are highly intellectual, the required knowledge, by some standards, obscure, and its execution elitist and/or aristocratic. For when do the required intellectual efforts begin to render the enterprise effete? And secondly, is it not profoundly paradoxical that the utopian force of a text's own supranational intertextuality can only be formulated on a 'national' screen, by ironizing texts that are national (and probably not known in other countries) and referring to 'international' texts (which the intended audience might not know)? This question gains importance when we consider the fact

---

11   For a discussion and differentiation of this term "literary diplomacy" with reference to the self-conception of imagology see Goerlandt, chapters 1 and 8.

12   The existence of a traditional 'utopian' dimension in Schmidt's text has long been discarded as a chimera in the 'meta'-utopian interpretations of poststructuralist aesthetics. See Goerlandt, chapter 8 for a refutation of this stance.

that Arno Schmidt, one of Germany's most important postwar authors, has received almost no critical attention and has only been able to claim a small readership abroad, for being 'too difficult' and 'too German.' This problem undoubtedly is related to the problematical translatability of this kind of performative meta-utopias which is visible already in the title of the novel, *Die Gelehrtenrepublik*. To be able to function in the same way, translations of this novel would have to draw on a completely different set of intertexts. To make such *international* adaptations, however, we have to know and respect each other's *national* literatures. There's the rub – and the challenge Schmidt puts on us readers.

Works Cited

Albrecht, Wolfgang. "'Lichtfreund' in der Epoche des Kalten Krieges: Arno Schmidts Verhältnis zur Aufklärungsbewegung und sein aufklärerisches schriftstellerisches Engagement." *Aufklärung nach Lessing: Beiträge zur gemeinsamen Tagung der Lessing Society und des Lessing-Museums Kamenz aus Anlaß seines 60jährigen Bestehens*. Ed. Wolfgang Albrecht, Dieter Fratzke, and Richard E. Schade. Kamenz: Lessing-Museum, 1992. 123-47.

Bowen, Huw V. *War and British Society: 1688–1815*. New Studies in Economic and Social History 35. Cambridge and New York: Cambridge University Press, 1998.

Buchholz, Friedrich and Christian von Massenbach. *Historische Denkwürdigkeiten zur Geschichte des Verfalls des preußischen Staates seit dem Jahre 1794* sowie *Gallerie Preußischer Charaktere*. Ed. Hans-Werner Engels. Frankfurt am Main: Zweitausendeins, 1979.

Dictionary of Greek and Roman Biography and Mythology. Ed. William Smith. Boston: Little, Brown, and Company, 1867. July 2007. <http://www.ancientlibrary.com/smith-bio>.

Engels, Hans-Werner. "Nachwort: Christian von Massenbach: Notizen zu einem vergessenen Preußen." Buchholz and Massenbach, *Historische Denkwürdigkeiten*. 1979. 771-873.

Eskildsen, Kasper Risbjerg. "How Germany Left the Republic of Letters." *Journal of the History of Ideas* 65.3 (2004): 421-32.

Finke, Reinhard. "Der Traum der Vernunft gebiert Gespenster: Zu Arno

Schmidts 'Massenbach/Historische Revue.' *Arno Schmidt: Das Frühwerk III: Vermischte Schriften: Interpretationen von 'Die Insel' bis 'Fouqué.'* Ed. Michael Matthias Schardt. Aachen: Rader, 1989. 10-21.

Fischer, Susanne. "Auf gepackten Koffern zwischen den Stühlen: Flüchtlinge im Werk Arno Schmidts." *Zwischen Heimat und Zuhause: Deutsche Flüchtlinge und Vertriebene in (West-)Deutschland 1945–2000.* Ed. Rainer Schulze, Reinhard Rohde, and Rainer Voss. Quellen und Darstellungen zur Geschichte des Landkreises Celle 6. Osnabrück: Secolo, 2001. 171-83.

Goerlandt, Iannis. *Schulen zur Allegorie: Nationale Bilder in Arno Schmidts utopischer Prosa.* Bielefeld: Aisthesis, 2008. Forthcoming.

Helmes, Günter. "Von 'Formindalls' und andere 'Hominiden': Überlegungen zu Arno Schmidts 'Die Gelehrtenrepublik.'" *Arno Schmidt: Das Frühwerk II: Romane: Interpretationen von 'Brand's Haide' bis 'Gelehrtenrepublik.'* Ed. Michael Matthias Schardt. Aachen: Rader, 1988. 216-55.

Hölderin, Johann Christian Friedrich. "An die Parzen." *Stuttgarter Hölderlin-Ausgabe.* Vol. 1. Ed. Friedrich Beißner. Stuttgart: J.G. Cottasche Buchhandlung Nachfolger, 1946. 241.

Höppner, Stefan. *Zwischen Utopia und Neuer Welt: Die USA als Imaginationsraum in Arno Schmidts Erzählwerk.* Klassische Moderne 2. Würzburg: Ergon, 2005.

Japp, Uwe. "Zweimal deutsche Gelehrtenrepublik: Klopstock und Arno Schmidt." *Literatur und Geschichte 1788–1988.* Ed. Gerhard Schulz, Tim Mehigan, and Marion Adams. Frankfurt am Main: Peter Lang, 1990. 263-84.

Joachimsthaler, Jürgen. "Schlesiophobie: Arno Schmidt und seine 'Bezugslandschaft.'" *Eine Provinz in der Literatur: Schlesien zwischen Wirklichkeit und Imagination.* Ed. Edward Białek, Robert Buczek, and Paweł Zimniak. Beihefte zum *Orbis Linguarum* 19. Wrocław: Zielona Góra, 2005. 287-302.

Klopstock, Friedrich Gottlieb. *Die Deutsche Gelehrtenrepublik: Ihre Einrichtung: Ihre Geseze: Geschichte des lezten Landtags: Auf Befehl der Aldermänner durch Salogast und Wlemar. Herausgegeben von Klopstock.* Ed. Rose-Maria Hurlebusch. *Werke und Briefe: Historisch-kritische Ausgabe VII-i.* Hamburger Klopstock-Ausgabe. Berlin and New York: de

Gruyter, 1975.
Kohl, Katrin. "Die deutsche Gelehrtenrepublik 1774: Essay by Friedrich Gottlieb Klopstock." *Encyclopedia of German Literature*. Ed. Matthias Konzett. Chicago and London: Fitzroy Dearborn, 2000. Vol. 2. 601-02.
——. *Friedrich Gottlieb Klopstock*. Stuttgart and Weimar: Metzler, 2000.
Lowsky, Martin. "Europäer Arno Schmidt oder Der Autor namens 'Timon d'Arsch.'" *Komplizierte Gefilde*. Ed. Guido Erol Öztanil. Schriftenreihe der Gesellschaft der Arno-Schmidt-Leser 7. Wiesenbach: Bangert & Metzler, 2007. 37-58.
Manthey, Jürgen. "'Nimm ock ... zwee=e': Arno Schmidts (nur skurrile?) Ostpolitik." *Arno Schmidt: Leben im Werk*. Ed. Guido Graf. Würzburg: Königshausen & Neumann, 1998. 126-43.
Mayer, K. Otto. "Die Feenmärchen bei Wieland." *Vierteljahresschrift für Literaturgeschichte* 5 (1892): 374-408; 498-533.
Miller, James E. "Horse Latitudes." *The Encyclopedia Americana: International Edition*. Vol. 14. Danbury, CT: Grolier, 1996. 408b.
"Moira." *Dictionary of Greek and Roman Biography and Mythology*. Vol. 2. 1109b-1111a. July 2007. <http://www.ancientlibrary.com/smith-bio/2217.html>.
Müller, Götz. *Gegenwelten: Die Utopie in der deutschen Literatur*. Stuttgart: Metzler, 1989.
Muret-Sanders: Enzyklopädisches english-deutsches und deutsch-englisches Wörterbuch: Hand- und Schulausgabe. 2 vols. Ed. B. Klett and E. Klatt (vol. 1) / H. Baumann and E. Klatt (vol. 2). New York: Ungar, 1931.
Müther, Karl-Heinz. *Bibliothek Arno Schmidt: 1949–2001*. 2003. July 2007. <http://www.gasl.org/muether/mueges.pdf>.
Preller, Ludwig. *Griechische Mythologie*. 2nd ed. 2 vols. Berlin: Weidmann, 1860-61. July 2007. <http://www.gasl.org/refbib/Preller__Mythologie.pdf>.
Pynchon, Thomas. *Mason & Dixon*. New York: Henry Holt, 1997.
Rauschenbach, Bernd. "Das übernächste Buch." *Arno Schmidts Lilienthal 1801, oder Die Astronomen*. Ed. Bernd Rauschenbach and Susanne Fischer. Bargfeld: Arno Schmidt Stiftung, 1996. 7-12.
Reemtsma, Jan Philipp. "Arno Schmidts Nachkriegsdeutschland." *Über Arno Schmidt: Vermessungen eines poetischen Terrains*. Frankfurt am Main:

Suhrkamp, 2006. 98-117.

———. "Der Vorgang des Ertaubens nach dem Urknall: Krieg und Nachkrieg im Werk Arno Schmidts." *Über Arno Schmidt*. Frankfurt am Main: Suhrkamp, 2006. 118-55.

Ringmayr, Thomas. "Arno Schmidts *Gelehrtenrepublik*: Ein historischer Zukunftsroman aus der Gegenwart." *Arno Schmidt am Pazifik: Deutschamerikanische Blicke auf sein Werk*. Ed. Timm Menke. München: Edition text + kritik, 1992. 49-63.

Sawyer Hogg, Helen. "Le Gentil and the Transits of Venus, 1761 and 1769." *Journal of the Royal Astronomical Society of Canada* 45 (1951): 37-44; 89-92; 127-34; 173-78. July 2007. <http://www.phys.uu.nl/~vgent/astrobib/outofoldbooks.htm>.

Schmidt, Arno. *The Egghead Republic: A Short Novel from the Horse Latitudes*. Trans. Michael Horovitz. Ed. Ernst Krawehl and Marion Boyars. London and Boston: Marion Boyars, 1979.

———. "Die Gelehrtenrepublik: Ein Kurzroman aus den Roßbreiten." *Bargfelder Ausgabe: Werkgruppe I: Romane Gedichte Erzählungen Juvenilia: Studienausgabe Band 2*. Bargfeld and Zürich: Arno Schmidt Stiftung and Haffmans, 1986. 221-351.

———. "Massenbach: Historische Revue." *Bargfelder Ausgabe: Werkgruppe II: Dialoge: Studienausgabe Band 3*. Bargfeld and Zürich: Arno Schmidt Stiftung and Haffmans, 1990. 7-104.

———. "Republica Intelligentsia: A Novella from the Horse Latitudes." *Collected Novellas: Collected Early Fiction 1949–1964, Volume 1*. Trans. John E. Woods. Normal, IL: Dalkey Archive Press, 1994. 301-429.

———. "Das schönere Europa: (*Zur Erinnerung an die erste große wissenschaftliche Gemeinschaftsleistung unseres Kontinentes, den Venusdurchgang von 1769)*." *Bargfelder Ausgabe: Werkgruppe II: Dialoge: Studienausgabe Band 1*. Bargfeld and Zürich: Arno Schmidt Stiftung and Haffmans, 1990. 265-75.

———. "Das schönere Europa: (*Zur Erinnerung an die erste große Gemeinschaftsleistung unseres Kontinentes)*." *Bargfelder Ausgabe: Werkgruppe III: Essays und Biographisches: Studienausgabe Band 3*. Bargfeld and Zürich: Arno Schmidt Stiftung and Haffmans, 1995. 313-16.

Schweikert, Rudi. "Arno Schmidts Lob des Lexikons: Gesammelte Liebeserklärungen.*" Das gewandelte Lexikon: Zu Karl Mays und Arno Schmidts produktivem Umgang mit Nachschlagewerken*. Aus dem poetischen Mischkrug 2. Wiesenbach: Bangert & Metzler, 2002. 189-205.

Sterne, Laurence. *Tristram Shandy: An Authoritative Text, the Author on the Novel, Criticism*. Norton Critical Edition. Ed. Howard Anderson. New York and London: Norton, 1980.

Theile, Harold, ed. *Europa ist jung*. Bonn: Europa-Verlag, 1978. 37-42.

Troebst, Stefan. "Begrüssung [sic] und Einführung in das Zwischenbilanzkolloquium." Introductory Speech to the Colloquium *Einheit in der Vielfalt? Grundlagen und Voraussetzungen eines erweiterten Europas* (Leipzig, January 22-24, 2004). July 2007. <http://www.uni-leipzig.de/zhs/kolloquium-volkswagenstiftung/vortraege/begruessung.pdf>.

Verne, Jules. *Die Propellerinsel: Roman*. Trans. Wolf Wondratschek. Frankfurt am Main: Fischer, 1970.

Willer, Stefan. "'Die scheinbar erdenfernste aller Wissenschaften': Arno Schmidts astronomische Orientierung." *Gestirn und Literatur im 20. Jahrhundert*. Ed. Maximilian Bergengruen, Davide Giuriato, and Sandro Zanetti. Frankfurt am Main: Fischer, 2006. 225-39.

Wolf, Thomas. *Einmal lebt' ich wie Götter'!!! ... : Nachforschungen zu Arno Schmidts 'Gelehrtenrepublik.'* Frankfurt am Main: Bangert & Metzler, 1987.

Ortwin de Graef (K.U.Leuven)

Epistle to the Europeans (On Not Reading Kipling)*

There are nine and sixty ways of constructing tribal lays, / And-every-single-one-of-them-is-right! (Rudyard Kipling, "In the Neolithic Age")[1]

But what is the peculiarity of a good bad poem? A good bad poem is a graceful monument to the obvious. (George Orwell, "Rudyard Kipling")

The thesis I want to advance in this essay is pretty trivial: the success of a literary artefact's contribution to the formation of (collective) identities depends on the extent to which it manages to elude reading by commanding thoughtless assent. If it weren't so trivial, we might call it the propaganda paradox; as it is, we should perhaps just call it the propaganda principle. The reason why I nonetheless propose to advance this principle yet again is that it is so often and so stubbornly denied – most significantly so by way of deferential expressions of admiration for the putative performative power of literature as a discourse that is properly untouched by the propaganda principle and whose effectiveness depends on the accuracy of its articulation of the constitutive elements of identity formation.

    The case I want to consider is a core classic of the British Imperial canon. If that seems unlikely to further advance the cause of European integration, that is probably a good thing. Indeed, one of the admittedly uncontroversial points I would like to draw from this case is that the notion of integration is fatally flawed by its family resemblance to the retrograde notion of the nation. Conversely, and slightly less trivially, I would like to suggest that Europe – the very idea – has a historical chance to haunt both nation and integration into the non-state of nature where they belong – a chance, to be sure, which continues to be lost, and will remain so as long as we (who, we?) persist in refusing to read.

---

*   This paper has benefited greatly from discussions with Benjamin Biebuyck, Gert Buelens, and Sigi Jöttkandt, my colleagues on the Fund for Scientific Research – Flanders (Belgium) research project "A Critique of Literary Ethics: Metaphor, Metonymy, and Synecdoche in Anglo-American Poetry and Prose of the Nineteenth Century."
1   See Orwell 193 n.1.

Who, we? Let us say, provisionally, *We Europeans*, alluding to the title of a 1935 book by Julian Huxley, A.C. Haddon, and A.M. Carr-Saunders, subtitled *A Survey of "Racial" Problems*, which sets out to present the then available "scientific facts [...] on the subject of 'race' in man [...] in the light of established scientific principles" (7). A vintage piece of committed popular science writing, the book distinguishes what the authors refer to "by the non-committal phrase 'group sentiment'" ("the sentiment which animates tribal and national units alike") from notions of "race," authoritatively rubbishing the sinister "claims to 'racial unity' [...] in recent nationalist controversy," and singling out for cool ridicule the notion of the "chosen people" typically informing such discourse (15, 19). By way of illustration, the authors note that "some of the noblest claims made for the British, by Mr. Kipling for instance, are closely similar to the claims made for the tribes of Israel by the authors of certain Biblical books," and suggest as evidence a comparison between "The White Man's Burden" and a passage from *Isaiah* in which the Lord proposes to give Israel "for a light to the Gentiles" (20). Passing over the complication that Kipling's "White Man" is not particularly British, while those he sets out to release from the "bondage" of their "loved Egyptian night" are typologically cast as anything other than Gentiles,[2] I want to turn to another poem Kipling wrote at about the same time which explicitly mentions the Gentiles in such a way that the close similarity suggested in Huxley's comparison collapses into identity – assuming we know what that means – and the chosen people are troped beyond recognition.

But before turning to this alternative text, I want to dwell for a moment on the significance of Kipling's quotability in Huxley's text. His "noblest claims for the British" are indeed just quoted, juxtaposed to a quotation from the Bible without further comment other than that allowance should be made "for differences of atmosphere and language" (19). What is important here is that any potential irony we might imagine in this juxtaposition of the Bible and Kipling is indeed left to our imagination – and any such imagination should be checked by an appreciation of Kipling's status at the time *We Europeans* was published, one year before his death. His greatest triumphs as one of the most popular poets in world history (recorded also by his being awarded the Nobel Prize in Literature in 1907) lay some decades behind him

---

2   For a recent update on "The White Man's Burden," see Brantlinger.

then, but placing his writing alongside Scripture was not as absurd then as it may seem to us now. Who, we? Perhaps it still should not be more absurd to quote Kipling than it is to quote Scripture. Huxley and his fellow authors, at any rate, leave any potential venom in the comparison unvoiced. Their express ridicule is reserved particularly for Madison Grant, whose 1916 *The Passing of the Great Race: The Racial Basis of European History* launched the so-called "Nordic theory" which would prove to be so germane to the Nazi imagination. Implicitly, this ridicule must also affect both Kipling and the Bible, but that implication is not spelled out. This would appear to allow for a difference more substantial than that of "atmosphere and language" obtaining between Kipling and the Prophets – a difference between, on the one hand, the poet-prophets or prophet-poets and, on the other, the unsound scientists, whose work Huxley likens to false Scripture: "We all know that the Devil can quote Scripture for his own purpose: today we are finding that he can even invent a false Scripture from which to quote" (7). False Scripture, it would seem, must be read; Scripture, including Kipling, is only quoted. "Lest we forget!" He always does have the best tunes.

The Diamond Jubilee celebrations of 1897 offered Britain ample opportunity to congratulate itself on the state of its Empire. Occasions such as this are always likely to bring out the worst in any Poet Laureate, as invariably they did in Alfred Austin, who had been appointed to the position, vacant for four years since Tennyson's death, in 1896. Kipling had been either denied the post or had refused it, and resented command performances anyway, but after some prompting he nonetheless reluctantly produced his "sentiments on things" a couple of weeks after the celebrations, in a poem published in *The Times* on the same page as a message from the Queen thanking the people for their jubilations.[3] "Recessional" was a runaway success and became "the most popular poem in the English language over the first half of the twentieth century" (Kucich 60; also Parry 79); according to Kipling's recent biographer David Gilmour, the poem effectively won its author recognition as unofficial Imperial Laureate, "a national symbol, a one-man embodiment of the Empire with a talent for anticipating a public sentiment (as well as encouraging and

---

3 For information on Kipling's Diamond Jubilee writing, see Newsom, Judd, Keating 114-17 and Gilmour 119-25. The phrase "my sentiments on things" occurs in the letter to *The Times* accompanying the manuscript of the poem and is quoted in Birkenhead 185-86.

perhaps moulding it) just before it became apparent" (124). Still according to Gilmour, "Recessional" (alongside the other anthems Kipling composed around this time) "demonstrates Kipling's extraordinary gift for persuading people that what they were reading was how they felt" (119). This assumes, of course, that people were indeed reading when they read what they felt – that the people was reading when it felt what it read. A closer look at the text and its reception suggests that this assumption is highly debatable, that feeling the feeling precisely requires the suspension of reading.

But, what, first, is the feeling, what are the "sentiments on things," the "idea" which, as Kipling himself remarked, "must have been in the air or men would not have taken to the rhymed expression of it so kindly" (quoted in Gilmour 123). Unsurprisingly, it is a pretty simple idea, neatly caught in Kipling's own summary statement in the letter accompanying the manuscript: "We've been blowing up the Trumpets of the New Moon a little too much for White Men, and it's about time we sobered down" (quoted in Birkenhead 186). Not a very hard idea to have – pride before a fall, beware of hubris, how the mighty are fallen, look on my works, ye mighty, and despair, whatever. Yet that is not how it reads in "Recessional." The poem comes in five six-line stanzas, the first four stanzas each ending (with one minor variation) on the imploring couplet "Lord God of Hosts, be with us yet, / Lest we forget – lest we forget!" The four lines preceding the rhyming couplets address God "beneath whose awful Hand we hold / Dominion" and envisage the future dissolution of Empire alongside the misconduct of its subjects, while the final stanza asks for "Thy Mercy on Thy People, Lord!" None of this seems especially arresting or challenging – easy to feel, until we begin to read.

The phrase Kipling, by his own account, "wrote the poem around" (Judd 38) is the mantra "Lest we forget," which is repeated eight times, and which prompts yet again our idiot question: who, we, exactly? Stanza 4 comes closest to articulating an answer by taking recourse to the us-them-scheme that invariably accompanies collective identity-constructions. But that is not to suggest this expression of "group sentiment" also makes sense.

> If, drunk with sight of power, we loose
>   Wild tongues that have not Thee in awe,
> Such boastings as the Gentiles use,

> Or lesser breeds without the Law –
> Lord God of Hosts, be with us yet,
> Lest we forget – lest we forget!

The sentiment is clear enough: if we get carried away, Lord, and start to speak like they do, please have mercy. But who they? The "Gentiles." And, or or, "lesser breeds without the law."

The latter phrase has always been a bit of an albatross for Kipling commentators, and not just for his admirers among them. George Orwell, for instance, whose candid characterization of Kipling as a "morally insensitive" and "aesthetically disgusting" "jingo imperialist" with "a definite strain of sadism in him" (184) leaves little to be desired, nonetheless goes out of his way to set the record straight on what he describes as this "interesting instance of the way in which quotations are parroted to and fro without any attempt to look up their context or discover their meaning":

> This line is always good for a snigger in pansy-left circles. It is assumed as a matter of course that the "lesser breeds" are "natives," and a mental picture is called up of some pukka sahib in a pith helmet kicking a coolie. In its context the sense of the line is almost the exact opposite of this. The phrase "lesser breeds" refers almost certainly to the Germans, and especially the pan-German writers, who are "without the Law" in the sense of being lawless, not in the sense of being powerless. (184-85)

Orwell does not explain how exactly he has arrived at this almost certainly almost exactly opposite alternative reading, but then Orwell is not a literary historian, let alone a Kipling scholar, and can afford to move on to higher perceptions. Yet professional historians and Kipling scholars so far have not convincingly succeeded in moving beyond Orwell's homely hermeneutical appeal to context. C.A. Bodelsen, for instance, blithely dismisses the 'pansy-left' interpretation as "a curious example of the tenacity of obviously mistaken readings, for the context makes it quite clear that it is aimed at power-drunk militaristic Great Powers" (335), while the historian Denis Judd merely remixes Orwell's "almost certainly" into a "not necessarily"-"surely"-riff:

> The "lesser breeds without the law" were not necessarily, as was so quickly assumed by critics of the poem, the black or brown citizens of Britain's empire. The poet is surely here referring both to foreigners and to those British citizens and subjects, no matter what their origin or ethnicity, who were unable or

unwilling to see what needed to be done in the national interest and what perils and spectres lurked in the shadows. (41)

Judd interestingly spells out the indifference to the trope of ethnicity which also informs Orwell's interpretation, stating in so many words that lesser breeds can be British too. Another historian, Robert Tombs, follows suit (admittedly in passing and in a different context), asserting, again without argument other than context quotation, that the meaning of the phrase is "not inferior races, but nations (not excluding [Kipling's] own) that indulged in demagogic extremism and relied on force uncontrolled by moral values" (503-04).

The consensus among commentators appears to be, then, that it is somehow obvious that "lesser breeds" cannot possibly mean inferior "natives" or "races," principally because of the context, stupid. Kipling's appeal to group sentiment here would therefore seem to by-pass the racial fallacy of the chosen people, suggesting that belonging to the chosen people is a matter of choice rather than being chosen. Ethnicity does not enter into it. Except, that is, in the term "Gentiles," which is the Vulgate translation, carried over into the Authorized Version, of the Greek "ta ethne," which itself translates the Hebrew "ha goyim."[4] That, too, is part of the context, and despite the Bible-thumping of his hermeneutico-historical apologists, it really does not help to make Kipling's meaning more manageable. And lest I be misunderstood, let me just insist that Kipling-bashing is a game I take no interest in – I am only trying to read what he wrote, which, for what it is worth, is more than can be said of most readers of "Recessional."

Consider David Gilmour's attempt to settle the matter. He recognizes that "lesser breeds without the law" "was an unfortunate and perhaps tasteless choice of phrase," but insists that it should not be interpreted as a "racial slur" (122). But what then *does* it mean, if anything? Gilmour turns to Scripture for enlightenment and singles out Paul's Epistle to the Romans as "[t]he relevant biblical text": "For as many have sinned without law shall also perish without law: and as many have sinned in the law shall be judged by the law [...] For when the Gentiles, which have not the law, do by nature the things contained in the law, these, having not the law, are a law unto themselves"

---

4 For an interesting reflection on the term "ethnic" which reminds us that the *OED* traces its current usage to Huxley's *We Europeans*, see Arac 265-66.

(2:12, 14). And lest we have forgotten what this means, Gilmour spells out the relevance:

> As the epistle's context makes clear, the Gentiles are the Roman rulers who, being without the Law of Christ, act as they please. Kipling transformed the Gentiles into their modern equivalents, the Kaiser and his henchmen, and the "lesser breeds" into the German people and anyone else, especially the Americans and perhaps also the Boers, whom he considered guilty of boastful lawlessness. (122)

What wonderful powers of transformation are here. Orwell would have had a field day on "the Kaiser and his henchmen" as an exhibit for "Politics and the English Language," and it might have given him some welcome pause for thought about his own insouciant translation of the "lesser breeds" as "the Germans." It would certainly have further fuelled his doubts "whether the blimps have ever read [Kipling] with attention, any more than they have read the Bible" (Orwell 188).

Gilmour, blimp or not, clearly hasn't bothered. The only reference he submits for his understanding of the Epistle to the Romans is a letter to the editor published in a 1967 issue of the *Kipling Journal* by one of his predecessor-biographers, the long-serving and, by his own admission, long-suffering Kipling scholar C.E. Carrington.[5] Carrington's letter makes interesting reading, beginning as it does by establishing a distinction between those who do and those who do not read: "Those of us who read the works of Kipling are perpetually tormented by the eminent literary critics who pontificate about him without having read them." The "lesser breeds without the law"-phrase is a case in point: "Your readers will not need to be told, as leader-writers for *The Times* must still be told, that Kipling could not possibly have meant to allude to the colonial peoples – whatever he did mean – by these famous words." Readers who read know what the phrase does not mean. But, once more, wearily, what then *does* it mean? Carrington, preaching to the converted, can afford to move into confessional mode: "I have been correcting the error in essays, and on platforms, without visible effect, for many years; and I am ashamed to confess that I have missed the clue." This clue, he goes on, was already revealed

---

5   I owe a debt of gratitude to David Page, the *Kipling Journal*'s current editor, who has kindly supplied me with this Carrington piece and other relevant materials from the journal, including interesting commemorative pieces on the occasion of Carrington's death in 1990.

in a 1930 book by R. Thurston Hopkins, who pointed out that the phrase was "directly lifted" from Paul's Epistle to the Romans, as Carrington then demonstrates by quoting verses 12 and 14 from the second chapter of the Epistle, copied later by Gilmour,[6] and by adding his final gloss:

> Throughout this epistle, so relevant to the problems of our own age, St. Paul refers to the Roman ruling class as "the Gentiles," to whom the "oracles of God" have not been committed. The pagan Romans in their arrogant boastings, are the "lesser breeds," and, of course, so are their modern counterparts.

Of course. Paul's Epistle sets up the familiar us-them-scheme conducive to group sentiment, and Kipling just copies the set-up, translating the boasting Gentiles into a generic modern lawless "them" and claiming the "us"-slot for the law-abiding true Brits. Just so. And this, according to Gilmour, is how Kipling's audience would indeed have read him: "The biblical language and allusions appealed to people who had been educated not only through the Classics but through the Gospels, the Epistles and the Hebrew prophets as well. They understood the message and they accepted it" (118). Just so: if they understood and accepted it, it must have been because they never read it. It is time, God forbid, that we turn to Scripture.

We have an extraordinarily successful poem that by all accounts managed to capture or even mould British group sentiment at a time when the Empire was at its height and, therefore, inevitably, courting decline. "Recessional" somehow manages to mediate this sentiment by articulating it into memorable verse, verse aspiring to the memorability of the Scripture it invokes, verse committed, apparently, to serve the letter of the Law. But at the level of the letter, what it achieves is an irredeemable perversion of the authorized version. Paul's Epistle to the Romans is a deeply tricky text, true to the trickiness of the mission it serves. Nothing could be easier or more beside the point than to confront Kipling's appreciative contemporaries as imagined by Carrington, Gilmour and others with state-of-the-art biblical exegesis, pointing out that Paul's "Gentiles" are *not*, *pace* Carrington, the boastful "Roman ruling class," sadly untouched, *pace* Gilmour, by the "Law of Christ." The point being that all that is needed to make the point of this point is to take a closer look, barely reading, at the verses Carrington quotes and Gilmour copies in

---

6   Though Gilmour, unlike Carrington who sticks closely to the Authorized Version, twice drops the second "as" in the phrase "as many as" in verse 12.

the immediate context both appeal to – ultimately, not even that context is required, the text will do.[7]

What does it mean, for instance, in and for Paul, that the Gentiles are "without law," "a law unto themselves"? For Gilmour it seems self-evident: they are "without the Law of Christ" and just do as they like. Yet that is pretty precisely *not* what the Epistle writes. True, the "oracles of God" (3:2) have only been committed to the Jews, not to the Gentiles, but that is emphatically not the point. Here is the immediate context for the phrase:

> [9] Tribulation and anguish, upon every soul of man that doeth evil, of the Jew first, and also of the Gentile; [10] But glory, honour, and peace, to every man that worketh good, to the Jew first, and also to the Gentile: [11] For there is no respect of persons with God. [12] For as many as have sinned without law shall also perish without law: and as many as have sinned in the law shall be judged by the law; [13] (For not the hearers of the law are just before God, but the doers of the law shall be justified. [14] For when the Gentiles, which have not the law, do by nature the things contained in the law, these, having not the law, are a law unto themselves: [15] Which shew the work of the law written in their hearts, their conscience also bearing witness, and their thoughts the mean while accusing or else excusing one another;) [16] In the day when God shall judge the secrets of men by Jesus Christ according to my gospel.

The Law that the Gentiles are unto themselves is not some non-principle allowing them to "act as they please," as Gilmour would have us believe, it is none other than the Law itself, now fulfilled through the offices of the Messiah. It is the Law which the Gentiles do not have only in the sense that it has not been taught to them as it has been to the Jews, but which they nonetheless manage to perform. If anybody is guilty of boasting, Paul adds, it is the Jews, not the Gentiles:

> [17] Behold, thou art called a Jew, and restest in the law, and makest thy boast of God, [18] And knowest his will, and approvest the things that are more excellent, being instructed out of the law; [19] And art confident that thou thyself art a guide of the blind, a light of them which are in darkness, [20] An instructor of the foolish, a teacher of babes, which hast the form of knowledge and of the truth in the law.[8]

---

[7] The only commentary on "Recessional" I have come across which devotes some proper, if passing, attention to what Paul actually writes is Keating 116.

[8] Later in the letter, admittedly, the Gentiles, for good measure, are warned not to boast either.

Full of themselves as "light to the Gentiles," elected by God, the Jews fail to see that the Gentiles are ahead of them, performing the Law without even knowing it. They act as they please only in the sense that they do what comes naturally, and what comes naturally to them is the law they have not heard, let alone read, but which is written in their heart.

"Such boastings as the Gentiles use, / Or lesser breeds without the Law" – what can Kipling have been thinking of? Hopkins, Carrington, Gilmour, and others are most probably right in hearing an echo of Paul in these lines; but as even a superficial scan of the Pauline text indicates, they are spectacularly mistaken in assuming that this echo also makes self-evident sense. Or, more accurately, in assuming that the perfect sense the phrase does make actually involves reading it. Like the Gentiles, they understand, accept, and perform the good message without even knowing it, executing the law of meaning which holds that any part shall always be justified by the whole and that every word is always already resolved by the totality of Scripture as essentially unwritten.

It is entirely fitting that this manifest failure to read should be grounded in a claim to reading a letter on the law which is written where it cannot be read. A delirious letter which, according to one recent commentator, "suffers the nemesis of rhetoric, as the flood of language takes over from the meaning," but whose "lapidary antitheses" (among them the "sinned without law"/"sinned in the law"-line) have nonetheless been characterized as "the closest we have to the voice of God" (Goulder 499), a letter written by a post-Jewish Jew projecting the unread Law of the ever-dissolving Jewish nation (in the beginning, in Genesis 12:2, the Jews too were set, by God, to become a *goy*, a nation, ethnic, Gentile) into the heart of the Gentiles, the nations to be united under Christ, he (who, he?) who became and thereby denied the word by turning it into the flesh (X marks the spot) which the ever-forming Jewish nation kept confusing with the law of difference, as witness its performance of difference as circumcision, separating the guide *goy* from the infant *goyim*.

But what can Kipling have been thinking of? Has he read the Letter to the Romans? Or has he, too, merely understood it? (Or, between brackets, should we entertain the notion, easily googled but hard to pin down, that he was somehow working under the sway of British Israelism and employed the implied distinction between the British and the Gentiles not as a convenient mythopoe(t)ic trope but as historical fact, in the belief that the Anglo-Saxons are the Ten Lost Tribes of Israel expelled by the Assyrians in the 8th century BC and then displaced to the British Isles? In which case his allusion to Paul amounts to a perverse re-writing of Scripture, denouncing all Gentiles, Judaeans or Jews included, as impostors without the real law of the one original Israeli covenant, which effectively confirms the Hopkins-Carrington-Gilmour reading, be it at the cost of Christianity itself. Dan Brown anyone? Close brackets.)

"Lesser breeds without the Law": in Paul, to be without the Law is not to have heard the Law, but not to have heard the Law is ultimately, and astonishingly for a lawgiving letter such as this, immaterial. The verse typically forgotten is Romans 2:13: "For not the hearers of the law are just before God, but the doers of the law shall be justified." Such is the self-suspending non-logic of essential ideology: the conversion of performative prescription into the arch-oxymoron of natural law.[9] The truth of the law is its performance prior to its performative production. The mission of the legislator is not to transmit the law but to establish it as always already having been there, untouched by material, i.e., linguistic, transmission, as when it is said that it has been established that such (and such) is the case, and the point of the statement is that it does not materially affect the case and instead aspires to radical redundance.[10] The truth of the law is its denial of the truth that it has to be given in order to be received, that it cannot be forgotten if it hasn't been gotten. This denial is performed when the law styles itself as begotten, transmitted not in writing but by life itself, inscribed beyond inscription and circumcision into the hearts of the goyim-Gentile-ethnic-nations: all of them, but only ever just the One.

---

9   For an instructive reading of Kipling's "Law" close to my concern here, see Bivona, especially 86-87. Bivona tantalizingly uses Romans 2:14-15 as an epigraph to his chapter on Kipling but fails, so to speak, to establish the law of the allusion.

10   "Do we then make void the law through faith? God forbid: yea, we establish the law" (Romans 3:31). "It is notable that Kipling does not seem to realize, any more than the average soldier or colonial administrator, that an empire is primarily a money-making concern. Imperialism as he sees it is a sort of forcible evangelizing. You turn a Gatling gun on a mob of unarmed 'natives,' and then you establish 'the Law,' which includes roads, railways and a courthouse" (Orwell 186).

"Recessional" has it right, but no-one is reading. "Breeds" is indeed an "unfortunate" term, destined never to be read. Kipling's apologists – including, of all people, Orwell – go out of their way to deny the referential accuracy of the term: breeds are natural collective entities bonded by bodily fluids; nations or natives or peoples are historical collective entities denying, or being denied, their linguistic constitution through the imagination of the inscriptions they live by as transcriptions of breed bonds. Nations are built on the systematic confusion of reading with breeding: they are always without the law because the law that they are unto themselves is the imaginary unwritten law of nature in which the law as law always already aspires to lose itself so as to become what it irrevocably abandons at the time, every time, of inscription.

All breeds are equal in that, as breeds, they are without the law. If some breeds are lesser than others, such as the Gentiles, and we are all Gentiles, that is not because they are without the law but because when breeds meet they are haunted by inscription and deny themselves the denial of the law, the law of the law, and re-imagine themselves, as opposed to the opposite breed, as having heard, even as having read, the law. Not that this differentiation makes any difference, for no nation can survive reading its own law. Which is why, as Paul writes, as Kipling miswrites, they boast about it, and then boast about not boasting about it. Anything to avoid reading. Anything to avoid exile and alienation.

"Lest we forget." Forget what, exactly? Though nations define themselves as repositories of collective memory, as nations they owe their existence to oblivion. "Lest we forget" to forget what makes memory possible in the first place: lest we begin to read – God forbid – that We are not of One Blood, that Blood doesn't enter into it, that God is the thing we invent to forget that the law is still waiting to be read. Unto itself, the law is never a law. But that is not how it works. "Recessional" works by producing a surface commanding recognition, a specular phantasm sustaining the referential illusion that it represents the blood of the first person plural in whose pronoun it speaks. In textual fact, it represents what is really written, not in the living heart but in the dead letter of difference which lays any natural we to waste and abandons us to the post-human burden of reading. But that, in turn, as they say, is history: the great unread.

It is tempting to wrest a moral from this story of a text that manifestly succeeded in giving shape to the sense of an Empire by blindly recycling bits of a text that managed to give shape to one of the greatest hyper-Empires in human history, against all odds, including its own eccentricities, for better or worse. Let us not resist that temptation. Let us take courage from the fact that our Constitution (who, we?) is not ratified and remains to be read. And by all means let our Constitution name Christianity and its crazes and crises as constitutive of Europe, lest this unreadable heritage be assumed and forgotten in the rapture of final understanding.

Works Cited

Arac, Jonathan. "Chinese Postmodernism: Towards a Global Context." *boundary 2* 24.3 (1997): 261-75.

Birkenhead, Lord. *Rudyard Kipling*. London: Weidenfeld and Nicholson, 1978.

Bivona, Daniel. "Kipling's 'Law' and the Division of Bureaucratic Labor." *British Imperial Literature, 1870-1940: Writing and the Administration of Empire*. Cambridge: Cambridge University Press, 1998. 69-98.

Bodelsen, C.A. Review of *Rudyard Kipling, Realist and Fabulist* by Bonamy Dobrée and *Rudyard Kipling's India* by K. Bhaskara Rao. *The Review of English Studies* (New Series) 19.75 (1968): 334-37.

Brantlinger, Patrick. "Kipling's 'The White Man's Burden' and Its Afterlives." *English Literature in Transition, 1880-1920* 50.2 (2007): 172-91.

Carrington, C.E. "The Lesser Breeds." *Kipling Journal* 164 (1967): 14.

Gilmour, David. *The Long Recessional: The Imperial Life of Rudyard Kipling*. London: Pimlico, 2003.

Goulder, Michael. "The Pauline Epistles." *The Literary Guide to the Bible*. Ed. Robert Alter and Frank Kermode. Cambridge: Harvard University Press, 1987. 479-502.

Huxley, Julian S., A.C. Haddon, and A.M. Carr-Saunders. *We Europeans: A Survey of "Racial" Problems*. Harmondsworth: Penguin, 1939.

Judd, Denis. "Diamonds Are Forever? Kipling's Imperialism." *History Today* 47.6 (1997): 37-43.

Keating, Peter. *Kipling the Poet*. London: Secker and Warburg, 1994.

Kucich, John. "Sadomasochism and the Magical Group: Kipling's Middle-

Class Imperialism." *Victorian Studies* 46.1 (2004): 33-68.

Newsom, George. "'Recessional' and 'The White Man's Burden'." *Kipling Journal* 255 (1990): 13-24.

Orwell, George. "Rudyard Kipling." *My Country Right or Left, 1940-1943. The Collected Essays, Journalism, and Letters of George Orwell.* 2nd vol. Ed. Sonia Orwell and Ian Angus. London: Secker and Warburg, 1968. 184-97.

Parry, Ann. *The Poetry of Rudyard Kipling: Rousing the Nation.* Buckingham: Open University Press, 1992.

Tombs, Robert. "'Lesser Breeds without the Law': The British Establishment and the Dreyfus Affair, 1894-1899." *The Historical Journal* 41.2 (1998): 495-510.

Herbert Grabes (University of Gießen)

Prodesse et Delectare: The World of National Literatures and the World of Literature

Just imagine there are many wonderful books and hardly anyone knows that they exist. This is not very likely, we can nowadays say. Though we may not know their authors and titles, there is no problem, for we can easily change this. After all, over the ages a great number of literary histories have been written that we can consult directly or via the internet, to which much of the information they provide has been transferred. So the *prodesse*, the 'being useful' which Horace in his *Ars Poetica* attributed to the poets, certainly applies to literary histories. The fact that what these histories present is normally a rather broad canon of the literature of a particular nation seems to be no drawback as such sources are consulted almost exclusively by those who study or have studied the national literature in question. There are, of course, also histories of European literature or even world literature. Their number, however, is very small in comparison, and not many people apart from the relatively small number of students of comparative literature seem to buy and read them. This is deplorable particularly regarding European literature, because there has been a continuous mutual influence between writers in the various European countries, but neither this nor the fact that there is an enormous quantity of books published in translation (which were thus originally part of another national literature) seems to have much of an impact. How this situation has arisen, why it continues to exist, and whether it is an immutable condition are matters that deserve some attention.

There had, of course, already been catalogues of famous authors in classical Antiquity. For example, the catalogue of the famous library of Alexandria compiled by Kallimachos of Cyrene in the third century BC included all the names of the important authors who were known then, arranged alphabetically under different genres, with each entry giving a brief autobiography, a list of works with their titles and incipits, dates of composition and number of lines, as well as a commentary on the likelihood of the authenticity of the manuscript used and on its physical condition. And the *De viris illustribus* by Gaius Suetonius Tranquillus, written in the second century AD under the emperor Hadrian, listed authors 'by profession' under one of five sections comprising poets, orators, historians, philosophers, and grammarians and rhetoricians, and provided information on descent, teachers and education, talent and character, social position, writings, and – if relevant – date of death. I mention this chiefly because this entry structure served not only as a model for the early histories of Christian religious writers but also for the early modern national catalogues and histories of writers compiled during the Renaissance, and it is even discernible in some literary histories of the 19th century.

The earliest religious or patristic historical catalogue, entitled *De viris illustribus*, like that of Suetonius, was written by the Church Father Jerome at the end of the fourth century and presented 135 Christian authors chronologically, from Saint Paul to Jerome himself. It was extended and continued principally by Gennadius of Massilia in the 5th century, by Isidore of Seville and Ildefonso of Toledo in the 7th century, and by Sigbert of Gembloux and Honorius Augustodunensis in the 12th century. The title given to it by Honorius, *De luminaribus ecclesiae*, is the one that fits it best, because these were all histories of religious writing, not of literature in any modern sense.

When investigating the origins of present-day literary histories, we will find that the first attempts were made at the time of the Renaissance. Most impressive – due to its comprehensive transnational canon – was the *Bibliotheca Universalis* published in 1545 by the Swiss humanist Conrad Gesner. With its inclusion of some three thousand authors of Greek, Latin, and Hebrew works it was an imposing catalogue, yet not a proper history, because the authors were not arranged in their historical sequence but listed alphabetically. Gesner's work nevertheless became famous throughout Europe because there had not yet been a compendium of this kind. Before, all there was were library catalogues, primarily those of monastery and cathedral libraries.[1] The transnational character of Gesner's work remained, however, an exception. The rise of literary histories in early modern times and later is closely connected with the formation of the modern European nation-states. The collection and presentation of a national literature with a long tradition

---

[1] See, for instance, Bateson, Botfield, Ker, *Mittelalterliche Bibliothekskataloge Deutschlands und der Schweiz*, and *Mittelalterliche Bibliothekskataloge Österreichs* in the bibliography.

was considered (internally) as an important factor in the creation of national identity and (externally) as essential to the burgeoning spirit of competitiveness with the literature of Classical antiquity and the literatures of the other early modern nation-states.

In Johannes Trithemius's *Catalogus illustrium virorum Germaniae* from 1495 we encounter the first more comprehensive work registering the authors of a particular nation. And what Trithemius had done for Germany, Claude Fauchet did in the second half of the 16th century for France with his *Recueil de l'origine de la langue et poésie française, rime et romans*, which was published in 1581. In Britain – on which I will concentrate in the rest of this essay – the urgent need to have a collection and historical record of the writing of the nation had a particular reason in the later years of the reign of King Henry VIII: the dispersal and at least partial destruction of library holdings caused by the dissolution of the monasteries. John Leland, antiquary and keeper of the Royal Library, after a long search for the library's dispersed holdings between 1534 and 1541, in the years 1542 to 1545 wrote a compendious chronological sequence of no fewer than 674 biographies of British writers under the title *Libri quatuor de viris illustribus* – a work which, according to his "newe yeares gyfte" of 1545 to King Henry, was to show

> that not alonely the Germanes, but also the Italianes themselfe, that counte as the Grekes ded full arrogantly, all other nacyons to be barbarouse + unlettered, sauinge their owne, shall haue a dirct occasyon, openly of force to say. That *Brytannia prima fuit parens, altrix (addo hoc etiam, et jure quidem optimo) conservatrix eum virorum magnorum, tum maxime ingeniorum.* (that Britain came first, as I may add with very good justification, in being parent, foster mother and supporter of these great and most creative men.) (C 7ᵛ)

Leland's work, though known to and used by subsequent historians in manuscript form, was not printed until 1709, so that the first national history of writing to be actually printed and made public in England was John Bale's *Illustrium Majoris Britanniae Scriptorum Summarium* from 1548. It comprises 500 regular entries and an additional 105 in two appendices. While the canon is quite similar to Leland's, Bale, who had become an ardent Protestant, used his history not only to demonstrate that the true creed resting on nothing but the Scriptures was never forgotten in Britain, but also to pillory those who had defended papal policy and the Roman tradition. Yet this tendency to submit the writing of literary history to an ideological purpose beyond patriotism became only really dominant in the much enlarged second edition, the *Scriptorum Illustrium maioris Brytannie, quam nunc Angliam & Scotiam uocant: Catalogus*, which was published in two volumes in the years 1557 and 1559, during Bale's exile at Basle under the reign of the Catholic Mary Tudor. Bale is nevertheless eager to point out the patriotic nature of his task by stating that he presents "praestantissimos scriptores Angliae" in order that they be known and valued also "ultra Oceanum" (*Scriptorum* α 3^v) – that is, on the Continent.

Bale's strongly Protestant bent must have been a major motivation for the Catholic priest John Pits to write a third compendious history of English writing, published 1619 in Paris under the title *Relationum Historicarum de Rebus Anglicis Tomus Primus*. Only 365 of the 1570 entries were new, and Pits took most of the factual information from Bale, as Bale had in his time taken it from Leland. More important, of course, is the fact that he praises authors who wrote in favor of the Roman tradition, and while he blames Bale for railing against the defendants of what in his view was the true religion, he himself deals much more drastically with those he holds to be schismatics by not mentioning them at all – that is, by trying to eliminate them from history altogether. Nevertheless, he also expressly states his patriotic motivation in writing that he is raising from obscurity "insulae nostrae scripta [...] ad Dei gloriam, Ecclesiae splendorem, & patriae honorem" (5).

All in all, one gets the impression that without the rise of the modern European nation-states we would not have national literary histories, and this means we would not have the most important records of the treasure of writing in Europe. In order to gauge the full importance of this statement, one needs to keep in mind that all these early histories are not histories of literature in a narrower sense but histories of written culture. They aim at quantity and cover authors and works of all kinds in order to demonstrate the high cultural standard of the nation. They are a mine of information for the cultural historian because the authorial entries often enough contain ample descriptions of the cultural and social conditions under which the writers made their contributions to the cultural development of their country. Yet the fact that they are written in Latin has increasingly become an obstacle to general familiarity with them. At least in Britain, alongside these learned histories of writing, a much narrower canon of 'poets' – or rather writers of fictional texts – developed from the late 16th century onwards and was presented to a broader readership in several "Histories of English Poetry" that appeared between the late 17th and the early 19th century.[2]

The chronological arrangement of authors that we find not only in these early histories but also until well into the 18th century has been considered to be at best a proto-form of literary history, inasmuch as it is held to betray a lack of a synthesizing theory of history. From the point of view of the later theories of evolution, revolution, or the workings of a Hegelian *Weltgeist* this seems indeed to be the case; but on the basis of a postmodern sceptical distrust of *grands récits*, such an additive structure may even be less deceptive than the later ones. For one thing seems clear: no author means no book; literary history is primarily made by authors and only secondarily by literary historians. The degree to which the biography of authors determined what they came to write about is, of course, another question; but when, for instance, composers of music, painters, or architects play an important role in cultural history, literary authors even beyond Shakespeare should not be excluded.

The subsuming of authors and their works under categories like epochs, movements, or genres began in the many histories of national literature in the 19th century. The canon of these histories is still wide, sometimes so wide that they seem to attempt to once again function as histories of national written culture. What they comprise are authors and works in all domains of writing which are held to be examples of such excellence as to have contributed to the national treasury of writing, though *belles lettres* or what until the late 18th century was called 'poetry' received most attention.

When I stated that without the rise of the modern European nation-states and the ensuing competition among them we would have no histories of national literatures and know much less about the rich treasury of literature written in Europe, this is best demonstrated by the openly patriotic and sometimes even nationalist motivation of the authors of 19th century literary histories which defined the genre as we know it today. The extreme degree to which the desire to serve the nation formed the primary motivation for the writing of these histories, at least in Britain, has been convincingly

---

2   See Winstanley, Johnson, and Hazlitt in the bibliography.

demonstrated by Margit Sichert. From William Chambers and George Lillie Craik, Thomas Budge Shaw, William Spalding, Thomas Arnold, Henry Morley, and Stopford Brooke to George Saintsbury at the very end of the 19th century we find again and again the conviction that an acquaintance with the treasure house of national literature will create and promote national identity and unity. Morley, for instance, was even convinced that English literature reveals the "religious sense of duty" of the people and that this is "to tell how England won, and how alone she can expect to keep her foremost place among the nations" (quoted in Sichert 204). The conviction that there was a close link between the nation and its literature continued into the 20th century, and while it is true that British histories of English literature written between the 1950s and today are much less openly patriotic, most of them are traditional in the sense that they have a very broad canon comprising all kinds of works held to be important for cultural history and suitable for the display of national excellence (see Grabes). They thus continue the tradition of the primacy of *prodesse*, of being useful for the creation of national identity and the strengthening of national pride. It is therefore surprising – but perhaps also significant – that in three more recent works, *The Routledge History of Literature in English: Britain and Ireland* from 1997, edited by Ronald Carter and John McRae, Michael Alexander's *History of English Literature* from the year 2000, and the *Brief History of English Literature* by John Peck and Martin Coyle from 2002, the authors have abandoned this pattern and limit their canon almost entirely to products of the imagination or *belles lettres*. They seem at least to indicate that *delectare* may become more important than it has been so far in most national literary histories.

This brings us to the question of what has been and what should be presented on a European scale. Regarding the earlier 19th century, Henry Hallam's *Introduction to the Literature of Europe in the Fifteenth, Sixteenth, and Seventeenth Centuries* from 1837-39 provides an impressive example. The title is much too modest, because in the 86 pages of the first chapter he takes the reader from Boethius early in the 6th century right through the earlier and high Middle Ages to Petrarch in the 14th century. Yet it is from chapter II onwards, "On the Literature of Europe from 1400 to 1440," when encountering the sections on the "Cultivation of Latin in Italy," the "Revival of Greek Literature," and the "State of Learning in Other Parts of Europe," on "Physical Sciences – Mathematics – Medicine and Anatomy – Poetry in Spain, France, and England – Formation of New Laws of Taste in Middle Ages – Their Principles – Romances," and on "Religious Opinions" that it dawns on the reader – especially when paying due attention to the ample footnotes – to what extent this product of 19th century scholarship, both in its objectives and in its execution, surpasses anything a single author has tried and achieved ever since. It is true that Hallam was in the favorable position of being able to devote most of his time to the task, yet one is nevertheless astounded by the extent of the reading he accomplished, and even more by the way in which he managed to turn the fruits of this research into a discouragingly learned and at the same time eminently readable history of written culture in Europe. And one has to say 'written culture' here instead of 'literature,' as the scope of Hallam's history is very wide indeed. Here, for example, are the chapter headings for Part III, "On the Literature of the First Half of the Seventeenth Century" (vols. II and III):

> Chapter I. History of Ancient Literature in Europe from 1600 to 1650.
> Chapter II. History of Theological Literature in Europe from 1600 to 1650.
> Chapter III. History of Speculative Philosophy from 1600 to 1650.
> Chapter IV. History of Moral and Political Philosophy and of Jurisprudence from 1600 to 1650.
> Chapter V. History of Poetry from 1600 to 1650.
> Chapter VI. History of Dramatic Literature from 1600 to 1650.
> Chapter VII. History of Polite Literature in Prose from 1600 to 1650.
> Chapter VIII. History of Mathematical and Physical Science from 1600 to 1650.
> Chapter IX. History of Some Other Provinces of Literature from 1600 to 1650.

When Hallam deals in each chapter with the relevant items from Italy, France, England, Germany, the Low Countries, and Spain, at times also from Portugal, Switzerland, or Denmark, his stunning knowledge becomes visible – even if he has to rely heavily on the work of other scholars and openly admits this.

What is further remarkable is Hallam's endeavor to stay free of nationalist prejudice and to arrive at a balanced judgement. In view of the common English pride in the Elizabethan period and the traditional reservations about Spain, it was, for instance, quite daring to say that "it is undeniable that, in most branches of erudition, so far as we can draw a conclusion from publications, Spain, under Philip II, held a higher station than England under Elizabeth" (2:61). And, inasmuch as learned works like his history are often sneered at by labeling them "mere positivist collections of facts," it is perhaps sobering to see that a historian like Hallam wrote on a general assumption that might well accord with our most recent dialogic models of the relationship between literature and society. Stressing the interdependence between the "national temper" and national literature, here is what he says in a paragraph on the chivalric romances: "The condition and the opinions of a people stamp a character on its literature; while that literature powerfully reacts upon and moulds afresh the national temper from which it has taken its distinctive type" (1:134). And it seems safe to say that it was this kind of interdependence, which led to characteristic differences between the national literatures of Europe, that motivated Hallam to look beyond England, and we can also say that even today it may be one of the reasons to become interested in a comparative history of European literature.

A quite different answer to the question of how to write a history of European literature was given, for instance, in the early 1930s by Laurie Magnus in his *History of European Literature*. His approach is clearly delineated in the preface of his comparatively short one-volume work by a long quotation of Edward Dowden:

> In an essay on "The Teaching of English Literature," Dowden declared that he "would have a student start with a *General Sketch of European Literature*, somewhat resembling Mr. Freeman's *General Sketch of European History* in its aim and scope and manner of treatment [...] When Boccaccio," he went on, "is spoken of in connection with Chaucer, when Tasso or Ariosto is spoken of in connection with Spenser, or Boileau in connection with Dryden or Pope, or Carlyle in connection with Goethe, he ought at least to be able to place Boccaccio and Tasso and Ariosto and Boileau and Goethe aright in the general movement of European literature, and in some measure to conceive aright the relation of each to the literary movement in our own country." (xi)

Here we see how the *prodesse,* the usefulness for the understanding of national literature, determines the approach chosen for the writing of a history of European literature. The interest in and occupation with the wider field of European literature is justified from the point of view of the study of national literature. Only by acquiring at least some knowledge of this wider field, it is argued, will one be able to assess the role of those important foreign works to which the national literature is indebted.

Beginning with Chaucer's going to Italy and meeting Petrarch in Florence in 1372, Magnus makes clear right from the start that he is writing above all for those acquainted with or studying English literature. This method of looking at European literature from the perspective of one's own national literature has, of course, the advantage of having a well-founded principle of selection: what is dealt with are above all those foreign authors and works that are known to have influenced the national literature, and the periods that will get most attention will be those in which the European link will be strongest. Apart from the time of Chaucer, Magnus accordingly concentrates on the Italian literature of the Renaissance, the Italian, Spanish, and French influences at the time of Shakespeare, what he calls "The French Rule and its Sequel" in the later 17th and 18th centuries, and on the period he terms "Revolutionary Europe" (surprisingly lumping together Goethe's and Wordsworth's writing on the French Revolution, the Hellenism of Byron, Keats, and Landor, and Russian literature from Pushkin to Dostoyevsky and Tolstoy). Magnus's approach can well be explained by the acute predominance of nationalist thought and feeling at the time of its conception. What we see now from a historical distance are, above all, its disadvantages. First, it is obvious that on this model one has to write a special history of European literature from the perspective of each nation; and, second, what will be presented are only those parts of the literature of the other European countries that have been of importance for the national literature in the past, with no other parts getting a chance to perhaps become of some influence in the future.

The last history of European literature I would like to comment on is amazing in more than one respect. First it has to be mentioned that its author, Michael Babits, is a gifted Hungarian poet, and the way in which he presents a great number of literary works from Homer to the early 20th century is, even in translation, a testimony to his powers of expression. Second, this manner of presentation leaves no doubt that Babits must have read all the works he describes in detail. Third, he wrote his history in the 1930s 'from the margins,' in Hungarian, and it is only due to the German translation from 1948 (as *Geschichte der europäischen Literatur*) that a broader readership could enjoy it. And fourth, this history is, indeed, written for *delectare,* for the particular kind of enjoyment that accompanies the process of discovering ever new ways of experiencing the world and the self in the great works of European literature. Holding that world literature consists above all of European literature, Babits writes about the relationship between national literature and world literature:

> It is said that literature "expresses the soul of the nation." Yes, it discovers and displays all the diverse emotional attitudes the children of one nation can adopt towards the world. This is of great importance: the nation thereby slowly becomes conscious of itself. Yet even greater and rarer is the discovery and expression of each new individual stance that raises to the level of consciousness a comment on the universe not only valid for a smaller community but for all mankind. World literature is the awakening of mankind to consciousness. (Babits 7, my translation)

I have quoted at length from Babits because it gives me the occasion to say a few words about what I hold to be a desirable project. When I put *prodesse,* the being useful, on the side of the national histories of literature, looking for an alternative that would promise more *delectare,* more delight, I could have had in mind Babits's dictum that "who writes the history of a national literature may consider the nation as more impotant than the literature. For the historian of world literature only literature is of importance" (Babits 5-6, my translation). Yet there is no European literature beyond the literature written within the different European nations, and one therefore may well make use of national pride to bring together the most precious literary products of Europe. What I am thinking of is a work designed as an enticement to read more of the most exciting works of literature from the various European countries, an invitation to the adventure of discovering the most interesting ways of seeing the world and the self created by the literary imagination, with language strained to its utmost limits. And to achieve a fair solution to the problem of selection, experts from every country should have the chance to offer those works for inclusion that are held to be its most important contributions. The result would quite obviously be a canon rather than a history of European literature. Some kinds of theorist will be bound to find any canon anathema, and perhaps a European one may be even more so, but faced with the alternative between becoming acquainted with a canon and knowing hardly anything at all beyond Shakespeare or Molière or Goethe I am in favor of a canon – only under the condition, however, that the principle of *delectare* will be more important than in most records of national canons.

Works Cited

Alexander, Michael. *History of English Literature*. Basingstoke: Macmillan, 2000.

Arnold, Thomas. *A Manual of English Literature, Historical and Critical. With an Appendix on English Metres*. London: Longmans & Co., 1862.

Babits, Michael. *Geschichte der europäischen Literatur*. Zürich and Wien: Europa-Verlag, 1948.

Bale, John. *Illustrium Majoris Britanniae Scriptorum Summarium*. Wesel, 1548.

———. *Scriptorum Illustrium majoris Brytannie, quam nunc Angliam & Scotiam uocant: Catalogus*. 2 vols. Basle, 1557-59.

Bateson, Mary, ed. *Catalogue of the Library of Syon Monastery Isleworth Cambridge*. Cambridge: Cambridge University Press, 1898.

Bayrische Akademie der Wissenschaften in München. *Mittelalterliche Bibliothekskataloge Deutschlands un der Schweiz*. 6 vols. München, 1918-62.

Botfield, Beriah, ed. *Catalogi veteres librorum Ecclesiae Cathedralis Dunelmi*. Surtees Society 7. Durham, 1874.

Brooke, Stopford Augustus. *English Literature*. London: Macmillan, 1876.

Carter, Ronald and John McRae. *The Routledge History of Literature in English: Britain and Ireland*. London: Routledge, 1997.

Chambers, William and Robert Chambers. *History of the English Language and Literature*. Edinburgh: William and Robert Chambers; London: Orr and Smith, 1836.

Craik, George Lillie. *Sketches of the History of Literature and Learning in England from the Norman Conquest to the Accession of Elizabeth*. 6 vols. London: Knight, 1844-45.

Fauchet, Claude. *Recueil de l'origine de la langue et poésie francaise, rime et romans*. Ed. J.G. Espiner-Scott. Paris: E. Droz, 1938.

Gennadius of Massilia. *Hieronymus Liber de viris illustribus – Gennadius Liber de viris illustribus*. Ed. Ernest Cushing Richardson. Leipzig:

Teubner, 1896.

Gesner, Conrad. *Bibliotheca Universalis*. Osnabrück: Zeller, 1966 [1545].

Grabes, Herbert. "Cultivating a Common Literary Heritage: British Histories of English Literature since World War II." *Modern Language Quarterly* 64.2 (2003): 239-54.

Hallam, Henry. *Introduction to the Literature of Europe, in the Fifteenth, Sixteenth, and Seventeenth Centuries.* London: John Murray, 1882.

Hazlitt, William. *Lectures on the English Poets, Delivered at the Surrey Institution.* Philadelphia, 1818.

Honorius Augustodunensis. *De luminaribus ecclesiae.* Ed. J.P. Migne, *Patrologiae cursus completus. Series Latina.* Vol. 172. Paris, 1844. 39-1270.

Jerome. *Hieronymus Liber de viris illustribus – Gennadius Liber de viris illustribus.* Ed. Ernest Cushing Richardson. Leipzig: Teubner, 1896.

Johnson, Dr. Samuel. *The Lives of the English Poets; and a Criticism on their Works.* 3 vols. Dublin: Whitstone, 1779-81.

Kallimachos. *The Alexandrian Library and the Origins of Bibliography [...] 324-222 BC. With a Supplementary Chapter by E. Cahen.* Trans. J. Loeb. London, 1931.

Ker, Neil. *Medieval Libraries of Great Britain.* Royal Historical Society, Guides and Handbooks 3. 2nd ed. London: Offices of the Royal Historical Society, 1956.

Ildefonso of Toledo. *De viris illustribus.* Ed. J.P. Migne, *Patrologiae cursus completus. Series Latina.* Vol. 96. Paris, 1844. 53-206.

Isidore of Seville. *De viris illustribus.* Ed. Carmen Condoner Merino. Salamanca: Consejo Superior de Investigacione Científicas, Instituto "Antonoi de Nebrija," Colegio Trilingüe de la Universidad, 1964.

Leland, John. *Commentarii de Scriptoribus Britannicis.* Ed. Anthony Hall. Oxford: Theatro Sheldoniano, 1709.

Magnus, Laurie. *A History of European Literature.* Port Washington, NY and London: Kennikat Press, 1934.

Morley, Henry. *A First Sketch of English Literature.* London, Paris, and New York: Cassel, Peter, and Galpin, 1873.

Österreichische Akademie der Wissenschaften in Wien. *Mittelalterliche Bibliotheken Österreichs.* 4 vols. Wien and Graz, 1915-66.

Peck, John and Martin Coyle. *A Brief History of English Literature.*

Basingstoke: Palgrave, 2002.

Pits, John. *Relationum Historicarum de Rebus Anglicis Tomus Primus*. Paris, 1619.

Saintsbury, George. *A Short History of English Literature*. London: Macmillan, 1898.

Shaw, Thomas Budge. *Outlines of English Literature*. London: John Murray, 1849.

Sichert, Margit. "Functionalizing Cultural Memory: Foundational British Literary History and the Construction of National Identity." *Modern Language Quarterly* 64.2 (2003): 199-217.

Sigebert of Gembloux, *Catalogus de viris illustribus*. Ed. Robert Witte. *Lateinische Literatur des Mittelalters* 1 (1974): 49-150.

Spalding, William. *History of English Literature, with an Outline of the Origin and Growth of the English Language. Illustrated by Extracts*. Edinburgh: Oliver and Boyd, 1853.

Suetonius, Gaius Tranquillus. *De viris illustribus*. Ed. Giorgio Brugnoli. Leipzig: Teubner, 1960.

Trithemius, Johannes. *Catalogus illustrium virorum Germaniam suis ingeniis et lucubrationibus omnifariam exornantium*. Mainz, 1495.

Winstanley, William. *The Lives of the Most Famous English Poets, or the Honour of Parnassus*. London: Samuel Manship, 1687.

Jeppe Ilkjær (Roskilde University)

The Late Europe: Elias Canetti and the Ordering of Time and Space in *Auto Da Fé*

When Elias Canetti received the Nobel Prize in Literature in 1981, he held a speech in which he emphasized that Europe had been the most important source of his authorship.[1] This is a surprising reference, not only because Canetti was born in a Jewish ghetto in the outskirts of the Ottoman Empire and carried a Turkish passport most of his life, but also because he constantly refers to this Europe as something which is delayed, something behind schedule or not in time. Europe is described as something that falls behind without Canetti ever stating exactly what it is trying to reach. Moreover, he relates this aged culture to four authors to whom he feels he owes his entire professional life and work: Karl Kraus, Franz Kafka, Robert Musil, and Hermann Broch. In different ways each of these authors belongs to the "World of Yesterday," as Stefan Zweig called the declining Habsburg Empire, and it is the characteristic atmosphere of this type of literature that gives us an idea of what it means for Europe to be somehow 'late.' Kraus describes the experience of living in the eleventh hour as being the last descendant in "the old house of language,"[2] and Broch makes use of terms such as "late homecoming," "dusk before night" and "mythical style" when describing contemporary European literature.[3] In this way, the meaning of the late Europe becomes, if not clear,

---

1   "This continent to which so many owe so much carries a great debt itself and it needs time to make up for its sins. We passionately wish to give it this time; a time in which one blessing after the other can spread itself over the earth; a time so victorious that no one in the whole world would ever have reason to curse the name of Europe again. Four men that I can't detach myself from have in my time belonged to this delayed, this real Europe." (Canetti, "Dank" 151). All translations from the German are the author's unless otherwise stated.

2   "I am just one of the Epigoni / living in the old house of language. // Yet, I have my own experience / I break out and I tear down Thebes. // Even though I come after the old masters, later, / I beat the fate of the fathers till the blood flows. // I speak of revenge, I will revenge the language. // I am an Epigon, an offspring. / Yet, you are the future Thebans!" (Kraus 79).

3   "But what a strange development of the human expression, since, apparently, it returns to its mythical source. Is this not like a late homecoming? And if it be such – does it not portend the dusk before the night? Is it not the curve that drops back into childhood?" (Broch, "Style" 249).

then at least less obscure: the old European culture, weak and condemned to decline, plays an important role for these Central European authors who see the destructive forces of global *civilization* making an end to the highly developed and advanced European *culture*. This divergence between civilization and culture is important, not only if we want to understand Central European literature written after the First World War in general and Canetti's works in particular, but also if we want to understand more about some of the current discussions about Europe and its future. This essay focuses on Elias Canetti and a small but important tradition of authors writing about Europe, not in the positive and instructive terms of a European civilization, but rather in terms of a European culture that is on the brink of disappearing.

If we look at the development of the ideas about Europe as they appear in this type of literature, what is remarkable is to what degree they are related to decline and destruction. After the First World War the field of literature was full of ideas concerning Europe.[4] Typically, these notions came from the countries that had suffered defeat or even experienced dissolution, as was the case with Austria-Hungary. Many Austrian authors and intellectuals pointed out the role of European culture as a connector between East and West, the past and the future, tradition and modernity. In their view, the Habsburg Empire had fulfilled this connecting role before the First World War, not only because it had been crucial for the stability of the geopolitical situation in Europe, but also since it had offered a cultural ideal that reached beyond nationalism – a challenge now being handed over to Europe. There was, however, a hesitant, almost sorrowful air about this assignment. When drawing a map of this kind of literature, it turns out that the geographical outline of the Habsburg Empire is considerably reduced, and it seems that nothing can prevent the liberalism and nationalism that undermined the old dynasty from destroying Europe as well.

Elias Canetti expresses some of the same concerns in his works. In his autobiography, he recounts playing with a jigsaw puzzle map of Europe, which he could put together blindfolded, identifying the countries by feeling their shape (*Tongue Set Free* 47). This geographical game is stamped on Canetti's memory because it was the last exchange he shared with his father.

---

4   For an indication of the different, but almost simultaneous responses to the question of Europe, see Lützeler.

Completing the jigsaw puzzle gave him a sense of wholeness. Looking back, however, Canetti's sense of wholeness seems to have disappeared with the same abruptness as his father's sudden death in 1912 while reading in the newspaper about the outbreak of the First Balkan War. It is characteristic for Canetti and the authors he mentions that they rarely speak of the creation of a European Utopia or a certain type of state; rather the idea of Europe is a way to reflect, observe, and write in the absence of such a social and national order.

Before proceeding to an investigation of how European lateness is described in Canetti's novel *Auto Da Fé* (1935), it is necessary to take a closer look at how Europe is being related to the decline and destruction of the Central European tradition. When the First World War came to an end, many Austrian authors, in looking back at the past, constructed an idealized version of Austria which they symbolically opposed to the new, modern world. In this mythical Habsburg Austria, the safety and warmth of the patriarchal society with its traditional hierarchies and multi-national harmony ensured the moral survival both of the individual and of certain collectives.[5] For the authors emphasized by Canetti in his Nobel Speech, however, this version of Austria contained at the same time an ironic double, an inverted image. A characteristic trait in their texts is that the central, organizing perspective has become obsolete. Instead, these texts primarily pay attention to a marginalized position, or, alternatively, they are literally using forms that are situated in the margins between the literary and the extraliterary in terms of genre and type. On the one hand, they use the spatial metaphor of the margin and thus express the feeling of living in a culture that has come to an end. On the other hand, they try to save whatever is left of this old culture in a new form. An example is Hermann Broch, who in his trilogy *The Sleepwalkers* (1931) describes the journey of the protagonist Joachim von Pasenow from the capital Berlin to Trier, in the provincial periphery of the German Empire. In this journey away from the center – which can also be decoded in a series of inserted essays moving the attention away from the central plot – the novel presents a great amount of different characters and describes their lives and deaths over a period of time ending with the First World War. This narrative form reflects the overall philosophical theme of

---

5   See Magris, *Mythos* 7.

the novel, i.e., the dissolution of values. In a remark on the novel Broch calls this form "poly-historic":

> It can be seen as part of the demonstration that the modern novel clearly shows poly-historic tendencies and, moreover, that in this respect it tries to act as a successor of philosophy. Of such poly-historic novels, Joyce's Ulysses cannot be stressed enough, just as André Gide and his great attempts to form the art of the novel in a new way, and not least, though in a different manner, Robert Musil, whom you all know. ("Grundlagen" 732)

We can rightly say that Broch's historical insight lies in the realization that he finds himself placed in an epoch that has no center. When religion is no longer the central value that organizes the inner life, then spiritual society is split up in a variety of autonomous value systems. According to Broch, the decisive downfall in European cultural history took place when the Middle Ages came to an end and when science and scientific thinking emerged during the Renaissance. The essay parts of *The Sleepwalkers* tell about this dissolution of values while the narrative shows us this dissolution. This multiple representation of Europe can be seen as part of a poly-historic tendency, which holds that European values can survive only by also taking into account marginal forms such as the essay.

The drift towards the periphery, not only on the level of literary form, but also in the historical sense of insignificance and distance from the center of power, or the geographical sense of spatial removal, is one of the distinctive marks of these Central European writers.[6] Thus, Musil not only represents the protagonist in his novel *The Man without Qualities* (1932) as the exponent of a certain way of reflecting and writing that makes use of the essayistic form to an even higher extent than Broch does; Musil's character also makes a journey from the historical center of activities in Vienna to the periphery in an unnamed Austrian province that is only marginally marked by history, and at last he moves completely out of the historical scene in the so called Garden-chapters, where the narrator talks about the "millennium Empire" and the "Empire of love."

One could suppose that it is merely Austrian literature that shows signs of decline and that only novels written in the German language use the drift

---

6 For a historical outline of the ties between the essay genre and the ideas of Europe, see Madsen.

away from the imperial center as a metaphor for a vanishing culture. This is emphatically not the case, as these characteristics seem to be significant for a great deal of the literature from the former Habsburg countries. Besides Musil, who grew up in the German-Czech town Brno, a first-class example is the Czech author Jaroslav Hašek, whose novel *The Good Soldier Svejk: and His Fortunes in the World War* (1921-23) describes a journey from Prague's warm inns along the Austro-Hungarian supply lines towards the front, which is throughout represented in a faint and unclear form. Another example is the Italian author Italo Svevo, who in his novel *Zeno's Conscience* (1923) again and again lets his protagonist smoke his last cigarette in an endless postponement of more important actions. One of the characteristics of this literature is exactly the large-scaled lack of action, heroism, and epic that characterizes the aftermath of an imperial picture of the world that does not exist any more. The protagonists always seem to get lost in endless contemplation and considerations instead of taking action. The kind of melancholy that is at stake in this prose has its most extreme manifestation in the novels of Joseph Roth, in which the old Habsburg provinces are depicted, but it can also be found in the works of a much more gloomy and enigmatic author such as Franz Kafka.

In Kafka's world Prague is never mentioned directly and his stories are stripped of identifiable local content and topical references: the city of Prague is always a mere decorative background, in quite the same sense as Canetti's Vienna. In Kafka's final novel, *The Castle* (1926), for example, places and names are consistently delocalized.

> "This village is Castle property, anybody residing or spending the night here is effectively residing or spending the night at the Castle. Nobody may do so without permission from the Count. But you have no such permission or at least you haven't shown it yet."
> K., who had half-risen and smoothed his hair, looked at the people from below and said: "What village have I wandered into? So there is a castle here?" (2)

The decline and downfall of an age-old European culture is important to Kafka's work, even though he does not belong to the authors who compulsively reflect on Europe in every other sentence. Without ever mentioning Judaism or the Habsburg Empire by name, Kafka is deeply engaged in exploring the complex and contradictory investment of educated, assimilated Jews in a society in which they were simultaneously an important economic force and cultural and religious aliens. Instead, seemingly endless buildings and odd constructions are described, and parallel to this endlessness, the space in which the protagonists are allowed to move is increasingly being limited.

The experience of being the sole remaining representative of a formerly celebrated European culture is characteristic of Broch, Musil, and Kafka. The experience can also be recognized among intellectuals such as Oswald Spengler and Karl Kraus, whose work *The Last Days of Mankind* (1926) is obviously about the decline of European culture. Paradoxically, this experience of being born too late and being alone is in many ways a common experience that can be detected in much of the literature and art from this period. Without turning to a simple form of mimesis, Carl E. Shorske, for example, has pointed out a connection between the general development in society and the emergence of specific works of art and literature (3). The tendencies of dissolution in the Habsburg Empire and the artistic representations of estrangement and identity crisis are intertwined. This way, many of the aesthetic and intellectual products can be said to transform political and societal changes into individual experience.

This transformation is also evident in the work of Canetti. The motif of destruction and downfall is central in the novel *Auto Da Fé* and subsequently continues to mark Canetti's imagination in the dramas *Wedding* (1932) and *Comedy of Vanity* (1934). Finally, it is reshaped and reborn in the autobiographical works *Tongue Set Free* (1977), *Torch in My Ear* (1980), and *Play of the Eyes* (1985). Turning to themes such as crowds, power, death, and metamorphosis, Canetti revived an entirely different side of the motif in the massive study on *Crowds and Power* (1960), a work which would require separate treatment. In *Auto Da Fé* Canetti describes the protagonist Peter Kien and his journey from the quiet rooms of a private library on the fourth floor into the noisy streets of Vienna, a chaos of hustlers, cripples, and beggars. The library is a European microcosm put together by important works from the history of thought from different nations and traditions. Given a voice, it becomes clear that though these nationalities and traditions despise each other, they despise everything that cannot fit in the bookshelves of the archive even more.[7] This is one aspect of the library, represented in the novel as

---

7   "At long last Kien turned his back on the fantastic inferno of German philosophy.

a small-scale model of European culture. The other aspect is related to Peter Kien, who lives in the library, but who distances himself from the German, the French, as well as the English tradition. In the novel Peter Kien is situated outside these different ideologies. He is a self-taught scholar and sinologist, and his profession provides him with a respectable way of abandoning social responsibility.[8] He measures everything from his obsession with books, their typography, size, style, and paper type. His 'knowledge' is home, as he states in the novel.[9] This intimate belonging to the library, which costs him his life in the closing scene when he burns along with all his books, runs parallel to the European history of thought, which in a certain sense can be said to come to an end with the First World War.

In this respect, it is interesting to look more precisely into how the library as a symbol of European culture is developed and transformed in Canetti's novel and how the self-taught scholar Peter Kien is transformed along with it. The vital element in the development is the fact that the library shrinks. After having married the plump housekeeper Therese Krumbholz, Peter Kien literally experiences that his liberty of action is being limited and that Therese lays claim on both his time and money. Kien draws up a contract that leaves Therese three fourths of the apartment if she promises to keep silent while they eat. One of the most important descriptions of this grotesque development is connected to the description of the library:

> In days of old, when every door stood open, a healing wind coursed through the library. Through the lofty skylights poured illumination and inspiration. In moments of excitement he had only to rise and stride fifty yards in one direction, fifty yards back again. The unbroken view of the sky was as uplifting as the invigorating distance. Through the glass above him he could see the condition of

---

He imagined that he would find compensation among the less grandiose and perhaps all too precise French, but he was received with a shower of raillery. [...] 'Go to the English!' they advised him. They were far too much interested in *esprit* to let matters come to a serious clash with him, and their advice was good." (Canetti, *Auto Da Fé* 87-88).

8   In his autobiography, Canetti singles out Eastern philosophy as the culprit for the asocial behavior on the part of many intellectuals of this era: "In renouncing sympathy for the world of one's immediate environs, one also surrendered responsibility for it." (*Play of the Eyes* 142). See also Donahue 76.

9   "Kien controlled his speech. Now and again his thoughts wandered towards knowledge. He seemed so near to it; how passionately he longed to spread himself on it. This was his home" (Canetti, *Auto Da Fé* 293).

the heavens, more tranquil, more attenuated than the reality. A soft blue: the sun shines, but not on me. A grey no less soft: it will rain, but not on me. A gentle murmur announced the falling drops. He was aware of them at a distance, they did not touch him. He knew only: the sun shines, the clouds gather, the rain falls. (59)

Peter Kien dreams about the majestic, open rooms of the library where he used to have the freedom to move as he wanted to and still keep a distance to the surroundings, and he becomes angry and irritated when he sees the closed doors that limit his freedom and cut him off from the rest of the library:

> But now the hermitage had dwindled. When Kien looked up from the writing desk, which was placed across one corner of the room, his view was cut off by a meaningless door. Three quarters of his library lay behind it; he could sense his books, he would have sensed them through a hundred doors; but to sense where once he had seen was bitterness indeed. (60)

While similar experiences of increasing isolation are unfolding in Kafka's descriptions of diminishing spaces, Canetti's claustrophobic description of the library at this particular time is one of the most significant manifestations of the cultural and mental nature of the shrinkage that is an integral part of the dissolution of the Habsburg Empire.[10] Equally important to this mindset is the fact that Kien, as the library shrinks and he gets locked up inside, has fantasies about the library growing to double its size due to the fortune he wrongly believes Therese has brought into the marriage. The grave discrepancy between the inner self and the world outside is forcefully illustrated by the fact that even after he has been expelled from the library, Peter Kien firmly believes that he carries all his books inside his head. Every night Kien unpacks the imaginary archive with great difficulty and every morning he deposits the books back inside his head. Here, the European library, and with it a vital cultural tradition, is reduced to a madman's illusion.[11]

---

10 Jacques Le Rider is very precise in his description of this matter: "'Central Europe' is not only an invention of the political language, a geopolitical *war game* of the superpowers of this world, serving to facilitate the rise of new markets, it is indeed also an everyday experience documented better than anywhere else in literature." (106).

11 The negative classification of Europe is also expressed by other characters in the novel. The dwarf Fischerle associates America with film actresses while Europe is represented as a home for cripples and beggars: "'Darling!' said the millionairess and pinched it, she loved long noses, she couldn't stand short ones; what's that man done with his nose, she said, when

Canetti's portrait of the protagonist Peter Kien confirms this picture of the European library as a secluded place that has long remained unspoilt and unaffected, but that now powerlessly experiences how disturbing forces break in. There is a progression in the novel that shows how Kien tries to manage the gradual reduction of space by inventing a myth that saves him and his library from reality and allows him to escape into the world of art and science through an attitude of nostalgia and denial. Exemplary for this strategy is the way Peter Kien imaginatively transforms the brutal caretaker Benedikt Pfaff into a lansquenet from the Middle Ages and refers to him as a "poor, late-born fellow" (105). Another time he turns himself into an old statue of an Egyptian high priest in order to escape from Therese (147). Kien thus applies the past as a protective shield against the present. The following passage from the chapter "Petrifaction" is interesting, because Kien here explains his escape from the closed rooms of the library into the open space of history:

> The present is alone responsible for all pain. He longed for the future, because then there would be more past in the world. The past is kind, it does no one any harm. For twenty years he had moved in it freely, he was happy. Who is happy in the present? If we had no senses, then we might find the present endurable. We could then live through our memories – that is, in the past. In the beginning was the Word, but it *was*, therefore the past existed before the Word. He bowed before the supremacy of the past. The Catholic Church would have much to be said for it, but it allowed too little past. [...] A Catholic priest is surpassed by any Egyptian mummy. Because the mummy is dead, he may think himself superior. But the pyramids are no more dead than St Peter's, on the contrary, they are much more alive, for they are older. [...] A time will come when men will beat their senses into recollections, and all time into the past. A time will come when a single past will embrace all men, when there will be nothing except the past, then everyone will have one faith – the past. (145)

What the citation suggests is that the past that Peter Kien takes refuge in has become a fortress that protects its inhabitants against all enemies. This

---

they went for a walk in the streets together, all noses were too short for her, she was beautiful and American, she was a blonde, like in the films, she was gigantically tall and had blue eyes, she only travelled in her own car, she was afraid of trams, because there you met cripples and pickpockets, who would steal your millions out of your pocket, a crying shame; what did she know of his former crippledom in Europe?" (Canetti, *Auto Da Fé* 335).

is a brief description of an attitude that was widely spread among European authors and intellectuals at the time and which we can call 'historicism,' even though Canetti is careful not to mention this disposition by name.[12] In Kien's eyes, the individual is a pawn, an insignificant instrument in the general development of mankind. While the ordinary man takes his existential condition and the importance of his personal experiences and petty struggles for granted, Kien surveys things from a higher plane, and he learns that our ability to protect ourselves against the dangers and annoyances of the present will be stronger if we base it upon the contemplation and interpretation of human history. In the character of Peter Kien, the historicist attitude is radicalized to the extreme: the criticism directed against civilization and the feeble celebration of history result in a narrow point of view that presents itself as a privileged insight.

In another passage, Kien's brother George looks back upon their childhood, and we learn that Peter has always been afraid of losing his ability to see (383). With crushing irony Canetti describes his protagonist as being born old and with the wish to withdraw from the present. This historical escapism is fundamental to the Habsburg myth mentioned earlier, as it appears in literature and is scrutinized by Canetti and his contemporaries. The lateness ascribed to Europe is clearly being ridiculed and scorned, yet it is still suggested that there are certain elements of beauty and truth that are hidden in this endangered world and that deserve to be preserved. The originality of the Austrian authors and intellectuals lies then in such conflicts between a fierce break with the past on the one hand and the duty of memory on the other, which is symptomatic of the work of Hugo von Hofmannsthal, between destruction of all traditional idols and the manic flight into an inner space, as can be seen in the work of Freud, and finally between decomposing analytic empiricism and the predisposition to use absolutes, as is the case in the philosophy of Wittgenstein.[13]

Age is a recurrent motif in the works of many post-First World War Viennese authors. In Canetti's novel, age stands for tradition, nostalgia, and

---

12   Oswald Spengler, Stefan George, and Egon Friedell are typical examples of this attitude towards history that focuses on the decline and downfall of European Culture.
13   Claudio Magris has described this conflict in Austrian literature in more detail (*Weit von wo* 150).

a longing for old times. This also holds true for the old state of Austria, as Stefan Zweig states in his life story *The World of Yesterday*:

> Austria was an old State, dominated by an aged Emperor, ruled by old Ministers, a State without ambition, which hoped to preserve itself unharmed in the European domain solely by opposing all radical changes. Young people, who always instinctively desire rapid and radical changes, were therefore considered a doubtful element which was to be held down or kept inactive for as long a time as possible. (33)

According to Zweig, what early 20th century literature on Europe has in common is not a specific European space but more likely a certain common age. There is a quite obvious tendency in much literature to reject every youthful *Sturm und Drang* and to favor the status quo. This attitude towards age is of course opposed to the political ideas about revolution and radical change that were spread widely in the years after the First World War and to those currents in art and literature that disregarded tradition and celebrated everything new. Peter Kien's distaste for youth, as something that has to be disposed of, should be viewed in this context:

> Young children ought to be brought up in some important private library. Daily conversation with none but serious minds, an atmosphere at once dim, hushed and intellectual, a relentless training in the most careful ordering both of time and of space, – what surroundings could be more suitable to assist these delicate creatures through the years of childhood. (10)

A thorough knowledge of the past is not passed on to the present as a natural heritage. Historical knowledge has to be cultivated and appropriated in isolation and according to a strict life model – such is Peter Kien's innermost belief. He thinks that action can stem only from longing and desire and that it can lead to nothing but chaos and disorder. His own character is a fine example of an inner life in which all tensions and conflicts are suppressed and confined to a vivid inner dialogue, rather than finding expression in fierce action. Over the years this model has turned into an odd symbiosis between uselessness and wisdom, a lack of ability to act that has been converted into clever caution and strategic thinking. Such is the case with the understanding between Peter Kien and Benedikt Pfaff: Kien pays the caretaker to make sure that nothing can disturb the library's peacefulness. In the final scene, however, the novel's irony towards the moderation and self-control that is inherent in this life model becomes obvious. Peter Kien laughs hysterically in the act of setting fire to his library.

If my view is correct, the stance towards Europe as 'something late' is one side of the European idea. The other side of this idea is then to save the best from European history, which is the objective of a particular European literature of which I have given some paradigmatic examples, so that not only ruins and rubble remain. On the one hand, we find the empty notion of Europe, the burned library, whereas, on the other hand, elements of beauty and truth are hidden underneath this damaged location or in its periphery. If we look back at the road we have travelled, we can now also understand that patience towards the delayed Europe which was announced in Canetti's Nobel Speech and which was connected to this particular Central European literature, the delayed Europe being just another way of portraying the old and weak Europe that cannot keep pace. The old and dying Europe can only be revived by seeking new life in the periphery and by giving marginal forms their due. Such is precisely the identifying mark of this literature. It is this dialectic that is at the heart of Canetti's work, which does not imply that behind the national and imperial state forms there is somehow a more real, authentic, or natural European culture. Still, for Canetti the collapse of civilization and the social order of the nation state that deprived him of his nationality did not leave him without a cultural and traditional orientation. On the contrary, it is precisely this situation that allowed him to become a truly European author.

Works Cited

Broch, Hermann. "The Style of the Mythical Age: An Introduction to Rachel Bespaloff's 'Iliad.'" *Dichten und Erkennen.* Zürich: Rhein-Verlag, 1955. 249-64.

——. "Über die Grundlagen des Romans *Die Schlafwandler.*" *Die Schlafwandler.* Frankfurt am Main: Suhrkamp, 1979. 728-33.

Canetti, Elias. *Auto Da Fé.* London: Pan Books, 1978.

——. *Tongue Set Free.* New York: Farrar, Straus, and Giroux, 1983.

——. *Play of the Eyes.* New York: Farrar, Straus, and Giroux, 1986.

——. "Dank: Rede bei der Verleihung des Nobelpreises für Literatur." *Wortmasken.* Frankfurt am Main: Fischer, 1995. 151-52.

Donahue, William Collins. *End of Modernism: Elias Canetti's Auto Da Fé*. Chapel Hill: The University of North Carolina Press, 2001.

Kafka, Franz. *The Castle*. New York: Schocken Books, 1998.

Kraus, Karl. *Worte in Versen*. München and Wien: Albert Langen – Georg Müller, 1964.

Le Rider, Jacques. *Mitteleuropa: Auf dem Spuren eines Begriffes*. Wien: Deuticke, 1994.

Lützeler, Paul Michael. *Hoffnung Europa: Deutsche Essays von Novalis bis Enzensberger*. Frankfurt am Main: Fischer, 1994.

Madsen, Anders Klinkby. "De hjemløse europæere." *Passage* 49 (2004): 103-9.

Magris, Claudio. *Der habsburgische Mythos in der österreichischen Literatur*. Salzburg: Otto Müller Verlag, 1966.

———. *Weit von wo: Verlorene Welt des Ostjudentums*. Wien: Europaverlag, 1974.

Musil, Robert. *The Man without Qualities, Volumes I-III*. London: Secker and Warburg, 1960.

Shorske, Carl E. *Fin-de-Siècle Vienna: Politics and Culture*. New York: Vintage Books, 1981.

Zweig, Stefan. *The World of Yesterday*. Lincoln: University of Nebraska Press, 1964.

Iulius Hondrila (K.U.Leuven)

Prague in Victorian Fiction: An Imagological Approach

Re-thinking Europe as a space of the dynamic cultural interplay of evolving identities in a continuously changing historical context is closely connected to the re-imagining, analysis, and understanding of the 'self-other' relations between Europeans throughout history. In this context, it is revealing to look at the role played by literary representations in processes of identity formation, in constructions of national awareness and of cultural difference, and in the dissemination of images of the 'self' and of the 'other' (i.e., auto- and hetero-images). Historically, literature has been one of the most powerful tools in constructing lasting auto-and hetero-images of places and people (Leerssen, "History and Method" 6). As a consequence, many scholars within the fields of literary and cultural studies have tried to deconstruct and critically analyze literature's role in processes of national identity formation. As Joep Leerssen points out, literary discourses are "by no means the least important ones when it comes to the formulation and dissemination of national stereotypes" ("Rhetoric" 281). Imagology, a research program that emerged in Western Europe in the aftermath of the Second World War and that built on the foundations of comparative literature, tries to deconstruct and analyze the literary hetero- and auto-images concerning character and identity as cultural discursive constructs constitutive of national identification patterns, or stereotypes, along with the mechanisms that make them possible (Leerssen, "History and Method" 5). As identities are fluid and transformative perceptions born in the interplay between 'self' and 'other,' between hetero- and auto-images, they are inextricably linked with images. The imagological approach requires both historical *contextualization* in the study of images as dynamic results of cultural diversity and interaction and in-depth *analysis* of the image qua image, i.e., qua persistent pattern of perception and representation (Barfoot 285-86). Literary depictions of the relationship between the Western European 'self' and the Eastern European 'other' are a case in point. The post-1989 context of European integration and EU enlargement has led to a renewed scholarly interest in past and present cultural encounters between Eastern and Western Europe. My aim in this article is to show the extent to which today's encounters are still shaped by past representations.

In order to demonstrate this, I will focus on Victorian literary representations of Eastern Europe(ans). Historically, Victorian literature is particularly significant. It was produced at a time when the British Empire was at its political and military zenith, and it therefore enjoyed a wide audience in and beyond Britain (Dolin 100). Furthermore, it coincided with a British 'rediscovery' of Eastern Europe, particularly after the revolutions of 1848, Britain's involvement in the Crimean War (1853-56), and the struggles for national emancipation throughout Eastern Europe in the second half of the century. Within this framework, the depictions of Prague, in those days the capital of the Habsburg province of Bohemia, and of its inhabitants (Czechs and Czech Jews) in the works of the English writers George Eliot and Anthony Trollope offer an opportunity to witness the way some parts of Eastern Europe were perceived in Britain at that time. George Eliot's *The Lifted Veil* (1859) and *Daniel Deronda* (1876), and Anthony Trollope's *Nina Balatka* (1867), *The Eustace Diamonds* (1871-73), and *Phineas Redux* (1873-74) are among the most prominent literary works of the period that depict Eastern Europe(ans). Eliot and Trollope are considered to belong to the elite of Victorian fiction, in so far as their literary status and output is concerned. The correspondence between these two prominent Victorian writers also indicates a personal friendship, and their literary works sometimes bear witness to the influence they had on each other (Escott 183-85). They both visited Prague and are likely to have found inspiration in each other's portrayals of the city (Hennesy 191-92). While their references to the nationalist struggles for independence there and throughout (Eastern) Europe are largely sympathetic, Prague appears in their novels as a backward and sometimes uncanny place. Their ambiguous depictions thus convey a sense of exoticism but at the same time also a certain uneasiness and fear of similar movements of emancipation throughout the British Empire, and indeed within Britain itself, and, most importantly, also of massive immigration from Eastern Europe (Winder 253-54).

The choice of Prague as the *topos* to demonstrate the persistence of heteroimages regarding Eastern Europe is, I am aware, far from obvious. After 1989, Prague has become a favorite tourist destination and one of the most prosperous cities in the whole of Europe. The picture of Prague today appears to be the complete opposite of that depicted in Eliot and Trollope's works. Can we then maintain that there are still parallelisms between past representations and today's perceptions? How does the threat of 'villainous Jews flooding England,' as is sometimes suggested in these novels, apply today, when only a few thousand members of that community can be found in Prague? Where are the thousands of Austrian-oppressed Czechs 'flocking to invade England', seeing that after 1989 Czechs not only gained their independence, but that they also recently have joined the EU and are already boasting a higher GDP per capita than some of the older EU member-states?

I would argue that, whereas (most of) the signifiers have changed, the signified persists. In travel literature Prague is now referred to not only as 'the Golden City,' but also as "the Capital City of Pickpockets" (Pinkava). It may be the Roma instead of the Jews this time, but they are equally intent on robbing the benign Brits of their possessions – and now, they can travel freely to Britain and even work there. That gypsies have replaced Jews in the British imagination regarding fears of invasion from 'the East' seems to be illustrated by the constant depictions in the British media of 'threatening waves of millions of Roma flooding the Kingdom' (Kundnani). Similar mechanisms engender similar fears. I therefore believe that it is worthwhile to analyze these national imagemes, i.e., these blueprints of discursively established character attributes concerning a given nationality or group of people (Leerssen, "Rhetoric" 279). I will particularly look at what I call 'the concentric circles of Eastern European otherness,' by which I refer to Prague, Czechs, and Czech Jews, as reflected in the depiction of Prague and its inhabitants. In doing so, I will analyze the mechanisms used by Eliot and Trollope in the construction of Prague imagemes as reflections of the interplay between Czech hetero-images and English auto-images. As I will point out, these imagemes are often characterized by an ambivalent polarity, present in both Eliot's and Trollope's works: how to reconcile a genuine spirit of tolerance and openness towards the 'other' with deep-seated pulsations of xenophobia and anti-Semitism? How to square a liberal and out-going cosmopolitanism with a nostalgic attachment to tradition and home?

The presence of Eastern Europe in British literature is not obvious. Historically, Britain had not been particularly involved with Eastern Europe although this started to change in the aftermath of the 1848 revolutions and the Crimean War. However, it is colonial history that has mostly occupied the British imaginary; it is the 'oriental other' that has generally provided the image of otherness *per se*. Eastern Europe was less known, and the limited knowledge that circulated was partly related to the Eastern Europeans who found refuge in England from persecutions in their own countries. Many of them were Jews, and they mostly settled in London (Winder 226-49). This immigration was accompanied by the emerging perception among Brits that most of these migrants were at best a bunch of swindlers, and at worst a pack of criminals threatening to undermine the empire, "the very lowest of mankind," as Coleridge put it (Winder 231). The widely read novels of Eliot and Trollope played an important role in the consolidation of these perceptions (165). They had a large audience at home, and from 1841 onwards, due to the German publisher Tauchnitz's cheap one-volume reprints in English, in addition to the many easily available translations, there was also an increasing European audience (O'Gorman 233).

Nor was Eastern Europe a major tourist destination for Victorian authors. Eliot and Trollope, however, formed an exception to the rule: they were both indefatigable travelers and both of them visited Prague; Eliot in 1858 and 1870, Trollope in 1865. They were also keen supporters of Czech struggles for national emancipation, and equally harsh critics of Czechs' intolerance towards Jews, their so-called unenlightened attitudes and general backwardness. At the same time, their visits left them with a deep sense of a genuine old European tradition preserved among Czechs and of an ancient Jewish tradition preserved among the Jewish community of Prague (Holt Hutton 254-55). Thus, they perceived Prague both as an authentic depository of centuries-old Judeo-Christian culture (Karl 286), "a singularly suitable environment immemorially associated with congenial traditions" (Escott 232), and as an ossified place where Austrian occupation arrested many developments. Prague was then perceived as being somewhere in between the 'savage,' more or less colonized 'East' and the enlightened, progressive 'ruling Britannia.'

Apart from many similarities, there is an important difference in their depictions of Prague. Towards the end of his literary career, Trollope adopted a devastatingly critical attitude regarding the imminent decay of a Britain swamped by (mostly Eastern European) Jews and other foreigners, underscoring "the danger outsiders pose to traditional values" in Britain (Tracy 161). Eliot, for her part, attempted a more 'positive' way out. She diagnosed the situation in a very similar way (Dolin 183-84, 226), but found the key elsewhere, to wit in nationalism. She was "one of those who believe that Judaism is not only a religion, but a nationality also" (Kaufmann 87). In her last novel, *Daniel Deronda* (1876), and in her last published book, *Impressions of Theophrastus Such* (1879), she explicitly declared that the best way to dispense with the 'undesirables' was to make them realize that the fulfillment of their dreams did not lie in 'a good British career,' but in the (re)establishment of a country of their own.

Written at a moment when, as Robert Tracy points out in his introduction to the novel, Trollope's status was fairly well established, his creative powers and personal reputation at their peak, *Nina Balatka* echoes the author's attempt at local coloring (Escott 231), at "descriptions of scenes and places, which has not been usual" for him (Trollope, *An Autobiography* 133). Trollope wrote his novel "immediately after" he visited Prague. Remarkably, upon reading the novel, Blackwood, his publisher, thought that Trollope had "thrown a perfectly foreign Prague atmosphere about all his characters so perfectly un-English that there is the sort of air of hardness about the story that one feels in reading a translation" (quoted in Hall 286). Prague did make a particularly strong impact on Trollope. At the time of the story, Prague was the capital of Bohemia, a province of the Austrian Empire, and thus a city under foreign rule. When Trollope visited Prague, Austrian rule had imposed German as the only legal language, had banned the use of Czech in schools and the publication of Czech newspapers, and had thereby increased political, linguistic, and ethnic tensions close to breaking point (Tracy in Trollope, *Nina Balatka* xi). Trollope was outraged by the Austrian barracks which were housing an army of occupation ready to immediately suppress the slightest Czech movement towards independence. The revolutionary events of 1848, which also affected Eastern Europe (Joll 112-18) – and particularly Prague, which was bombarded by the imperial forces of occupation, and where Czech nationalist demonstrators were shot down – were probably still fresh in readers' minds.

Regarded by some critics as "a problem Jew story" (Escott 223), the novel is a good example of English national auto-imaging accomplished through the hetero-imaging of the Czech 'others.' Trollope presents this 'otherness' through the authorial lens of an English writer familiar with Prague 'as it was and as he saw it,' and through the participating voices of an exclusively Czech cast in a novel entirely set in Prague. The novel portrays the difficulties besetting the love of a Czech Catholic girl, Nina Balatka, for her Czech Jewish friend, Anton Trendellsohn. Overcoming all prejudices and hindrances, the two lovers finally escape Prague, heading for a more tolerant place, in all likelihood London. In his depiction of the city and of Czech Catholic and Jewish life in Prague, Trollope demonstrates a thorough knowledge of the local traditions and cultural history. The familiarity with Czech and Jewish names, as well as repeated scenes featuring Nina on Charles Bridge, reveal Trollope's careful study of the geography and cultural history of Prague (Tracy in Trollope, *Nina Balatka* 385-92). These elements are instrumental in conveying a deep sense of immediateness, reality, and participation to the English reading audience, while at the same time contributing to the extrapolation of those aspects meant to emphasize the 'otherness' of Trollope's Eastern European cast.

The foreignness of the place is strongly underlined: "The aspect of the place is such as to strike with wonder a stranger to Prague" (5). Czechs are said to live in an obsolete world. The prevalent tone used by them when displaying their rabid hatred for Jews mostly runs along the lines of "Oh, I hate them! I do hate them! Anything is fair against a Jew" (77). Sophie Zamenoy, Nina's aunt, "could still hate a Jew as intensely as Jews ever were hated in those earlier days in which hatred could satisfy itself with persecution" (3). The obfuscated medievalism displayed by the Czechs in the novel is in profound dissonance with Trollope's liberalism and was unquestionably regarded as deeply un-English by his audience (Cheyette 30). The hetero-image of Czechs that is thus created – an unenlightened, oppressed and in their turn oppressive people – places them in an anachronistic periphery and at the same time assists in the contrastive construction of a tolerant and emancipated auto-image for the English reader. Equally, the subliminally disturbing parallelisms and fears awoken among the English audience blur 'the concentric circles of otherness,' underscoring the eminently ambiguous effectiveness of the imagemes thus created. As L.J. Swingle points out, what Trollope seems to be aiming at in his depiction of 'the concentric circles of otherness' mapped throughout *Nina Balatka* is "neither vindication of prejudice nor condemnation of prejudice, but rather cultivation of the unsettling idea that it is not safe to make prejudgements in either direction about the justice of prejudice" (128). Nina represents the felicitous exception here. She is constant in her love, devoted, defiant of prejudices and willing to pay the highest toll, be it her life or conversion to Judaism, in order to stay together with her Jewish lover, despite his hesitations and distrust. Her enlightened example, however, strengthens the exotic and uncanny obsoleteness of her compatriots even more. As James R. Kincaid observes, the novel's setting in Prague seemed to suggest to Trollope "civilizations with highly unsteady principles and therefore less stability than England" (145-46). Hall, who observes that the Czech Christians in the novel "are far more deeply prejudiced, more venal, dishonest, unscrupulous, inhuman" than their Jewish fellow countrymen, arrives at the essential point of the novel: its unequivocal indictment "of the old world anti-Semitism of Eastern Europe" (288).

The fact that Trollope depicts Prague almost as an anthropological site of Eastern European hetero-images places it on almost the same footing with exotic and primitive abodes of 'otherness' spread throughout the British Empire, although when visiting the British colonies Trollope tends to think of Prague as "romantic" (*South Africa* 2.171). At the same time there seem to be different degrees of 'otherness' among Eastern Europeans, with Czechs and Czech Jews crying, as it were, for maximum alterity. What appears to be clear is that the Czechs are infinitely less accommodating in their treatment of Jews than the English, whereas Czech Jews are clearly more exotic than their English counterparts (Rosenberg 282). This both reinforces the English reader's auto-image of superiority, and inculcates panic at the not too remote prospect of being confronted with a significantly large migration of these undesirable Eastern Europeans (Endelman 81; Cheyette 30). The causes for the possible migration are suggested subliminally: Jews will migrate because of Czech discrimination and Czechs will do so because of Austrian persecution. Indeed, the novel ends with Nina and Anton leaving Prague for a city "greater than Prague," most likely London, often described by Anton as one of the most tolerant places in the world (167, 191, 123). Therefore, what must have been perceived as a dreadful prospect by the English audience was the fact that these most un-English people might eventually lead to a fundamental challenge of the very enlightened ideals of rationality and tolerance that formed such an indivisible part of the English auto-image (Endelman 150-59).

Featuring for the first time in *Nina Balatka*, the Prague/Bohemian *topos* was carried on by Trollope in the third and fourth of his famous Palliser novels, *The Eustace Diamonds* (1871-73) and *Phineas Redux* (1873-74). In both novels, a not negligible role is played by the Czech Jewish swindler-*cum*-Rev. Joseph Mealyus/Emilius. Mercenary, deceitful, and hollow, he will suitably end up marrying the most prominent charlatan in the novels, Lizzie Eustace, who loves the "scheming hypocrite" precisely because he is able "to lie readily and cleverly, recklessly and yet successfully" (*The Eustace Diamonds* 762). Of doubtful origins – so doubtful that even T.H.S. Escott, Trollope's friend and biographer got these origins wrong: "partly Jew, partly Pole, and wholly scamp" (280) – he is thought in the beginning to be a Hungarian Jew, but in the last pages his true identity is revealed: "a Bohemian Jew," a polygamous "impostor" who came from Prague "to make a fortune" in England (767). He seems to be part of the 'exodus' of Czech Jews from Prague foreseen in *Nina Balatka*. As to the quality of the Czech Jewish émigré there can be no doubt: he is a mock preacher fooling the credulous (365), artful and coarse when uncomfortable (428), "a greasy, fawning, pawning, creeping, black-browed rascal," "utterly untrustworthy," with "an oily pretence at earnestness in his manner" and "a foulness of demeanor about him" which can only inspire "abhorrence of his society" (639). Another important reason why such "nasty, greasy, lying, squinting" Jews, "creatures to loathe" from Prague/Eastern Europe pose a real threat to the English 'self' is that, unlike their English rivals (Lord Fawn being the perfect example), who are emasculated, undecided, sickly, and cowardly, these foreigners possess "a certain manliness" which makes them successful in conquering English ladies and thus threatening the very essence of 'Englishness' (710).

For the reading audience, there is little comfort in the fact that Mr. Emilius, the bigamous impostor, is finally deserted by Lady Eustace after she learns that he has deceived her. The existence of his Czech wife "out in a strange country" is finally proven (*Phineas Redux* 357). Lady Eustace's friends embark on a trip to Prague where they find the wife, who admits having been "acquainted" with "a certain Yosef Mealyus," "a Jewish money-lender in the city." She now lives "somewhat merrily in Prague" on his spoils from England. An English clerk is sent to Prague to prove the bigamy, but later they find out that "he had been poisoned at his hotel," "though the poison had probably been nothing more than the diet natural to Bohemians" (358-59, 471). From Czechs feeding on poison to Transylvanians feeding on blood is but a small step. Important here is that Prague proves to be a murderous place sheltering Jewish bigamists, crooks, falsifiers, and criminals. The story develops into a full-fledged thriller when the English 'gentleman' in charge of the 'truth-finding campaign' is found murdered in London. The "cormorant" bigamist has now also become a murderer. In the end, the "horrid Jew" (386) is found guilty of bigamy, but not of murder, though Trollope ensures the reader that Mr. Emilius did commit that crime (390). A key witness at the trial is a Czech blacksmith "who naturally can't speak a word of English, and unfortunately can't speak a word of German, either" (528). He is brought from Prague by an impressive English crew who undertake "a roving tour through all the wilder parts of unknown Europe, Poland, Hungary, and the [Romanian] Principalities for instance" (511-12). In the end, despite the English public's "strong desire to prove 'the incubus' to have been a murderer, so that there might come a fitting termination to his career in Great Britain," he gets away with "penal servitude for five years" instead of being convicted to the gallows (573-76).

By 1875, when he had written *The Eustace Diamonds* (1871-73), *Phineas Redux* (1873-74), and *The Way We Live Now* (1875) – his most bitter and furious satire on the moral stench and decay of England, according to Frank Kermode (*The Way We Live Now* xxii) – Trollope's worst apprehensions had apparently come to fulfillment under the sign of the so-called "Melmotte era" (Sutherland in *The Way We Live Now* vii-ix). Thus, the foreign financier of uncertain origins who invades London represents not only the cause, but also the symptom of the moral gangrene that had been corrupting English society for a while. The network of mostly Jewish swindlers who permeate all levels of English private and public life in the novel, many of them reflections of real-life characters in Trollope's time, ominously reminded the reading audience that the most somber prophecies of *Nina Balatka* had indeed come true. By presenting a shattering picture of the condition the "paper kingdom" finds itself in, a kingdom where valueless pieces of paper create and destroy names, careers, families, and destinies, Trollope draws the final lines of a portrait he started with *Nina Balatka* and continued with *The Eustace Diamonds* and *Phineas Redux*, a portrait which delineates a devastating auto-image of Britain via the parallelisms offered by its Eastern European hetero-image (Tracy 158-84). Britain's decadence, which, in Trollope's opinion, started already in the aftermath of the Crimean War, is also due to Eastern European migration (Halperin 159-60, 236).

Let us now turn to George Eliot. Several entries in Eliot's journal from July 1858 convey her impressions recorded during her visit to Prague. We learn that she was struck by the Jewish burial-ground and the old Synagogue, noticed "a lovely dark-eyed Jewish child," whom she was glad "to kiss in all its dirt," and visited "the smoky old synagogue with its smoky groins," where "an intelligent Jew" was their cicerone and read them "some Hebrew out of the precious old book of the Law" (quoted in Haight 263). In an almost identical description, the synagogue later figures in *The Lifted Veil* (1859). The protagonist of the novel is Latimer, a young man educated in Geneva, who is "cursed with exceptional intelligence, afflicted with clairvoyance, suffering from the miseries of true prevision." This latter quality extends to a precise view of his own death (Haight 296). The narrative is situated in the immediate aftermath of the 1848 revolutions. Written at a bleak time in Eliot's life, the novel's conclusion reflects Eliot's determination at the time to "be a stranger and a foreigner on the earth for ever more" (Eliot, *Selections* 71). Latimer, a possible *alter ego* of Eliot's, is also "a wanderer in foreign countries" (Eliot, *The Lifted Veil* 42). The novel is centered on Latimer's vision of Prague, a vision of doom and of his own death. Eliot uses the Eastern European city she knew very well as the central symbol for her deep-seated anguish regarding the ultimate meaning and interchangeability of life, death and art (*The Lifted Veil* xx).

The word 'Prague' resonates strangely in Latimer's mind and triggers his first cauchemaresque vision of the city. Scorched by sun and dust, immutably ossified in its long-arrested development, Prague echoes Latimer's nihilistic *Weltanschauung*. Fallen into desuetude, captive to its pre-Enlightenment past, this city of "tanned time-fretted dwellings" that lead towards the "worn and crumbling pomp of the palace," represents a shocking sight (9). Trollope described the city in similar terms in *Nina Balatka*, noticing "the narrow crooked streets," "narrow passage," "gloomy wooden stairs, at the foot of which there hung a small lamp, giving just light enough to expel the actual blackness of night," leading to the rich Trendellsohns' "pinched-up, high-gabled," deserted-looking house, standing proof of their carelessness and slackness (9).

Depicted as perfect reflections of Latimer's spiritual and psychological decay, the inhabitants of Prague bring the morbid ill-boding otherness of the place to its climax. Dwellers of "a long-past century arrested in its course," they "live on in the stale repetition" of their memories, walking specters of an immolated past, trivial ephemerae "infesting" the Eastern European Pompeii they swarm in, "grim, stony beings," fathering "ancient faded children" (9). Doomed "to be ever old and undying," these revenants live on perpetually in the rigidity of their centuries-old habits, somnambular hallucinations of a diseased Demiurge whom they worship "in the stifling air of the churches" (9). This description defines a particular type of otherness characteristic of Prague: it is a backward, hardened, unenlightened place, torn up by religious hatred, but also, by virtue of its *ancienneté*, an authentic repository of lost traditions.

Eventually, Latimer confronts his vision with the reality of Prague by visiting it. Suitably, he arrives there at night, in a hot and dry season. He visits the old Jewish synagogue and his vision is confirmed: under the "blackened, groined arches" the Jewish guide reads him from "the Book of the Law" in "its ancient tongue," inducing the "shuddering impression" that "this strange, surviving withered remnant of medieval Judaism" is "of a piece" with his vision. Hurrying towards his anticipated doom, Latimer receives the final confirmation on Charles Bridge: a "patch of rainbow light on the pavement transmitted through a lamp in the shape of a star" (22-23). The star-shaped light projected onto the pavement reflects his withering feeling of "shrivelled death-in-life" that permeates his being in the old Jewish synagogue (9-10, 22-23). The scene reproduces *ad litteram* Eliot's own experience in Prague (91). Eliot uses the Czech-Jewish symbolism as a reminiscence of a decaying past projected onto the future, thus setting up a clear hetero-image of Prague and Czechs as archaic, underdeveloped, and anachronistic, but at the same time strange depositories of forgotten traditions. In doing so, she challenges the English auto-image which is constructed along a deterministic belief in an ever-enlightening linear progress, but which risks losing the "vital connexion with the past," a past that in England can only be recalled "by an effort of memory and reflection" (Eliot, *Selected Critical Writings* 283). At the same time, she launches a lasting hetero-image of Eastern European backwardness.

Though barely mentioned in the novel, Prague is decisive in the 'Jewish plot' of *Daniel Deronda* (1876). In this plot, Daniel Deronda is a model English gentleman who discovers his Jewishness after having already and repeatedly manifested his elective affinities with Jews of all walks of life in London. He will eventually emigrate to Palestine in order to help establish a Jewish state, accompanied by his Eastern European Jewish wife Mirah Lapidoth, whom he met in London. Mirah, a Jewish singer and Deronda's companion in his Zionist project, comes "a long way, all the way from Prague" (170), where she had lived with her father in a dark place, hardly lit by "the strange bunches of lamps" (186-87). Consistent with its image in *The Lifted Veil*, Prague is again portrayed as a nightmarish city. It appears in the form of Mirah's memories of her father's corruption, as he "never observed the Laws, but lived among Christians just as they did" (Herzog 52), as the place where he tried to sell her to a Viennese Count from whom she finally managed to escape to England, the ghost of the past preventing her from being truly free. After their marriage, Deronda and Mirah leave for Palestine to help establish a Jewish state. What is thus redeemed in the end is not Prague, but its (Judaic) cultural legacy. As in *Nina Balatka*, this legacy is best preserved abroad, in England or in a future state for the Jews. Prague is irrevocably interred in the dusty memory of its past, though subliminally it is still the preserver of ancient Jewish tradition.

In *Daniel Deronda* Eliot uses the 'Jewish plot' in a larger attempt to revive the national character of Victorian Britain (Tischler Millstein 1). I here want to question those interpretations of the novel that choose to see Eliot's "separateness with communication" (Eliot, *Daniel Deronda* 620) as an inclusive and conciliatory modern cosmopolitanism. I believe that her Zionist project is based on three cornerstones: genuine sympathy for the oppressed and persecuted, a firm belief in racial homogeneity and in a cohesive identity built on shared memories, traditions, and culture, and finally a real apprehension regarding the pervasiveness of less-God-than-Mammon-oriented Jews. Eliot's "separateness with communication" is a type of anti-assimilationist nationalism that may grow into universal sympathy (Waterman Ward 110). Her concept of cultural identity remains, however, racially based (Anderson

45). Rural traditionalism is the alternative to a deracinated and decadent cosmopolitanism (Eliot, *Selected Critical Writings* 274). Ultimately, it is only in the higher sphere of art that these conflicts are resolved: Deronda's Jewish mother and the German-Slavic-Semite Klesmer, both artists, belong to the privileged few who overcome the 'nationalist-cosmopolitan dichotomy' and find fulfillment in art and, in Klesmer's case, in inter-religious marriage. The marriage between Klesmer and Catherine Arrowpoint, an English aristocrat, proves that a certain elite may transcend ethnicity, religion, and prejudices. But this is not Eliot's answer for the many.

To prove this point, I would argue that Deronda and Mirah's final 'dismissal' to the Promised Land, notwithstanding Eliot's genuine attempts to understand and sympathize with the plight of Jews, reflects her deep-seated belief about the viability of cosmopolitanism, overtly expressed in "The Modern Hep! Hep! Hep!," the last essay of her last book published in 1879, *Impressions of Theophrastus Such*: "it is a calamity to the English, as to any other great historic people, to undergo a premature fusion with immigrants of alien blood" (158). After criticizing "the marring of our speech," Eliot points out, in the same vein as Trollope, that this linguistic catastrophe is still "a minor evil compared with what must follow from the predominance of wealth-acquiring immigrants, whose appreciation of our political and social life must often be as approximative or fatally erroneous as their delivery of our language" (159). Eliot's solution, however, is not persecution, against which she fought all her life, but the resuscitation of nationalist feeling among all those oppressed undesirables, and particularly Jews, many of Eastern European extraction, so that they may return and build anew *their* country: "but in a return from exile, in the restoration of a people, the question is not whether certain rich men will choose to remain behind, but whether there will be found worthy men who will choose to lead the return" (163). Emigration, not immigration, Eliot suggests, is the way out, so that both Britons and Eastern European Jews may be happy.

The aim of this essay has been to propose a different way of re-thinking Europe, by undertaking an imagological investigation of the relationship between the English 'self' and the Eastern European 'other,' as reflected in the construction of persistent auto-and hetero-images. I have chosen those works written by two of the most prominent Victorian writers, George Eliot and Anthony Trollope, in which the Czech city of Prague plays an instrumental role in conveying to the British audience complex but distinct images of a largely unknown European 'other' and of itself. If Eliot and Trollope differ in many ways in their depictions of Eastern Europe(ans), in one respect they agree: they share an equally strong apprehension about the detrimental effects of increased immigration from Eastern Europe to Britain. However, they place this process against the background of what seems to them a morally, socially, and politically deteriorating British society. I therefore believe that the relevance of an imagological analysis of these texts can hardly be understated today, when similar signs of anxiety at the new EU-citizens from Eastern Europe migrating to Britain are once again making themselves apparent throughout the Isles.

Works Cited

Anderson, Amanda. "George Eliot and the Jewish Question." *The Yale Journal of Criticism* 10.1 (1997): 39-61.

Barfoot, C.C., ed. *Beyond Pug's Tour: National and Ethnic Stereotyping in Theory and Literary Practice*. Amsterdam: Rodopi, 1997.

Cheyette, Bryan. *Constructions of 'The Jew' in English Literature and Society: Racial Representations, 1875-1945*. Cambridge: Cambridge University Press, 1993.

Dolin, Tim. *George Eliot*. Oxford: Oxford University Press, 2005.

Eliot, George. *Daniel Deronda*. Oxford: Oxford University Press, 1984.

———. *Selections from George Eliot's Letters*. Ed. Gordon Haight. New Haven: Yale University Press, 1985.

———. *Selected Critical Writings*. Ed. Rosemary Ashton. Oxford: Oxford University Press, 1992.

———. *Impressions of Theophrastus Such*. Iowa: University of Iowa Press, 1994.

———. *The Lifted Veil* and *Brother Jacob*. Ed. Sally Shuttleworth. London: Penguin Books, 2001.

Endelman, Todd M. *The Jews of Britain: 1656 to 2000*. Berkeley and Los Angeles: University of California Press, 2002.

Escott, T.H.S. *Anthony Trollope: His Public Services, Private Friends, and Literary Originals*. Honolulu: University Press of the Pacific, 2004.

Haight, Gordon. *George Eliot: A Biography*. London: Penguin Books, 1968.

Hall, N. John. *Trollope: A Biography*. Oxford: Clarendon Press, 1991.
Halperin, John. *Trollope and Politics: A Study of the Pallisers and Others*. London: Macmillan, 1977.
Hennesy, James Pope. *Anthony Trollope*. Herts: Panther, 1973.
Herzog, Annabel. "Tale of Two Secrets: A Rereading of Daniel Deronda." *Differences: A Journal of Feminist Cultural Studies* 16.2 (2005): 37-60.
Holt Hutton, Richard. *George Eliot as Author and George Eliot's Life and Letters*. Kila, Montana: Kessinger Publishing, 2005.
Joll, James, ed. *Britain & Europe: Pitt to Churchill 1793-1940*. London: Oxford University Press, 1967.
Karl, Frederick R. *George Eliot, Voice of a Century: A Biography*. New York and London: Norton, 1995.
Kaufmann, David. *George Eliot and Judaism: An Attempt to Appreciate 'Daniel Deronda'*. Honolulu: University Press of the Pacific, 2005.
Kincaid, James R. *The Novels of Anthony Trollope*. Oxford: Oxford University Press, 1977.
Kundnani, Arun. "The Media War against Migrants: A New Front." *IRR News* 21 January 2004. August 2007. <http://www.irr.org.uk/2004/january/ha000008.html>.
Leerssen, Joep. "The Rhetoric of National Character: A Programmatic Survey." *Poetics Today* 21.2 (2000): 267-92.
———. "History and Method of Imagology in Literary Studies." 2006. August 2007. <http://cf.hum.uva.nl/images/info/historymethod.html>.
O'Gorman, Francis, ed. *A Concise Companion to the Victorian Novel*. Oxford: Blackwell, 2005.
Pinkava, Vaclav. "Without Prejudice." *Central Europe Review* 1.3 (1999). August 2007. <http://www.ce-review.org/99/3/pinkava3.html>.
Rosenberg, Edgar. *From Shylock to Svengali: Jewish Stereotypes in English Fiction*. California: Stanford University Press, 1960.
Swingle, L.J. *Romanticism and Anthony Trollope: A Study in the Continuities of Nineteenth-Century Literary Thought*. Michigan: The University of Michigan Press, 1990.
Tischler Millstein, Denise. "Lord Byron and George Eliot: Embracing National Identity in Daniel Deronda." *Forum: The University of Edinburgh Postgraduate Journal of Culture and the Arts* 1 (2005). August 2007.

<http://forum.llc.ed.ac.uk/issue1/Millstein_Byron.html>.

Tracy, Robert. *Trollope's Later Novels*. Berkeley and Los Angeles: University of California Press, 1978.

Trollope, Anthony. *The Way We Live Now*. Oxford: Oxford University Press, 1982.

———. *Nina Balatka* and *Linda Tressel*. Oxford: Oxford University Press, 1991.

———. *The Way We Live Now*. London: Penguin Books, 1994.

———. *An Autobiography*. London: Penguin Books, 1996.

———. *Phineas Redux*. London: Penguin Books, 2003.

———. *The Eustace Diamonds*. London: Penguin Books, 2004.

———. *South Africa*. Vol. 1-2. Gloucestershire: Nonsuch Publishing Ltd., 2005.

Waterman Ward, Bernadette. "Zion's Mimetic Angel: George Eliot's Daniel Deronda." *Shofar: An Interdisciplinary Journal of Jewish Studies* 22.2 (2004): 105-15.

Winder, Robert. *Bloody Foreigners: The Story of Immigration to Britain*. London: Abacus, 2004.

Bart Keunen (University of Ghent)

European Identity from Normality to Immanence

The discipline of comparative literature has a long tradition of research on the topics of national identity and its relation to literature. While it was certainly also concerned with supranational relations between national literatures, for a long time the cultural identities of nations and ethnic groups were considered the very core of the discipline. The frame of reference of many 19th and prewar 20th century comparatists was very much indebted to the German idealist tradition – Herder's and Hegel's concept of *(Volks)geist* in particular. As Paul Michael Lützeler's work shows, the 'imagined community' of Europe was indeed an important theme within this old-fashioned branch of 'cultural studies.' In the course of its development as an academic discipline, comparative literature increasingly distanced itself from its idealist ancestors and came to focus on the semiotics of literary language. In recent decades, however, new forms of research have rediscovered the concept of identity in the wake of poststructuralist French philosophers and their heirs in literary theory. Nowadays, identity formation is again conceived as one of the most important aspects of literary communication in such fields as postcolonial studies, gender criticism, and cultural materialism. Still, the scholars working within these theoretical frameworks will no longer affirm a direct link between literature and nationality or transnationality but will instead note that literature is only indirectly useful to make statements about nationality and cultural identity.

Newer forms of comparative literature concentrate on social processes that have little to do with the construction of (supra)national identities; post-Foucauldian concepts such as 'power' and 'normalization' are nowadays conceived as the basic mechanisms of identity formation and are responsible for the fact that older debates on *Weltliteratur* or national identity are considered more or less irrelevant. A consideration of the relationship between literature and cultural identity is nevertheless still possible in contemporary comparative literature. The study of literature can offer some insight into the cultural toolkit used in the course of Western history, and these insights can then be used to gain a new perspective on the politics of identity in general. A modest contribution of contemporary comparatists to questions concerning Europe and its cultural identity seems to consist in the study of the toolkit behind some of the ideological strategies deployed by the European subject since the advent of modernity. A key concept in this kind of analysis would be 'the ethical impulse' that is inherent in writing strategies. As Thomas Pavel argues, literature is a cultural product that continually raises moral issues:

> the novel raises, with extraordinary precision, the philosophical question of whether moral ideals are inherent in their world, for, if they are, why do they seem so remote from human behavior, and if they are not, why does their normative value impose itself so clearly on us? For the novel to raise this question is to ask whether, in order to defend their ideals, humans should resist the world, plunge in to try to defend moral order, or concentrate on trying to correct their own frailties. (3)

Throughout literary history, most writers tried to stage moral problems in their work; and by studying the implicit moral ideals writers tend to promote, one almost automatically becomes attentive to reflections on cultural topics as well. Some of the moral ideals which emerged in the course of Western literary history will be discussed in this essay in order to illustrate the attitude of writers towards traditions and cultural identity. Rather than presenting a catalogue of ideals that can be used to establish a foundation for a European cultural identity, I will sketch two critical positions concerning idealist versions of the concept of cultural identity. Both positions integrate modern, anti-traditionalist moral norms in their critique of idealist conceptions of 'normality.' The first position consists in a radical refusal of all forms of idealist thinking and is to be found within vanguard circles of the early 20th century. The second position tends to a somewhat ambivalent critique of traditionalist ideologies and can be labelled 'liberal' or reformist.

The issue of 'avant-garde and politics' is an ideal starting point to capture the scope of the late modern attitude towards collective identity construction. The process of political modernization is one of the most important contextual factors in studying the avant-garde. This process consists in the foundation of parliamentary democracy and political parties, the establishment of modern states, and the growing importance of citizenship and international political decision-making. But the process is relevant for a more fundamental reason: political modernity is a cultural condition that reproduces a paradoxical mix of power conceptions, a condition that confronts modern man with, on the one hand, the appeal of individual sovereignty and, on the other hand, the necessity of collective kinds of sovereignty. This paradoxical condition seems to impel the avant-garde artist to confront the question of personal as well as of social identity formation. Individual sovereignty is defined by most avant-garde artists as a subversion of normality, while collective power is seen as the symptom of Western ideals of normality, a conception of personal and social identity that would, according to Jürgen Habermas, gradually become hegemonic during the 20th century.

In *Empire,* the provocative work of political philosophy by Antonio Negri and Michael Hardt, we find a statement that can easily be applied to the political positions of avant-garde movements. Negri and Hardt state

> that modernity should be understood not as uniform and homogeneous, but rather as constituted by at least two distinct and conflicting traditions. The first tradition is that initiated by the revolution of Renaissance humanism, from Duns Scotus to Spinoza, with the discovery of the place of immanence and the celebration of singularity and difference. The second tradition, the Thermidor of the Renaissance revolution, seeks to control the utopian forces of the first through the construction and mediation of dualisms, and arrives finally at the concept of modern sovereignty as a provisional solution. (140)

At the beginning of the second part of their study, Negri and Hardt assert that we can distinguish between two Europes, or rather between two tendencies in European modernity. Modernity is, on the one hand, the historical tendency towards fragmentation and an almost anarchic liberation of thought and, on the other hand, the opposite inclination towards totalization, normalization, and exclusion. The former tendency can be regarded as a Nietzschean sovereignty directed at the power of the individual will (freedom of speech, freedom of association, freedom of settlement, etc.), while the latter must be seen as an adaptation to forms of rational order (the state, public morality, ideological belief systems, technocratic or bureaucratic rationality – all the strategies within Western civilization mentioned by Foucault, Deleuze, Weber, and other Horkheimers). Regarding European avant-garde movements from the viewpoint of this paradox allows us to detach the social attitudes of avant-garde artists from the specific ideological and party-political debates and contexts in which they were embedded. In spite of the heterogeneous nature of the political alliances they enter into, avant-garde artists demonstrate that they are trying to free themselves from totalizing interpretation systems and prescribed action schemata. Their position is intimately related to the process of political modernization because, in accordance with the demands and restrictions of modern forms of society, they insist on the role of individual growth and of an ever problematical norm of individuality. They contribute to the dominant tendency of political modernization because they view social change as a project that has to depart from the possibilities of man. The cultural position of radical artists in the 20th century can be explained both as a symptom of the modernization process as it asserts itself on an individual level and as a critical comment on the collective forms of modern life.

The most notable way in which political modernity emerges in avant-garde writings is through the critical stance vis-à-vis the established forms of collective sovereignty and vis-à-vis 'normality' as a social identity construction. I could quote countless statements by artists that illustrate the pre-eminent commonplace in avant-garde research, i.e., the idea that the political attitude of the avant-garde fundamentally consists in a radical anti-establishment stance. The overt rebellion against various forms of collective sovereignty is not only negative but equally reveals the implied, 'positive' understanding of power; the avant-garde artist unearths the "idea of the immanence of power in opposition against the transcendent character of modern European sovereignty" (Hardt and Negri 164). Although different artists present different images of the 'transcendent' enemy and although the ideals that are defended and the ideologies that are rejected can switch places in various movements (take the position of internationalism and nationalism in Dada and futurism, for example), the underlying logic remains virtually identical: it consists essentially in the call for a community of autonomous sovereign individuals that frees itself from organized forms of power and their detrimental effects on individuals. Richard Huelsenbeck is a good example of the resistance toward the 'transcendent' aspect of power. Around 1920, he expressed his cult of freedom in exalted terms ("The dadaist is the freest man on earth") (Huelsenbeck, *Almanach* 6) and, in his autobiography from the thirties, he rephrases the love for freedom in terms of sovereignty: "[Der Dadaist] nimmt für sich die Souveränität in Anspruch" (quoted in Bru 305).

The tendency to emphasize individual sovereignty is supplemented by a critique of several forms of transcendent power constellations. The navigation between different political alternatives and, above all, the never-ending condemnation of 'wrong' alternatives are typical for 20th century artists. Tzara's comments on Bolshevism illustrate this: "Le communisme est une nouvelle bourgeoisie partie de zéro; la révolution communiste est une forme bourgeoise de la révolution. Elle n'est pas un état d'esprit, mais une 'regrettable nécessité.' Après elle, l'ordre recommence" ("communism is a new bourgeoisie starting all over again; the communist revolution is a bourgeois revolution. It is not a spiritual state, but a 'regrettable necessity.' After it, order starts over again") (quoted in Pop 318). Tzara's attitude demonstrates the importance of the paradox of modernity for the political stance of avant-garde art. The political condemnations are permeated by statements on the intersection between individual and collective sovereignty. Transcendent power is put under suspicion not in the service of a specific ideological alternative, but because of the notion of social identity that is inherent in all existing ideologies. The notorious avant-garde hatred of the bourgeois exemplifies this suspicion and can in a sense be viewed as a projection of the collective logic of sovereignty onto an individual attitude (that of the bourgeois). The *Bürger*, the *Spießer* frequently represents the interiorized collective sovereignty that is assumed to typify the ruling class in advanced societies. This position involves a mentality that displays a rigid fondness of 'normality,' a mentality of moralism, self-discipline, law-abidance, and prudence, a mentality that perfectly supports the rational societal order aspired to by modern societies. Given that 'the bourgeois' could surface everywhere and is in fact part of the personality structure of the modern individual, an unambiguous positive choice for a specific societal blueprint could never gain a consensus within the avant-garde community.

Within the frame of this historical meditation, avant-garde movements figure as a late modernist cultural phenomenon. Late modern subjects experience collective sovereignty and the forms of identity it generates as problematic. Normality in particular is seen as the result of contemporary power mechanisms. Instead of the ideal of normality, avant-garde artists invoke a picture of collective identity that is temporal and in a permanent state of revolution. Moreover, a perfect collective identity is born out of individual sovereignty and thus has to avoid conflict with the immanent laws of personal experience. This attitude toward personal and collective identity would certainly have seemed absurd to pre-modern man. For centuries, Western man conceived his individual identity as essentially related to collective forms of identity formation.

In order to clarify the exceptional position of the avant-garde writers, let us dwell upon pre-modern conceptions of literary communication and identity formation found in pre-modern cultures. In these cultures, we find a close link between narrative form (the epic is paradigmatic here) and a notion of personal identity that is grounded in metaphysics. Simplifying somewhat, we can say that the epic can be related to 'community religions' – a concept with a strong tendency towards the absolute in terms of community, tradition, and ancestors. Collective sovereignty is legitimized by metaphysics and, as a result, individual sovereignty is devaluated as a mere function of this metaphysics. In his recent study *The Mind and Its Stories*, Patrick Hogan formulates the values of heroism in ancient World Literature as follows: "the triumph of the hero is a triumph of the entire nation. The condition of the individual is generalized to the group" (225). And the reverse is also true: the condition of the group is generalized to the individual. The hero in epic works is a stand-in for 'normality.' Of course, the epic hero has often been depicted as a sovereign individual, but his individual agency is always a function of collective sovereignty. For instance, at first sight the adventures of the chivalric hero seem to affirm the hero's individual sovereignty when they in fact only acquire meaning within a broader framework. For the knight who sets out on an adventure, every single act has a metaphysical meaning; opposing forces never arise by accident. Just as the *Geist* in Hegel can only materialize due to the (apparently) Other, so the transcendent value system also materializes in the romance thanks to the (apparent) sovereignty of the hero. Like the Messiah in Christian eschatology, the epic hero is an enforcer of the law, a sacred individual who transforms the world of selfish individuals into a new world. At the end of the epic, the hero helps the eschatological development to come to an end; in the narrative closure the hero and the world come to the point where the final truth of the value system can be revealed. The narrative ending is crucial to an epic because it is by means of a representation of the final state of the world that this genre is made useful for the construction of social identity. The final state of the world is very often based on a conception of a sacred past, of an original state. In the epic, moral values do not emerge through a historical process in which social values are created – rather, they have a stable position outside of time (Keunen 95). This eschatological thought pattern determines the explicitly nationalist nature of some epics. National traditions belong to the core of the value systems propagated in epics, and as such they are fundamental for the work of social identity construction that the epics undertake. According to Bakhtin (but also Georg Lukács), in the epic the "normative national tradition" is at stake. Typical for epics is the "devaluation of the future" (Bakhtin, "Forms of Time" 148) and of progress, because what is foremost at stake is the "absolute national past" (Bakhtin, "Epos" 12). Epics are all about "tradition, sacred and sacrosanct, evaluated in the same way by all and demanding a pious attitude toward itself" (16).

The eschatological – and in a sense nationalist – closure is the point of culmination of a concept of sovereignty based on metaphysics. Yet the modernization of the Western world gradually forced European man to take a more modest stance. As mentioned earlier, modernity has essentially to do with the acceptance and celebration of immanence. In late medieval cities and in early modernity, a new image of human existence appears, an image the major traits of which are growth, self-development, and faith in the sovereignty of individual action. In several of his texts, particularly in his study of Rabelais, Mikhail Bakhtin states that Rabelais, through his parody of medieval customs, dismisses the religious medieval image of mankind in order to shape his own 'human' view of existence. To a certain extent, Rabelais experiences the medieval worldview as 'unnatural' and purposefully chooses a world in which the material bond between mankind and the world can be represented as viable and natural. In order to conceptualize this bond, Rabelais draws on cultural traditions that had been dormant for a long time in the unwritten material culture. Typical for those folk traditions is a concept of time that becomes extremely powerful in modernity, namely the concept of what Bakhtin calls idyllic time. The conception of time in rural societies is of course determined by labor in the fields, by the rhythm of the periods of sowing, growing, harvesting, and resting. This collective concept of time is further reflected in the course of human life ('birth-growth-death' in its most elementary form). As a result, growth processes and individual development become the main focus: "Insofar as individuality is not isolated, such things as old age, decay and death can be nothing more than aspects subordinated to growth and increase, the necessary ingredients of generative growth" ("Forms of Time" 207).

This time concept becomes the core of the work of Rabelais and, a few centuries later, of one of the most characteristic genres of high modern literature, the *Bildungsroman*. In pre-modern societies, social identity was seen as an eternal present, as an original state that had to be reaffirmed by the individual. In contrast, modern man sees social identity as something evolving, as a continuous discovery and colonization of the future – a process that is monumentalized in the *Bildungsroman*. Individual agency is likewise redefined: it becomes the most important instrument in the shaping of society and in the creation of the future. The "novel of emergence," Bakhtin writes, illustrates a world in which

> man's individual emergence is inseparably linked to historical emergence. In such novels as *Gargantua and Pantagruel, Simplicissimus*, and *Wilhelm Meister*, individual man is no longer within an epoch, but on the border between two epochs, at the transition point from one to the other. This transition is accomplished in him and through him. He is forced to become a new, unprecedented type of human being. What is happening here is precisely the emergence of a new man. The organizing force held by the future is therefore extremely great here [...] It is as though the very foundations of the world are changing, and man must change along with them. (Bakhtin, "The Bildungsroman" 23-24)

Bakhtin helps us move toward a better understanding of the relation between bourgeois identity formation and social identity in capitalist societies. When he describes and analyzes the inflections that idyllic time has undergone throughout the history of modern literature, he comes to a conception of bourgeois individuality by pointing to the phenomenon of the "interiorized idyll." The idyll is a crucial genre for an understanding of social identity, as it is not only closely linked with the aesthetics of elite groups in almost all Western societies, but it is also used in many narratives as an emblem of community values. In this sense, idyllic scenes often function in adventure stories as both opening and closing scenes. While the eschatological pattern in epic literature that I described earlier sometimes takes the form of a return to an idyllic community, in modernity idyllic time becomes a factor of individual agency. Following Rabelais, authors like Rousseau aided the survival of the idyll by sublimating it as a philosophical ideal. The idyll in Rousseau does not embody some peculiar form of literary atavism but instead re-fashions social identity into a useful, incisive tool that can compensate for what Bakhtin calls "the isolated, egoistic bourgeois *individuum*" ("Forms of Time" 231, italics in original). Goethe equally reworked the idea of the idyll and looked for ways to constitute it as the basis for revaluating the cold, alien world of modernity.

Bakhtin's comments on Rousseau and Goethe demonstrate the same tension mentioned earlier regarding the historical avant-garde movements. Bakhtin sees an abstract, totalitarian form of sovereignty in the world of capitalism and at the same time notes that individual sensibility and the individual form of sovereignty can help to counter this tendency. Goethe, for instance, believed it "necessary to constitute this great world on a new basis, to render it familiar, to humanize it. [...] In place of the limited idyllic collective, a new collective must be established capable of embracing all humanity" ("Forms of Time" 234). While from this perspective the modern novel could be said to anticipate the radical stance of the historical avant-garde movements, such a conclusion would be all too hasty. From Franco Moretti's *The Way of the World*, his famous study on the *Bildungsroman*, we can learn that the celebration of the future and of individual freedom was already betrayed as early as the beginning of bourgeois cultural hegemony. The abstract idea of a new, democratic, and progressive collective identity based on the idea of individual growth and autonomy was almost immediately countered by what Norbert Elias has called the "civilization process." Modern subjects do not see themselves as devoted citizens by divine or military order, but they rather like to cultivate the image of a person who acts morally in a spontaneous way. In essence, this attitude is a symptom of a phenomenon that Elias dubbed "emotional and moral self-coercion." The *Bildungsroman* exemplifies this fundamental tendency: far from being saviors of the metaphysical order, modern heroes are extrapolations of our tendency towards self-coercion. In a sense, they seem to be emblems of unbound freedom and of a life that is more adventurous than that of ordinary people, but their attitude is, in fact, more ambiguous. They not only represent human freedom, but they also illustrate the troubles experienced in a world that forces individuals into the "social correctness" of self-coercion.

Moretti diagnoses this tendency as the "comfort of civilization." Modern man desires psychological regularity and is ready to sacrifice his individual sovereignty to a new transcendent identity construct: "The clash between individual autonomy and social integration" becomes, according to Moretti, the pretext for an "elusion of whatever may endanger the Ego's equilibrium" (12). In a rich reflection on the intersection of personal and social identity and on the tension between what I have called individual and collective sovereignty, Moretti comes to the following conclusion: "The image of the escape from freedom, which places the desire to 'belong' within the individual psyche itself, is, as it were, its solution [...] socialization is no longer felt as a mere necessity but as a value choice: it has become 'legitimate'" (67). This tendency towards social correctness is the other side of the idyllic ideals of modern man. Idyllic time not only stands for growth and development but also for normality, regularity, and repetition. Just as idyllic community life repeats itself in the rhythm of seasons and generations, the interiorized idyllic space is a psychological world of strict moralism and dogmatic ideals. The interiorized idyll, in this sense, epitomizes the persistence of mythical thinking in a seemingly anomic and profane society. The *Bildungsroman* can be seen as a cultural tool for the achievment of a new social identity based on such a mythical idyllic conception. It can be viewed as a genre that cultivates immanent power, but also as an instrument for the construction of transcendent identities. If one reads Bakhtin against the grain, we can find confirmation for this statement. For Bakhtin, the perfect *Bildungsroman* had to be structured like the Hegelian thought-system. Such a novel is also a kind of eschatology, yet it does not describe the world in terms of messianic actions; instead, the Hegelian-eschatological patterns are preserved in the fate of the characters. Regarding this pattern, Bakhtin notes that "[a] man must educate or re-educate himself for life in a world that is, from his point of view, enormous and foreign; he must make it his own, domesticate it. In Hegel's definition, the novel must educate man for life in bourgeois society" ("Forms of Time" 234). Judith Butler has called this subject "Hegel's unhappy hero" (Salih 22), because the price he pays for the comfort of civilization is frustration: "before mediated self-reflection is achieved, the subject knows itself to be a more limited, less autonomous being than it potentially is" (Butler 8).

Further proof for the transcendent tendencies in the *Bildungsroman* can be found in the close link between the *Bildungsroman* and nationalist ideals. The desire for a new humanity that inspired Goethe goes together with a desire for a spiritual unity among citizens. This desire is in line with the developments of political modernization. In Negri and Hardt we find a useful description of the typical modern association of collective sovereignty with nationality:

> The transformation of the absolutist and patrimonial model consisted in a gradual process that replaced the theological foundation of territorial patrimony with a new foundation that was equally transcendent. The spiritual identity of the nation rather than the divine body of the king now posed the territory and population as an ideal abstraction. Or rather, the physical territory and population were conceived as the extension of the transcendent essence of the nation. The modern concept of nation thus inherited the patrimonial body of the monarchic state and reinvented it in a new form. (94-95)

Because of the nationalist re-writing of older forms of collective sovereignty, literature of the 19th and 20th century had to find new ways to be subversive. Moretti states that "the conflict between the ideal of *self-determination* and the equally imperious *demands of socialization*" (15, italics in original) inspired writers to counter power-constellations with explicitly anti-idyllic writings. Most novels of 19th and 20th century realism do not end with a return of idyllic harmony, but, in a modernist way, end in a state of ambiguity; although part of the disorder is eradicated, contingency in general survives. There is no explicit idyllic apotheosis. This anti-idyllic aesthetic can be seen as the beginning of a new era in literature. In essence, literature from the 19th century onwards will be anti-nationalist and anti-bourgeois, either in a mildly ironical way as in the great modernist novels, or in a radical manner, as in the attitude of *épâter le bourgeois* we find in many avant-garde writers.

Works Cited

Bakhtin, Mikhail. "Epos and the Novel." *The Dialogic Imagination*. Ed. Michael Holquist. Austin: University of Texas Press, 1981. 1-83.

———. "Forms of Time and of the Chronotope in the Novel: Notes toward a Historical Poetics." *The Dialogic Imagination*. Ed. Michael Holquist. Austin: University of Texas Press, 1981. 84-254.

———. "The Bildungsroman and Its Significance in the History of Realism." *Speech Genres and Other Late Essays*. Ed. Caryl Emerson and Michael Holquist. Austin: University of Texas Press, 1986. 10-59.

Bru, Sascha. "Dada as Politics." *Arcadia: International Journal of Literary Studies* 41.2 (2006): 296-312.

Butler, Judith. *Subjects of Desire: Hegelian Reflections in Twentieth-Century France*. New York: Columbia University Press, 1987.

Elias, Norbert. *The Civilizing Process: Volume I: The History of Manners*. Oxford: Blackwell, 1969.

Habermas, Jürgen. "Die Kulturkritik der Neokonservativen in den USA und in der BRD." *Die Moderne – ein unvollendetes Projekt: Philosophisch-politische Aufsätze, 1977-1990*. Leipzig: Reclam, 1990. 75-104.

Hardt, Michael and Antonio Negri. *Empire*. Cambridge, Ma.: Harvard University Press, 2000.

Hogan, Patrick Colm. *The Mind and Its Stories*. Cambridge: Cambridge University Press, 2004.

Huelsenbeck, Richard, ed. *Dada Almanach*. Berlin: Erich Reiss Verlag, 1920.

Huelsenbeck, Richard. "Die Dadaistische Bewegung. Eine Selbstbiographie." *Wozu Dada: Texte 1916–1936*. Ed. Herbert Kapfer. Giessen: Anabas, 1994. 33–41.

Keunen, Bart. *Tijd voor een verhaal: Mens- en wereldbeelden in de (populaire) verhaalcultuur*. Gent: Academia Press, 2005.

Lützeler, Paul Michael. *Die Schriftsteller und Europa: Von der Romantik bis zur Gegenwart*. München: Piper, 1992.

Moretti, Franco. *The Way of the World: The Bildungsroman in European Culture*. London: Verso, 1987.

Pavel, Thomas. "The Novel in Search of Itself: A Historical Morphology." *The Novel: Volume 2: Forms and Themes*. Ed. Franco Moretti. Princeton: Princeton University Press, 2006. 3-31.

Pop, Ion. "L'avant-garde roumaine et la politique." *Arcadia: International Journal of Literary Studies* 41.2 (2006): 313-30.

Salih, Sara. *Judith Butler. Routledge Critical Thinkers*. London and New York: Routledge, 2002.

Notes on Contributors

NELE BEMONG is a postdoctoral fellow of the Research Foundation Flanders (Belgium) at the K.U.Leuven. Her PhD dealt with the historical novel in Belgium in the 19th century. She has published articles on Stijn Streuvels, Mark Z. Danielewski, and different aspects of 19th century historical fiction. She is a member of the Executive Committee (2007-2009) of the European Network for Comparative Literary Studies.

MICHAEL BOYDEN is a postdoctoral fellow of the K.U.Leuven Research Fund and a visiting professor at University College Ghent. His PhD, which he is currently rewriting into a book, dealt with the development and self-legitimation of American literary history as a discipline. His current research focuses on bilingualism in U.S. immigrant memoirs. He is the founding editor of the *Review of International American Studies*.

DAVID DAMROSCH is Professor of English and Comparative Literature at Columbia University, and is a past president of the American Comparative Literature Association. He is the author of *The Narrative Covenant* (1987), *We Scholars: Changing the Culture of the University* (1995), *Meetings of the Mind* (2000), *What Is World Literature?* (2003), and *The Buried Book: The Loss and Rediscovery of the Great Epic of Gilgamesh* (2007). He is also the general editor of the six-volume *Longman Anthology of World Literature* (2004).

ORTWIN DE GRAEF is Professor of English Literature at the K.U.Leuven. He is the author of two books on Paul de Man (*Serenity in Crisis* and *Titanic Light*) and has published on Romantic and post-Romantic writing and literary theory. His current research deals with aesthetic ideologies of sympathy and the State in the post-Romantic condition.

MATTHIJS DE RIDDER is a research assistant at the Louis Paul Boon Documentation Center at the University of Antwerp and is currently pursuing a PhD in Dutch literature. His research focuses on the activistic countertradition in Flemish literature. He is the author of essays on Willem Elsschot, Gaston Burssens, and Louis Paul Boon, the co-editor of the *Collected Works* of Louis Paul Boon, and the editor of the *Collected Poems* of Gaston Burssens. He also works as a book critic for the Flemish newspaper *De Standaard*.

REINDERT DHONDT is a member of the research unit "Identity and Intercultural Relations" at the K.U.Leuven as a doctoral student and a teaching assistant in Hispanic literature. His research deals with the relation between the hybrid refigurations of the European baroque in Latin American literature and the recent rehabilitation of the baroque as a modern worldview. He has published articles on Reinaldo Arenas, Hervé Guibert, and Carlos Fuentes.

LIEVEN D'HULST is Professor of French and Francophone literature and of translation studies at the K.U.Leuven (and at K.U.Leuven, Campus Kortrijk). His current research topics include: translation in the Francophone Caribbean (1950-2000), the discursive construction of Flemish migrant communities in Northern France (1850-1900), literary relations in Belgium (19th century), and transfer procedures (including translation). He is review editor of *Target: International Journal of Translation Studies*, and co-director of the series "Traductologie" at Artois Presses Université (APU). He is also a member of the Executive Council (2007-2010) of the International Comparative Literature Association.

IANNIS GOERLANDT is associated with the University of Ghent. He obtained his PhD in 2006 with a study of the functions of national imagery in Arno Schmidt's utopian prose. His research focus is on narratology, imagology, paratextuality, and literary ethics. He has published articles on Arno Schmidt, David Foster Wallace, Max Goldt, and Einstürzende Neubauten.

HERBERT GRABES is Professor Emeritus of English and American Literature at the Justus-Liebig-Universität Gießen. He has published widely on literary theory, Renaissance English Literature, and 20th century American literature. He is the author of numerous books, such as *Fictitious Biographies: Vladimir Nabokov's English Novels* (1977), *The Mutable Glass: Mirror-Imagery in Titles and Texts of the Middle Ages and the English Renaissance* (1982), and most recently *Einführung in die Literatur und Kunst der Moderne und Postmoderne: Die Ästhetik des Fremden* (2004). He is co-editor of *The Yearbook of Research in English and American Literature* (*REAL*).

NAGIHAN HALILOĞLU is a PhD student at the University of Heidelberg. Her research is on narrative and identity in the postcolonial context. She has published articles on the work of Jean Rhys and on diasporic women's memoirs. She is currently also working on Turkish female writers such as Halide Edip and Elif Shafak.

IULIUS HONDRILA is a PhD student at the K.U.Leuven, where he is writing a thesis on the representation of Eastern Europe(ans) in British literature in the period between the Crimean War and the First World War. From an interdisciplinary perspective involving cultural history, imagology, Victorian literature, history, and philosophy, his research attempts to highlight mechanisms of cultural representation and identity formation in the interplay of constructed images of 'self' and 'other.'

JEPPE ILKJÆR is a doctoral student at Roskilde University and is currently pursuing a PhD degree in European Cultural Studies. His research focus is on Elias Canetti and issues of tradition, cultural boundaries, and identity formation in Central European literature. He has published articles on Elias Canetti and on autobiographical writing.

BART KEUNEN is Professor in Comparative Literature at the University of Ghent. He teaches graduate and postgraduate courses in European literary history, the sociology of literature, and comparative literature. He has published articles in the fields of urban studies, genre criticism, literary historiography, and literary sociology. Book publications include *Literature and Society: The Function of Literary Sociology in Comparative Literature* (with Bart Eeckhout, 2001), *Tijd voor een verhaal: Mens- en wereldbeelden in de populaire verhaalcultuur* (2005), and *Verhaal en verbeelding: Chronotopen in de Westerse verhaalcultuur* (2007).

SILVANA MANDOLESSI is a research assistant at the K.U.Leuven and is currently pursuing a PhD degree in Latin American literature. Her research deals with travel writing in Argentine literature (1920-1950). She has published articles on Witold Gombrowicz, contemporary Argentine literature, autobiography, and travel writing.

MARY STEVENS has recently completed a PhD in the French and Anthropology departments at University College London (UCL), exploring the reconfiguration of national identity in the *Cité nationale de l'histoire de l'immigration* in France. She is currently a postdoctoral researcher at UCL, working on a research council project that looks at the relationship between community archives and collective identity constructions. She has published articles on North African fiction (Assia Djebar) and on the politics and poetics of memory discourses in French museums and monuments, as well as several translations (Rancière, Stora).

MIRJAM TRUWANT is a research assistant at the K.U.Leuven and is currently pursuing a PhD degree in German Literature. Her research investigates images of authorship in German biographies of and by women writers (c. 1850-1920). She has published articles on Ödön von Hórvath, contemporary German literature, biography, and women writing.

BEATRIJS VANACKER is a research assistant at the K.U.Leuven and is currently pursuing a PhD degree in French Literature. She is working on a genetic and discursive analysis of the genre of the *histoire anglaise* in the broader context of the Anglomania-movement in 18th century France. She has published articles on the translation and adaptation of French novels into English and Italian, on 18th century *histoires anglaises* (Mme Riccoboni, Prévost, Crébillon, Mme Leprince de Beaumont), and on women writing (Eliza Haywood).

KARI VAN DIJK is pursuing a PhD degree at Radboud University Nijmegen. Her research looks at the innovative ways in which three female artists (Austrian writer Ingeborg Bachmann, American painter Elizabeth Murray, and Japanese-German writer Yoko Tawada) deal with the existential problematics of arriving at an androgynous subjectivity. She currently lives and writes in Trondheim, Norway, and has published both on Bachmann and Tawada. A publication on Peter Sloterdijk's *Sphären* trilogy is in preparation.

BEN VAN HUMBEECK is a doctoral researcher for the Flemish-Dutch Committee (VNC) at the K.U.Leuven. He is currently working on a research project which focuses on the development of the literary relations between Flanders and the Netherlands in the 1980s and 90s.

PIETER VERMEULEN is a postdoctoral fellow of the K.U.Leuven Research Fund. He has published numerous articles on critical theory (especially on the work of Geoffrey Hartman, Erich Auerbach, and Theodor Adorno) and on contemporary literature (especially J.M. Coetzee). He is also the co-editor, with Theo D'haen, of *Cultural Identity and Postmodern Writing* (2006).